Supervision and Clinical Psychology

2nd edition

Theory, Practice and Perspectives

Edited by
Ian Fleming and Linda Steen

Routledge
Taylor & Francis Group

LONDON AND NEW YORK

First published 2004 by Routledge
27 Church Road, Hove, East Sussex BN3 2FA

Second edition published 2012
by Routledge
27 Church Road, Hove, East Sussex BN3 2FA

Simultaneously published in the USA and Canada
by Routledge
711 Third Avenue, New York NY 10017

Routledge is an imprint of the Taylor & Francis Group, an Informa business

British Library Cataloguing in Publication Data
A catalogue record for this book is available from the British Library

Library of Congress Cataloging in Publication Data
Supervision and clinical psychology : theory, practice and perspectives / edited by Ian Fleming and Linda Steen. – 2nd ed.
        p. ; cm.
    Includes bibliographical references and index.
    ISBN 978-0-415-49511-0 (hardback) – ISBN 978-0-415-49512-7 (pbk.) 1. Clinical psychologists–Supervision of. I. Fleming, Ian, 1954– II. Steen, Linda.
    [DNLM: 1. Psychology, Clinical–organization & administration–Great Britain. WM 105]
    RC467.7.S87 2011
    616.890092–dc22

                                                                2010050167

ISBN: 978-0-415-49511-0 (hbk)
ISBN: 978-0-415-49512-7 (pbk)
ISBN: 978-0-203-80581-7 (ebk)

Typeset in Times by Garfield Morgan, Swansea, West Glamorgan
Paperback cover design by Andrew Ward
Printed and bound in Great Britain by TJ International Ltd, Padstow, Cornwall

Supervision and Clinical Psychology
2nd edition

Supervision is crucial to good professional practice and an essential part of training and continuing professional development. This second edition of *Supervision and Clinical Psychology* has been fully updated to include the recent developments in research, policy and the practice of supervision.

With contributions from senior trainers and clinicians who draw on both relevant research and their own experience, this book is rooted in current best practice and provides a clear exposition of the main issues important to supervision. New areas of discussion include:

- the impact of the recent NHS policy
- developments in supervisor training
- practical aspects of supervision
- a consideration of future trends

Supervision and Clinical Psychology, 2nd edition is essential reading for clinical psychology supervisors as well as being invaluable to those who work in psychiatry, psychotherapy and social work.

Ian Fleming and **Linda Steen** are joint Clinical Directors on the doctoral training programme in Clinical Psychology at the University of Manchester. Within their professional bodies they have played a leading role in the development of supervisor training, which has led to the recent establishment of a register for practice supervisors.

Contents

Figures

Tables

Notes on contributors

Gill Aitken trained as a researcher in the 1980s and worked full time as a lecturer in social psychology and communication until 1993. After qualifying as a clinical psychologist (1996) and Cognitive Analytic Therapy practitioner (2000) she worked in secure psychiatric settings, including as Lead Psychologist in Women's Services (2000–2006). Nominated by the Psychology of Women section, Gill accepted the BPS 2005 Distinguished Contributions to Professional Psychology award in 2006. Since 2006, she works freelance providing psychological assessments, therapy, supervision, training and consultancy to individuals, services and organisations across sectors, and also qualified as an executive and business coach (2009). To support Gill's ongoing human development and learning, in addition to continuing professional development, she engages with regular meditation, (silent) retreats, Buddhist study, improvised contact dance and in 2009 started training as a therapeutic yoga teacher.

Helen Beinart is Clinical Director of the Oxford Doctoral Course in Clinical Psychology, where she has worked since 1994. Clinically, she works with children, young people and their families in a primary care setting. She has worked in the NHS for the past 30 years as a clinician, service manager, consultant, supervisor and trainer. She is joint editor of *Clinical Psychology in Practice* (2009), along with P. Kennedy and S. Llewelyn.

Delia Cushway is Emeritus Professor of Clinical Psychology at Coventry University. She is an Associate Fellow of the British Psychological Society (BPS), a clinical and forensic psychologist chartered with the BPS and registered with the Health Professions Council (HPC). Delia has worked for 20 years in clinical psychology training and was Director of Clinical Psychology Training at the Universities of Coventry and Warwick until 2008. Her main clinical and research interests and publications are in the areas of reflective practice, supervision, stress and self-care, dream work and Gestalt therapy.

Maxine Dennis is a Consultant Clinical Psychologist and Adult Psycho-therapist based at the Tavistock Clinic. She has worked extensively within the NHS clinically and as Head of a primary care service. She is involved in the teaching, training and supervision of psychologists, psychotherapists and counsellors.

Ian Fleming is joint Clinical Director of the Clinical Psychology training programme at the University of Manchester and a Consultant Clinical Psychologist working with people with learning disabilities.

David Green is Clinical Director of the Doctorate in Clinical Psychology training programme at the University of Leeds. He has a long-standing interest in clinical supervision as a trainer, theorist and sometime researcher, and has published regularly on the topic. His current enthusiasm is for the use of sessional feedback measures in both therapy and supervision. Since the chapter was completed, David retired from his post as Clinical Director at the University of Leeds in 2010.

Jan Hughes is Director of Clinical Practice at the University of Sheffield, on the Doctor of Clinical Psychology programme. She has provided super-visor training for qualified clinical psychologists for a number of years, and has been commissioned by the Yorkshire and the Humber Strategic Health Authority to provide Improving Access to Psychological Therapy (IAPT) supervisor training since 2008. Since the chapter was completed, Jan has moved to the University of Leeds where she is Clinical Director.

Ian James (BSc, MSc, PhD, C.Psychol.) is a consultant clinical psychologist leading the Newcastle Challenging Behaviour Team, Older People's Services. Prior to this he worked in the Newcastle Cognitive and Beha-vioural Therapies Centre, where he was involved in the assessment of competence relating to therapy and supervision.

Caroline Leck (RMN, MSc) is a Clinical Nurse Specialist, working with patients who experience enduring and severe mental health problems. She had worked as a supervisor for several years prior to participation in the study reported herein, and had obtained her MSc for research on supervision.

Derek Milne (BSc, Dip. Clin. Psych., MSc, PhD, C.Psychol., FBPsS) is a Consultant Clinical Psychologist specialising in staff development. He is Director of the Newcastle University Doctorate in Clinical Psychology and is currently Consultant to the NTW NHS Trust programme of supervisor development.

Nimisha Patel is a Reader on the Doctoral Degree Programme in Clinical Psychology at the University of East London and Lead Consultant Clinical Psychologist and Head of Audit, Evaluation and Research at the Medical Foundation for the Care of Victims of Torture. She has previously worked in the NHS in a range of adult services in primary, secondary and tertiary settings, developing psychological services and practices with minority ethnic people. Since 1997 her specialist area has been in human rights and clinical psychology in the field of torture.

Rachel Procter (BSc) studied Psychology at Newcastle University and then worked as an Assistant Psychologist within a Child and Adolescent Mental Health Service in the North East of England. She has previous Assistant Psychologist experience in the field of Adolescent Forensic Services, and aims to further her career in psychology by completing a Doctorate in Clinical Psychology.

Laura Ramm (BSc) studied Psychology at Newcastle University.

Linda Steen is Joint Clinical Director of the University of Manchester Clinical Psychology training programme and a Consultant Clinical Psychologist in adult primary care at Manchester Mental Health and Social Care Trust. She has a longstanding interest and involvement in training and supervising. For the past 15 years, together with Ian Fleming, she has developed and delivered supervisor training and she regularly supervises qualified clinical psychologists and other health professionals.

Graham Turpin is Head of the Department of Psychology at the University of Sheffield and is currently seconded to the National Mental Health Development Unit, Department of Health, as National Advisor for Education and Training for the Improving Access to Psychological Therapies (IAPT) National Programme. He was formerly Director of the Clinical Psychology Unit at Sheffield, and a former Chair of the Division of Clinical Psychology and Director of the Professional Standards Unit (DCP), BPS. He is co-convenor of the IAPT Workforce Group and is linked to the Skills for Health projects around developing National Occupational Standards for Psychological Therapists, together with a Career Framework for practitioners working in Psychological Therapy Services and New Ways of Working for Psychological Therapists. His interests include training and workforce planning around applied psychology and psychological therapies.

James Weetman (BSc) studied Psychology at Newcastle University, before completing a PGCE with QTS in Primary Teaching. He is currently a primary school teacher in Sheffield, with a continuing interest in psychology in an educational setting.

Sue Wheeler is Professor of Counselling and Psychotherapy and Director of the Counselling and Psychotherapy programme at the University of Leicester. She is a BACP-accredited counsellor and UKCP-registered psychotherapist and Fellow of BACP. Her research interests include counsellor training, supervision and the professional development of therapists, and she is the author of many papers on these topics. Her books include *Difference and Diversity in Counselling: A Psychodynamic Perspective* (Palgrave, 2006), *Training Counsellors: The Assessment of Competence* (Cassell, 1996), *Supervising Counsellors: Issues of Responsibility* (Sage, 2001), co-edited with David King, and the *BACP Systematic Review of Supervision* (2007), co-edited with Kaye Richards.

Judith Wilkinson (BSc) studied Psychology at Newcastle University before going on to work as an Assistant Psychologist with the Central Norfolk Early Intervention Team. She has subsequently worked on a national 'early detection in psychosis' trial, evaluating the effectiveness of cognitive therapy in preventing or delaying transition. She hopes to further her career in psychology by completing a Doctorate in Clinical Psychology in the near future.

Maria Wilson (BA Hons, PGCE, Dip.Psych.) studied Psychology at Newcastle University and then worked as an Assistant Educational Psychologist in North and South Tyneside. She is currently studying for a Doctorate in Applied Educational Psychology at Newcastle University.

Foreword

Despite its title this is not just a book for clinical psychologists; its content applies to a much wider constituency. The notion that therapists or counsellors should have time to discuss, review and reflect on their work is an accepted professional wisdom, and supervision is usually seen as the primary vehicle for achieving this. This means that anyone who practises as a psychological therapist should have been supervised, making it a ubiquitous experience across professional groups. More than this, supervision is not restricted to individuals in training; even senior practitioners continue to seek out and to receive supervision, making it ubiquitous across the professional lifespan.

Given its ubiquity there are surprisingly few texts on supervision, and this book makes a valuable contribution to the field by addressing a broad range of theoretical and practical issues pertinent both to supervisees and supervisors. Many of the issues it addresses are challenges to and for our thinking – for example:

- What are the methods that supervisors should best employ in order to enable and sustain a supervisee's clinical practice? Reflection on the nature of clinical skills makes it immediately clear that their acquisition is far from straightforward, because clinical skills rest on both declarative and procedural knowledge. So, while underpinned by academic knowledge, competent clinical work depends on an ability to titrate this knowledge against an array of intra-psychic, interpersonal and socio-cultural factors, and apply skills responsively (in the sense of spontaneously), reflectively (in the sense that there is a degree of self-monitoring and appraisal) and reflexively (in that learning takes place on the basis of experience). This confronts supervision with an array of tasks, and the challenge is to identify the best and most effective sets of methods for achieving not just one but a multiplicity of aims.
- What is the evidence for the benefit of supervision? While supervision is specified as good practice by all the major professional bodies and training organisations, widespread acceptance of its value risks being

no more than an article of faith unless there is reasonable evidence that
it makes a difference. But asking the question presupposes that we are
clear about the 'benefit' we have in mind. For example, it makes sense
to ask what impact supervision has on supervisees – does it improve
their understanding of clinical matters, increase their confidence,
improve their capacity to manage complexity, and so on? But the more
stringent test is whether supervision results in therapy that is more
competently delivered and in improved outcomes for clients. This may
be a more difficult link to demonstrate, but it is critical because the
implicit rationale for offering supervision is the enhancement of client
outcomes. While it is true that there are many aims to supervision,
committing resources to it would be hard to defend if we realised that
its presence or absence made no difference to the quality of therapy
that clients receive or the outcomes they can expect.

- What is the appropriate process and content of supervision? Even brief
reflection makes it clear that this is a hard question to answer, because
'supervision' is an imprecise and protean term. For example, if supervision operates from the cradle to the grave of our professional careers
its focus should shift accordingly, from an initial emphasis on the
educational (training, teaching and learning) towards strategies for the
maintenance and enhancement of practice. Further, the structure of
supervision often echoes the model of therapy being employed, so that
while supervision in all modalities aims to impart knowledge and skills,
facilitate personal and professional development and offer support for
the supervisee, the manner in which these issues are approached will
vary, as will the emphasis placed on each area. There has been much
writing about (and advocacy for) different models of supervision, but
there are interesting questions to be asked about their differences and
similarities, and especially the extent to which there are common core
educational principles that might underpin the endeavour, regardless of
theoretical orientation.

It is easy to raise questions of this sort; more difficult is the task of
answering them. Between them the first two chapters from Ian Fleming/
Linda Steen and Sue Wheeler/Delia Cushway set out the supervisory terrain
from the perspectives of psychologists and other professions. Questions
about the models adopted by supervisors of different therapy modalities are
considered by Helen Beinart (Chapter 4) and David Green (Chapter 5),
with the impact of factors such as gender, culture, power and difference
detailed by Nimisha Patel (Chapter 7) and Gill Aitken and Maxine Dennis
(Chapter 8). A further set of chapters detail the governance of supervision:
research into supervision is considered by Derek Milne and co-authors
(Chapter 9), the training of supervisors by Ian Fleming (Chapter 6), and the
organisation of supervision in relation to IAPT by Graham Turpin

(Chapter 3). Finally there is the issue of implementation, with Jan Hughes' chapter (Chapter 11) focused on practicalities – never something to over-look – and Linda Steen (Chapter 10) discussing how innovative formats for supervision can be implemented.

What comes across from all these chapters is the enthusiasm of the authors and their thoughtfulness about supervision, making it all the more unfortunate that professional enthusiasm for supervision is not always echoed by local service arrangements, and outside training programme arrangements for supervision can be highly variable. In this respect the Improving Access to Psychological Therapies (IAPT) programme, now rolling out across England, sets a helpful tone by making supervision an inherent part of service organisation. In part this reflects the governance of the programme, which aims to achieve outcomes for clients equivalent to those found in clinical research trials: alongside initial training, ongoing supervision is seen as important to achieving this. In fact this emphasis echoes the usual pattern of research studies (on which our claims for the efficacy of psychological therapy are based), where regular supervision is a standard component in the organisation and delivery of therapy. This fact is not always appreciated, partly because there is no standardised system for reporting it (Roth, Pilling and Turner, 2010). It seems that researchers share an article of faith with clinicians: it is a rare trial that does not commit significant resources to the supervision of its therapists. The assumption, presumably, is that skilling-up therapists increases internal validity by maximising competence, and indeed there is good evidence that therapist variance (the variation in client outcome that can be attributed to individual therapist) is much lower in clinical trials than in most clinical settings. How we understand this is open to interpretation, but it seems reasonable to suggest that delivering interventions more skilfully may lead to better and more consistent outcomes, and if so then evidence-based practice is not just a matter of doing the right thing, but also of doing the right thing in the right way. This idea is at least part of the reason for developing 'competence frameworks' (Roth and Pilling, 2008), which set out to indicate the competences associated with the skilful delivery of a range of therapy modalities.

Included in the 'suite' of competence frameworks is a framework for the conduct of supervision across all modalities of psychological therapy (accessible at www.ucl.ac.uk/CORE/). This places a strong emphasis on the educational principles that underpin supervision and apply whatever the therapy being applied, but also identifies some of the assumptions and principles that will shape supervision of specific models. Many of the contributors to this book had input to the framework, either as members of the Expert Reference Group that oversaw its development or as the authors of source materials that were incorporated into the work. Their collective expertise is reflected in this book: all supervisors (from the most experienced, to those about to take their first supervisee) have much to gain from it.

Tony Roth
University College London
May 2010

References

Roth, A. D. and Pilling, S. (2008) Using an evidence-based methodology to identify the competences required to deliver effective cognitive and behavioural therapy for depression and anxiety disorders, *Behavioural and Cognitive Psychotherapy* 36: 129–147.

Roth, A. D., Pilling, S. and Turner, J. (2010) Therapist training and supervision in clinical trials: Implications for clinical practice, *Behavioural and Cognitive Psychotherapy* 38: 291–302.

Chapter 1

Introduction

Ian Fleming and Linda Steen

Welcome to the second edition of *Supervision and Clinical Psychology*. The first edition was written largely in 2002 and published in early 2004. This revised edition incorporates new knowledge and utilises the experience of supervision gained from both within and outside clinical psychology since 2002.

What has changed since the first edition?

Superficially, it might seem as if not a lot has changed since 2002 in the practice of clinical psychology in the UK. The vast majority of clinical psychologists – over 8000 – remain working in the public health system, the National Health Service (NHS); see Chapter 3. There has been some increase in the numbers of people working independently (either directly for themselves, or for private employers or so-called third-sector organisations) and this may be accounted for in part by the policy of outsourcing certain NHS services to the 'independent' sector.

There have been some changes to the organisation of clinical psychologists in the NHS, most apparently the dissolution of psychologist-managed psychology departments that cross specialisms. Moreover, as for all non-medical NHS staff, the career structure for clinical psychologists has changed since the introduction in 2004 of the NHS salary structure, Agenda for Change (AfC; DH, 2004). A clear career structure remains intact and it is still common to find unfilled posts that are hard to recruit to, although there is a tendency for a smaller proportion of posts to exist at Consultant grade (see, for example, Turpin and Llewelyn, 2009).

There has continued to be an expansion in the number of clinical psychology training places, with 623 places having been commissioned in the UK in 2009, although this increase has slowed. To illustrate, from 2000 to 2005 there was an increase of 198 training places; from 2005 to 2009 the number of places increased by 35 and, as noted by Graham Turpin in Chapter 3, far from expanding, in some regions of England there has been a reduction in training places since 2005 due to financial stringencies.

Nonetheless, there continue to be very high numbers of well qualified applicants for each place; the 2010 data for applications to UK clinical psychology training programmes show a 27% increase in applications as compared with 2009. Once qualified, most individuals appear to quickly find full-time employment, usually in a clinical area of their choice; the exception to this was in 2006 following the introduction of the AfC pay structure, when there were fewer full-time posts available within the NHS and, unusually, a significant number of trainees had to take locum or part-time jobs or seek employment within the private sector.

This picture of relative stability may be illusory, however, and significant changes to the organisation of clinical psychology services in the NHS may be in the offing. One example of this is the *Improving Access to Psychological Therapies* (IAPT) initiative. For many years the psychology profession has worked to be better recognised by the government, and within the past few years this has taken place. Lord Layard, Labour Life Peer and Emeritus Professor of Economics at the London School of Economics, through reading the research on psychological treatment for anxiety and depression championed clinical psychology as the key to therapy that would enable numbers of people to throw off their psychological distress and as a result be able to return to employment. Whatever the range of beneficial reasons underlying the practice of clinical psychologists, the basis of the Layard Report was firmly in the economic realm, with an emphasis on the overall gains for the exchequer when offset against the finances needed for new therapists. This was crystallised in the policy document entitled *Improving Access to Psychological Therapies* (IAPT; DH, 2009b). This contained an emphasis on therapists rather than clinical psychologists per se, because the understanding of the research demonstrating the effectiveness of cognitive behaviour therapy presumed a need for a limited form of uni-linear training as necessary to provide effective treatment – as opposed to the training in different psychological models required of clinical psychologists. There may be significant implications contained in IAPT for the continuing use of trained clinical psychologists.

The September 2009 report of the NHS Workforce Review Team 'suggests that there is room for growth on the clinical psychologist workforce over the next 5 years' and specifically refers to the 'increased requirement for clinical psychologists in both a training and service delivery capacity' resulting from IAPT (Workforce Review Team, 2009: 1). However, it should be noted that the data set (from the NHS Information Centre) that underpins the report includes within the category 'clinical psychology' all applied psychologists and some trainees and assistants. At the time of writing this is generating more heat than light amongst the profession. It also must be recognised that IAPT in its original incarnation applies to only one of the client areas in which clinical psychologists now practice, although in mid-2009/10 there had been an expansion of IAPT to working with children and their families, and some consideration of its application to working with other groups, including people who have learning disabilities. It is unclear in this case where any economic benefits may lie. These issues will be discussed at more length in Chapter 3.

This development has important implications for supervision and there are a number of strands to this. First, within the IAPT strategy – and indeed inseparable from the different levels ('intensities') of therapeutic input – there is an explicit reference to the use of supervision to ensure the quality of therapeutic delivery. Second, it is clear that there are differences between the approach to supervision envisaged within IAPT and the more inclusive form of supervision being developed in supervisor training. Here the priority would appear to be adherence to a manualised approach to treatment combined with problem-solving within that model. This '"high volume" and outcome-linked' (Milne, 2009: 51) case-based supervision has quite a different feel from clinical supervision; in the former, the emphasis is on client outcome, whilst the latter focuses on 'the personal and professional development of the individual' (BPS, 2006a: 4). In Chapter 5 David Green debates the issues involved in model-specific and more general forms of supervision. The first indicates the widespread presence of supervision, although the second has implications for the content and breadth of these skills.

It remains unclear whether we will continue to see greater demands for supervisor training as part of the organisation of professional training. Whatever the outcome, it is hoped that the momentum that has developed over the past decade will continue to press for better training and supervisory arrangements.

Supervision developments

It is interesting to reflect that a 2000 survey of clinical psychology trainers (Milne and Oliver, 2000) found little support for developing formal procedures such as supervisor certification, due largely to 'a cautious approach to a finite and fragile placement/supervisor resource' (ibid.: 300). In 2009 accreditation of clinical psychologist supervisors became a reality, with the introduction of the BPS Register of Applied Psychology Practice Supervisors (RAPPS). Although membership of the Register will not be a *requirement* for supervising, it will certainly act to focus attention on the content and form of effective training, the subsequent transfer of training into practice and research into supervision and supervisor training. Accreditation is discussed further alongside the training of supervisors in Chapter 6, where similar developments in other professions are also considered.

The introduction of the aforementioned AfC pay and grading structure and, more recently, the publication of *New Ways of Working for Applied*

Psychologists (BPS, 2007b; Lavender and Hope, 2007) appear to have had a positive impact on clinical psychologists' attitudes towards supervision as well as their supervisory practice. Whilst the majority of clinical psychologists have always had a favourable approach to supervision, particularly towards supervising trainee clinical psychologists, they could opt out of supervising if they so chose. Now, there is a clear expectation that all clinical psychologists will supervise others from an early stage in their career. Moreover, as the capacity to provide supervision is a key factor within the Knowledge and Skills Framework and is thus one of the criteria for career progression within AfC, it is not unusual for clinical psychologists to seek training in supervision as soon as they qualify, whereas previously it was much more usual for them to wait at least 2 years before training to take on the supervisory role.

The implication of the above is that in future there will be increasing demands on clinical psychologists to receive and provide supervision, both to members of their own profession and to others. This will place pressure on the traditional model of one-to-one supervision, and in Chapter 10 Linda Steen considers different supervision formats and those that might develop in the future.

Also, the introduction of the IAPT programme has led many clinical psychology trainers to have concerns about its potential impact on the supervisory resource for clinical psychology trainees, fearing that those clinical psychologists involved with IAPT training and supervision would have little additional time for supervising clinical psychology trainees. To date, this does not seem to have had a significant impact, although it remains to be seen what will happen in the immediate future.

Another important issue is that of *preparedness* for supervision, especially when a member of one profession supervises a member of another. Within the NHS, interprofessional learning and working are priorities for both education providers and healthcare organisations, and it is not unusual for clinical psychologists to both supervise and be supervised by other professionals. There does not appear to be a single view of supervision, however, and, for example, clinical and managerial supervision can be confused or seen as interchangeable. Moreover, as outlined in Chapter 10, some terms are used by different professionals to describe similar activities; notable amongst these are consultation, support, mentoring and coaching. In this book the emphasis is on clinical supervision, and particular models are discussed. Rarely does the process take on a didactic form, and yet this is sometimes what people in other professions receive and expect in their supervision. This misapprehension is not an insurmountable problem, but at a service level it does suggest increased clarity about the purpose of supervision, and at an individual level honest communication through the means of a *supervision contract*. This is highlighted in a number of the chapters in this book, for example Chapters 4, 10 and 11.

This book contains unambiguous recognition of the importance of the supervisory relationship and this is succinctly explored by Helen Beinart in Chapter 4. It is interesting to consider which elements are sufficient for effective supervision and how this relationship can be both established and maintained within different supervision formats, especially the distal ones such as telephone and email supervision. There is evidence that, where possible, participants who engage in some forms of remote supervision, such as on-line supervision, prefer to meet face-to-face initially in order to establish an alliance; this theme is developed further in Chapter 10.

We closed the first edition of our book by quoting Milne and James (1999), who were of the view that we were at an 'exciting stage' (ibid.: 36) in the development of supervisory practice. It is satisfying to report that since the first edition was published the increased interest in all aspects of supervision has been maintained. This is the case at all levels: research grows in strength, as exemplified by the work of Derek Milne and colleagues in Chapter 9; there is a keen emphasis on the reflection on supervisory practice, for example in the work of NHS Education for Scotland (NES), referred to in Chapter 6; there is a huge demand for training in supervisory skills from newly qualified clinical psychologists; and there is a recognition that at best supervisor training should commence in pre-qualification and extend to post-qualification continuing professional development.

There has been an increased focus on the evaluation of both supervision and supervisor training and there are a number of assessment tools that can be used. The issue of evaluation is discussed in a number of chapters alongside a call for the evaluation of the transfer of training into practice, although this is in its early stages.

Developments in clinical psychology training

At the time the first edition of this book was written, the BPS had just introduced a new, competence-based framework for clinical psychology training. This involved moving from an experiential model of training, in which trainees were required to have pre-defined experience on 'core' placements, to one that emphasised achievement of the competencies required for the roles and responsibilities of newly qualified clinical psychologists. The competencies were expressed as learning outcomes and transferred into the new Standards for Doctoral Programmes (BPS, 2010), which guide all aspects of clinical psychology training from the design of the curriculum, through placement experience, to the methods of monitoring progress and assessment. The particular relevance of the competence framework to this book is two-fold. First, it has given training programmes much more flexibility in the pathways through training, enabling the use of a much wider variety of clinical placements than previously, thereby maximising the supervisory resource. Second, three of the learning outcomes directly concern the practice of supervision, namely: 'using supervision to reflect on practice, and making appropriate use of feedback received' (ibid.: 2.3.7); 'understanding of the supervision process for both supervisee and supervisor roles' (ibid.: 2.3.8); and 'providing supervision at an appropriate level within own sphere of competence' (ibid.: 2.3.9). Whilst the practice and quality of supervision have always played a large role in pre-qualification clinical psychology training, the focus had mainly been on the supervisors' practice. The introduction of the competence framework, with its explicit focus on the aforementioned learning outcomes, has undoubtedly raised the profile of the practice of supervision as a two-way endeavour and has led to an increased emphasis during the pre-qualification period on training in how to receive and provide supervision.

Another important development within clinical psychology training has been the increased emphasis in recent years on trainees' personal and professional development (Hughes and Youngson, 2009) and their development as reflective practitioners (Stedmon and Dallos, 2009). In both of these areas, supervision plays a crucial role in helping the practitioner to reflect on self, other and process, and this is developed further in Chapter 2.

Professional developments

As mentioned previously, a desire amongst clinical psychology trainers to recognise the increased attention being paid to supervisory practice in clinical psychology has led to significant developments towards the accreditation of supervisory skills for clinical psychologists; these are described in detail in Chapter 6. It is pleasing to be able to report that agreement has been reached on a core set of learning outcomes for introductory supervisor training and that a process has been agreed whereby the acquisition and practice of these skills are validated by the body that professionally represents UK Psychologists, the British Psychological Society (BPS).

In 2010, the vast majority of UK Clinical Psychology training programmes were engaged in supervisor training and there appears to be a great deal of agreement about the content and organisation of this training. In addition, there is an increasing interest in a requirement for participants to demonstrate the transfer of this training into practice, although this has not been made a specific requirement of accreditation.

In addition to the potential pressures resulting from the wider service policies mentioned earlier, another potential influence on supervision and supervisor training derives from the changing role of the BPS, clinical psychology's professional body. In July 2009, the Health Professions Council (HPC) took on responsibilities for the regulation of practitioner psychologists. Whereas previously the BPS was responsible for accrediting clinical psychology training programmes, this approval role has also been taken on by the HPC. At the time of writing, the role of the Committee on Training in Clinical Psychology (CTCP), the BPS body that formerly took the lead for accreditation visits to training programmes, is under review. In Chapter 6, Ian Fleming describes the important part played by the CTCP in increasing the requirements for the training of clinical psychology supervisors. In the first edition, reference was made to the benefits that would accrue from further specification of these training requirements within the accreditation process. One possible effect of this increased role for the HPC will be a diminution in the responsibilities of the BPS, but this may be accompanied by a sharpened focus on the Society's role and, in particular, an increased level of activity connected to professional development.

The central role of the HPC concerns registration and the achievement of certain minimal standards to protect the general public. Despite a somewhat equivocal role in future, clinical psychology's professional body would seem to have an important *complementary* future role. The limited nature of the HPC's statements about supervision and supervisor training is discussed alongside actual developments in practice in Chapter 6 and further highlighted in Chapter 3.

Aim of increasing diversity within the profession: Implications for addressing the issues of diversity and power in supervision

It would be pleasing to be able to report that the membership of the clinical psychology profession has become more representative of the whole UK population. Despite the emphasis given to this aim by the BPS, however, there is little evidence to support this (BPS, 2004; Cape et al., 2008).

At the time of writing, an article has appeared in *Clinical Psychology Forum* examining the attraction to the profession of candidates from Black and ethnic minority populations (Shepherd, Vanderpuye and Saine, 2010). The authors conclude that the websites of different UK clinical psychology training programmes varied in terms of the adequacy of information provided and in their likely impact of attracting applicants from Black and ethnic minority backgrounds.

These findings do not preclude the establishment of good practice with respect to particular issues of power and difference in supervision. Indeed, two recently developed supervision competence frameworks – the Supervisor Training and Recognition (STAR[1]) competences, described in Chapter 6, and Roth and Pilling's (2008c) supervision competence framework – both include the ability to work with difference and diversity.

Issues of diversity and difference will feature in supervision and it would be poor professional practice to ignore these. Gill Aitken and Maxine Dennis (Chapter 8) and Nimisha Patel (Chapter 7) have revised and updated their chapters from the first edition, to incorporate new developments in practice and research.

Using knowledge and innovations from research

Although chapters in the earlier edition made full reference to appropriate research, the absence of a chapter devoted to the most recent research into supervision was a significant omission. We hope that this has been rectified in the second edition by the inclusion of the chapter by Derek Milne and colleagues (Chapter 9). Readers are likely to be familiar with the body of Derek's research into aspects of supervision that has busied him for many years, and his most recent work – reported in the chapter – has focused on training workers in supervisory skills that are relevant to the IAPT initiative.

There is evidence that research is informing supervisory practice in clinical psychology in the UK. The work of the STAR group was informed by research and commissioned projects of its own. Through its links with many providers of supervisor training and its sponsorship of small scale research projects, it was able to be informed by practice and research and to feed this back into proposals for supervisory practice. There is a lot of common ground between the competences for supervisor training adopted by the BPS and those commissioned by the American Psychological Association (Falender and Shafranske, 2004).

The practice of supervision

A major omission from the first edition was an illustration of the practice of supervision: What happens in supervision? What can go wrong? What does the experienced supervisor pass on to the novice? What is the *feel* of supervision? Jan Hughes was asked to make good this deficiency and in Chapter 11 she uses her experience of supervision to reflect on and unite themes explored in other chapters

Novice supervisors often struggle with the anxieties associated with becoming a supervisor. In our supervisor training in Manchester we aim to discuss this humorously by showing a quotation from Kaslow:

> the supervisor should be ethical, well-informed, knowledgeable in his/ her theoretical orientation, clinically skilled, articulate, empathic, a good listener, gentle, confrontative, accepting, challenging, stimulating, provocative, reassuring, encouraging, possess a good sense of humour, a good sense of timing, be innovative, solid and existing.
> (Kaslow, 1986: 6)

The resulting discussion helps individuals to find balance between, on the one hand, the excitement and the potential benefits of both giving and receiving supervision and, on the other hand, the real limitations in the range of tasks and roles that can be maintained within effective supervision.

The increased demands for supervision, referred to earlier in this chapter, have led clinical psychologists to consider the use of different formats, including the use of technology both to access and to provide supervision. For pre-qualification clinical psychology training, the BPS since 1995 has permitted the use of a range of supervision formats as adjuncts to one-to-one supervision. Post-qualification too, supervision guidance suggests the use of a number of different formats. There is some evidence within clinical psychology practice in the UK for a breaking away from traditional one-to-one formats, particularly amongst those clinicians whose therapeutic orientation is better suited to other formats, for example group supervision for those practitioners running psychotherapeutic groups. For those of us who are still wedded to the one-to-one format, we need to be prepared for changed demands and to have considered the advantages and disadvantages of different formats, of which there are many; this will be discussed in Chapter 10.

About the book

This book contains a collection of chapters on important aspects of supervision written by leading practitioners, researchers and trainers. As before, the focus will be on clinical supervision as distinct from line management supervision (BPS, 2006a), although several of the chapters refer to other types of supervision, including case management supervision (see Chapter 3).

In preparing this second edition we thought it essential to retain some of the important themes addressed in the first edition. To this end we have included chapters on models of supervision and the supervisory relationship, developments in supervisor training, the impact of gender, 'race' and culture on supervision and asked the authors to update their earlier text. We have complemented these chapters with others that are either new or heavily revised to reflect the changes in supervision over the past few years. Four of the chapters are completely new (Chapters 5, 9, 10 and 11) and others are updated to incorporate new research, experience and policy changes since the first edition was written 8 years ago.

We hope that this book will act for readers both as an academic source and as a guide to the current issues affecting the practice of supervision in clinical psychology in the UK. Although there is a focus on one profession, we have drawn on research and practice from other professions, as appropriate, and we are very pleased to have Chapter 2 by Sue Wheeler and Delia Cushway, which helps to set the scene for the rest of the book by placing the practice of supervision in context. We think that much of the content of this volume will be relevant to a wide range of practitioners within the helping professions, as they consider and develop their own particular supervisory requirements. We think that there is a lot of common ground in the supervision needed in different mental health and caring professions, in particular a specific agreed relationship that through reflection and feedback encourages a process by which one can review one's clinical work in order to improve future practice and ultimately have a positive impact on client outcome.

One of the themes of the first edition was a reflection at that time that the profession of clinical psychology needed to catch up with developments in supervision already rooted in other, related professions. Additionally and perhaps related to this, the book contained an emphasis on supervision of trainee clinical psychologists rather than the supervisory practice of qualified clinicians, as this was where most of the research had been carried out. The past 8 years has seen significant developments in both these areas, as is reflected in the current volume. The BPS requirements for the supervision of qualified clinical psychologists have been tightened to make this an *essential* requirement throughout the career span for all clinical psychologists (BPS, 2006a). Moreover, as part of clinical governance arrangements, many NHS trusts and clinical services now have in place supervision policies and guidelines. All of this has led to an expectation on the part of newly qualified clinical psychologists that receiving clinical supervision will be just as much an essential part of their job as will be seeing clients. The ability to make use of supervision is one of the core competences that trainee clinical psychologists must acquire during their training and this further ensures that they are prepared for this important aspect of their work on qualification.

One final remark: We think that supervision should be acknowledged as a truly enjoyable experience. Of course we should identify required competences and hone evaluation tools, but it is important not to forget the restorative powers of supervision for both supervisee and supervisor.

Note

1 The development of the STAR framework is described in detail in Chapter 6 and referred to in several chapters of this book. This framework was originally named 'DROSS' (Development and Recognition of Supervisory Skills) and details can still be accessed on the website of that name: http://www.leeds.ac.uk/lihs/psychiatry/courses/dclin/cpd/DROSS/dross_welcome.htm

Chapter 2

Supervision and clinical psychology: History and development

Sue Wheeler and Delia Cushway

Introduction

This chapter sets the scene for the rest of this book by looking at the historical development of clinical supervision in both counselling and psychotherapy practice and the practice of clinical psychology. It traces the ways in which supervision has evolved from an informal to strictly formal process and the influence of politics and government initiatives on its practice. Finally there is a brief summary of the recent developments in the creation of defined supervision competencies.

Supervision for clinical psychologists, psychotherapists, counsellors and other psychological therapists is now accepted as a routine aspect of good practice not only during training but for the duration of practice. Clinical governance requirements have had a profound impact on the day-to-day work and professional development of everyone employed by the National Health Service. It is through clinical governance that organisations ensure good practice, by making individuals accountable for setting and monitoring performance standards. Butterworth (2001: 319) summarises the value of clinical supervision to clinical governance:

> Clinical supervision focuses on matters of central importance in the provision of safe and accountable practice. The concept of clinical supervision is focused on: organisational and management issues, clinical case-work, professional development, educational support, confidence building and interpersonal problems.

Clinical supervision is enshrined in protocols for safe effective practice but is also highly valued by practitioners as both professional and personal support.

Supervision is defined in many different ways depending on the professional context in which it is practised. Inskipp and Proctor (2001a: 1) promote the importance of the relationship between the supervisor and supervisee in their definition of supervision:

A working alliance between the supervisor and counsellor in which the counsellor can offer an account or recording of her work; reflect on it; receive feedback and where appropriate, guidance. The object of this alliance is to enable the counsellor to gain in ethical competence, confidence, compassion and creativity in order to give her best possible service to the client.

Bernard and Goodyear (1998, 2004) have been in the forefront of supervision practice and research for many years and they define it as follows:

supervision is an intervention provided by a more senior member of a profession to a more junior member of that same profession. This relationship is evaluative, extends over time, and has the simultaneous purposes of enhancing the professional functioning of the more junior person, monitoring the quality of professional services offered to the clients seen, and serving as a gatekeeper for those who are to enter the particular profession.

(Bernard and Goodyear, 2004: 8)

More recently, Milne (2007: 437), himself a clinical psychologist, has extracted a definition of supervision from empirical studies, which is as follows:

The formal provision, by approved supervisors, of a relationship-based education and training that is work-focused and which manages, supports, develops and evaluates the work of colleague/s. The main methods that supervisors use are corrective feedback on the supervisee's performance, teaching, and collaborative goal-setting. It therefore differs from related activities, such as mentoring and coaching, by incorporating an evaluative component. Supervision's objectives are 'normative', 'restorative' and 'formative'. These objectives could be measured by current instruments.

For many years the British Association for Counselling and Psychotherapy (BACP) has made supervision a requirement for all practising counsellors and therapists, regardless of their length of experience. *The Ethical Framework for Good Practice in Counselling and Psychotherapy* (BACP, 2010) clearly states that 'There is an ethical responsibility to use supervision for appropriate personal and professional support and development and to seek training and other opportunities for continuing professional development' (p. 2). In 2008, the British Psychological Society (BPS) published their *Generic Professional Practice Guidelines* (BPS, 2008a), which include a section on supervision. The document defines supervision principles, roles and responsibilities and provides guidance for the supervision of trainees. It states that 'for some psychologists, especially those working in therapeutic settings, supervision is an *essential* component of the psychologists' continuing professional development' (p. 16), an unequivocal statement that supervision is no longer optional.

In 2007, a major innovation for the National Health Service has been the Improving Access to Psychological Therapies (IAPT) initiative that has been funded by the government to ensure that National Institute for Clinical Excellence (NICE) guidelines related to anxiety and depression can be followed. The initiative involved training thousands of new therapists in cognitive behavioural therapy (many of whom were expected to be clinical psychologists) and in low intensity and self-help therapies (many of whom were expected to be graduate psychologists) and the provision of new psychological therapy services nationwide. Supervision has been seen as crucial to the success of the IAPT services and, to support good practice of supervision, guidance notes (Turpin and Wheeler, 2008) were issued to support the development and sustainability of supervision provision to all therapists employed in the services. The notes emphasise the importance of supervision and include strong statements such as 'Supervision is a key activity, which will determine the success of the IAPT programme.' The notes set a minimum standard for the provision of supervision for both qualified staff and trainees that includes weekly supervision for a minimum of 1 hour with a trained supervisor, with trainees also required to attend a 1½-hour group each week.

The United Kingdom Council for Psychotherapy (UKCP) includes the requirement for supervision in its minimum standards for training (UKCP, 2008) but makes no mention of supervision in its *Ethical Principles and Code of Professional Conduct* (UKCP, 2009), and there is no overall statement to suggest that supervision is a career-long requirement. To be fair, each member organisation of UKCP is required to have its own ethical code that may say more about supervision requirements. The Sherwood Institute in Nottingham for instance, in its *Codes for Graduate Members*, clearly states that: 'Supervision provides a challenging and supportive context for members to share their work, enhance their effectiveness, and protect the client. Members should not practise without appropriate levels of supervision' (Sherwood Psychotherapy Training Institute, 2010: 5).

Clinical supervision has an important role to play in safeguarding the interests of patients and clients, and is increasingly being recognised and valued by a variety of professional groups. Kilminster and Jolly (2000) see clinical supervision as having a vital role in postgraduate medical education, but lament the limited amount of medical literature addressing supervision. Townend (2005) surveyed health professionals who were also cognitive behavioural therapists about their use of supervision. Some reported that supervisors sometimes have difficulties understanding the professional context of their work, but overall found a lot of satisfaction with inter-professional supervision.

The practice of supervision has become enshrined in good practice guidelines for professional groups, organisations and services and is widely promoted as an essential aspect of safe and ethical psychological therapy. This position has been achieved step by step as one professional group has taken the lead and others have followed. The next section of this chapter traces the history of supervision in general and then as it has evolved in clinical psychology in particular. Finally, the chapter is concluded with a summary of the most recent development of defined competences for supervision.

History of supervision

The supervision of clinical practice has had a place in the training of analysts, therapists and social workers particularly, since almost the beginning of therapeutic practice (Jacobs, David and Meyer, 1995). In his report of the case of Little Hans, Freud describes how he worked with the boy's father, who was conducting the therapy with his son. Max Graf, the father, had his own ideas about the development of his son's neurosis, but Freud used the relationship with Max Graf to further develop his own views on childhood sexuality. The supervision that is described is chaotic and intrusive, and there is a lack of clarity about the relationships fostered between father, son and analyst/supervisor. When thinking about Freud and his work, it seems inevitable that other therapists would wish to consult him and discuss their cases. Much of the communication was through letters and personal meetings, nothing that resembles the formal structures of supervision that are to be found today. As the demand for training in psychoanalysis grew, it became more important to move beyond the old apprenticeship model. Formal training courses were developed by an organising body, with the development of a syllabus, admissions criteria, criteria for assessment and other systematic education procedures. In the early days of therapy training it was custom and practice for trainees to discuss their cases with their own analyst. In 1924, the Congress of the Berlin Institute published the requirement that candidates have at least 2 years of clinical work as part of their education. The idea of supervision arose as analysts became tired of hearing about their patients' patients. Karl Abraham, Max Eitingon and George Simmel were some of the first supervisors at the Institute, but others soon followed (Jacobs et al., 1995).

By the 1930s the practice of social work as a professional activity had become established, and case-work had a more therapeutic aim than is the case today. The clients' individual psychodynamics were seen to contribute towards their current difficulties and were the focus of attention. In 1936, Robinson described the supervisor's task, which was to pay attention to ways in which the client and the supervisees were relating, in order to understand more about the client's interpersonal difficulties, rather than focusing on the personal history of the supervisee, as analysts had previously. Kadushin (1968) and Mattinson (1977) developed their own ideas about supervision, within the context of social work, which, although not widely influential with other professions at the time, have continued to influence models of supervision in vogue today.

In 1987, Hess articulated ways in which the practice of therapy and supervision are different and require different skills. He asserted that supervisors must be good therapists, but they need training to be good supervisors, as the focus of the endeavours is different. During the past four decades, interest in supervision has grown. In their classic text, *The Teaching and Learning of Psychotherapy*, Ekstein and Wallerstein (1972: 12) describe the practice of supervision:

> The supervisor is directly related to the student but has a quasi-indirect relationship to the patient. On one hand his responsibility is to teach psychotherapeutic skills to the student, but there is an additional responsibility in maintaining clinical standards and seeing that patients benefit from the service which is being extended.

With the exception of the work of Janet Mattinson, who worked with the Tavistock Clinic in London, the development of supervision in Britain seems to have followed on from research and practice developed in the USA. Many models of supervision have been derived by American researchers (Fleming, 1953; Hogan, 1964; Holloway, 1995; Litrell, Lee-Bordin and Lorenz, 1979; Loganbill, Hardy and Delworth, 1982; Stoltenberg, 1981), and it is only in recent years that British texts have appeared to provide models of supervision for British audiences. In 1989, Hawkins and Shohet published their classic text, *Supervision in the Helping Professions*, which offered a process model of supervision. Page and Wosket (2001) followed on with their cyclical model of supervision. Carroll (1996) offered an alternative model of supervision emphasising the seven generic tasks of supervision: creating the learning relationship, teaching, counselling, monitoring professional/ethical issues, evaluating, consulting and administration. Meanwhile, Inskipp and Proctor (2001a,b) have developed the work of Hawkins and Shohet and have been writing about and teaching supervision for two decades.

In a recent systematic review of the impact of clinical supervision on counsellors and therapists, their practice and their clients (Wheeler and Richards, 2007), over 1000 research articles related to supervision were reviewed, of which few had British authors. Hence when addressing the topic of supervision in Britain reference is always being made to American research literature, which informs our practice. Supervision is still predominantly only a requirement for counselling and psychotherapy trainees in the USA, hence most research literature refers to supervision with trainees.

History of supervision in clinical psychology

'It can be argued that the profession of clinical psychology in the UK has only recently become concerned with the role of the supervisor and the practice of supervision' (Fleming, 2004: 74). We probably need to look back at the history of the profession to see why this might be the case.

It can be seen from the previous section that the roots of supervision of clinical practice lay firmly within the psychoanalytic tradition. This may provide a first clue as to the relatively late uptake of routine supervision of their clinical work by qualified clinical psychologists. In the late 1950s and early 1960s clinical psychology struggled to free itself from the psycho-analytic stranglehold in order to become scientifically respectable. The adoption of the 'Scientist-Practitioner Model' has been key to the early development of clinical psychology. With the advent of radical behaviour-ism and its emphasis on the strictly observable, there arose a bitter feud and a split between adherents of the behavioural and psychoanalytic traditions, which still continues to this day in some quarters. Supervision was, at this time, associated only with the psychoanalytic tradition.

Clinical psychology has always been inextricably linked with the NHS and another important aspect of clinical psychology is its love/hate rela-tionship with the medical model and, in particular, psychiatry. Like psy-chiatrists and medical practitioners, psychologists saw themselves, when qualified, as autonomous practitioners. Thus, clinical supervision was seen by medics and clinical psychologists alike as only for those undergoing training. Autonomous practitioners were in no need of supervision. In this respect the different meanings of supervision and what is implied by it have done a disservice to clinical supervision as we know it today and as defined earlier in this chapter.

Since the advent of formal training courses in the late 1950s and 1960s there has been supervision of clinical psychologists in training, on their clinical placements within the NHS, by more senior qualified clinical psy-chologists. Trainees see patients/clients under supervision and the respon-sible clinician is the qualified clinical psychology supervisor. Historically, clinical supervision of trainees was more like case management with little attention given to process. Similarly there was limited impetus and scarce resources to promote the training of supervisors until relatively recently.

In the 21st century there has been a change in emphasis on the import-ance of clinical supervision influenced by several factors. There have been important drivers from within the healthcare system. In the 1990s there were a number of highly publicised failures in quality of care, largely within the medical profession. This has had two important consequences. First, there has been an emphasis on clinical governance, which aims to promote good practice and accountability. Clinical supervision for health profes-sionals is one way of improving quality and increasing accountability

(Fleming, 2004). Second, the quality failures within the medical sector led to a challenging of the notion of autonomous professionals, whom, once trained, were considered trained for life with no additional training or supervision. Within the NHS there has been an increased emphasis on Continuing Professional Development (CPD) for all health professionals. This was a British Psychological Society (BPS) requirement for practice (Golding and Gray, 2006) and is, of course, a Health Professions Council (HPC) requirement for professional registration (HPC, 2008a). There has thus been a growing requirement for clinical psychologists to demonstrate their ongoing CPD and their proficiency in increasingly important aspects of their job, such as supervision. There has also been a growing demand from within the NHS for clinical psychologists to act as supervisors to other mental health professionals.

Historically, clinical psychology trainers, who were responsible for providing training for clinical supervisors for their trainees, sometimes found it difficult to fill their supervisor training days, which tended to be more task and less process oriented. In particular, some clinical psychologists, often those who were quite senior and questionably sometimes more in need of supervisor training, were reluctant to attend. However, within the last 10 years and partly for the reasons outlined above, there has been a growing enthusiasm and demand for supervisory training. This has also been helped with the addition of supervision as a recognised task built into the 'Agenda for Change' grading structure. Many clinical psychologists have looked to their local training courses to provide increased training. Thus, the important contribution of a small group of clinical trainers, notably Dave Green, Ian Fleming and Linda Steen among others, was to establish national learning outcomes for clinical psychologists' supervisor training. The formation of the working group STAR (Supervisor Training and Recognition) and the work it produced has finally led to the formation of the BPS Register of Applied Psychology Practice Supervisors (RAPPS). The developments in supervisor training and accreditation are described elsewhere in this book.

There has also been an increased openness to a range of theoretical models within the profession that have influenced the growth of supervision. 'The range of theoretical models of therapy, and associated practice, have increased beyond imagination compared with 30 years ago' (Hall, Lavender and Llewelyn, 2003: 39). Notwithstanding the recent boost IAPT has given the cognitive behavioural perspective, which has always had a prominent place in clinical psychology, there has been an increasing interest and growth in mainstream clinical psychology of systemic approaches and integrative models such as cognitive analytic therapy. There have always been some psychoanalytically trained clinical psychologists, largely influenced by the Tavistock Clinic, who have stressed the importance of ongoing supervision, as well as those with a humanistic or personal construct theory orientation. Within all of these therapeutic orientations attention is paid to relationship and process issues and ongoing supervision is regarded as an essential part of the therapeutic process. As clinical training courses have broadened their therapeutic perspective, so reflective practice has become more integral, hand in hand with supervision (Cushway and Knibbs, 2004).

Another important factor within the profession has been the growth of reflective practice, with its emphasis on supervision as a way of helping the practitioner to reflect on self, other and process (Stedmon and Dallos, 2009). This increased emphasis led by the training community on personal and professional development, together with the acknowledgement of stress within the profession (Cushway and Tyler, 1996) and taking care of the person of the therapist as the 'instrument of therapy', have all been important. A special issue of *Clinical Psychology* (2003) had as its focus reviewing the use of reflection within clinical practice and discussing the development of reflective practice through training and supervision (Cushway and Gatherer, 2003). Gillmer and Marckus (2003) use the term 'personal and professional development' (PPD) to refer 'to that part of the curriculum that is dedicated to developing in trainees a capability to critically and systematically reflect on the work–self interface. This process is directed towards fostering personal awareness and resilience' (p. 23). Also within this special issue, Stedmon et al. (2003) present the concept of 'reflecting on reflections', and propose that this process 'forms the basis of a continuous cycle of critical evaluation of one's practice' (p. 31). It can thus be seen how clinical supervision, which is an important feature of this 'continuous cycle of critical evaluation of one's practice', came to occupy a more central role within the profession of clinical psychology. There has also been an accompanying shift in emphasis from quantitative to qualitative research methodologies on process, personal meaning and experience. These factors have all helped to foster recognition of the importance of supervision within the profession.

Alongside this, the number of clinical psychology trainees on courses grew steadily but slowly until around the millennium, when there was a rapid expansion for a few years in the number of training places funded. This had the effect of putting pressure on the number of training placements and supervisors available. This, in turn, may have fuelled the developing interest in the process and methods of supervision. Trainees who were on placements with psychodynamic supervisors often expressed more satisfaction with their supervision because of its emphasis on relationships and process issues. Trainees' demands for good supervision have also been influential.

This burgeoning interest in clinical process supervision, as opposed to case management, led to some clinical psychologists looking to their psychological therapy colleagues in other professions. The fact that the BACP has made supervision a requirement for all practising counsellors and therapists has not gone unnoticed by clinical psychologists and many have turned to the counselling and psychotherapy professions for supervisor training, for example courses run on the Hawkins and Shohet process model (Hawkins and Shohet, 2000). Thus, the counselling and psychotherapy professions, together with the growth of a British literature and models of supervision, have led to the development of supervision as a discipline. This has been influential in the growth and recognition of supervision for all qualified clinical psychologists.

Clinical psychologists have put considerable pressure on the BPS in recent years to create a register for supervisor recognition, which has been implemented from 2010. The directory will be an encouragement for clinical psychologists to undergo training in supervision and to develop their supervisory skills in the knowledge that such skills will be recognised and valued.

Recent developments in the definition of supervision competencies

There are numerous research studies that have sought to determine the qualities and experience that make for a competent supervisor. Falender and Shafranske (2004) have led the field in developing a competence-based approach to both supervisor training and supervision with the publication of their book that is based on theory and research. The book is a rich resource for training and evaluating supervisors, although, as with many American publications on the subject of supervision, the emphasis is on trainees. The authors have reported on their research into the best and worst supervisors that trainees have experienced. Factors that distinguished good supervisors from those perceived as bad included a capacity for conflict resolution, facilitating disclosure, paying attention to culture and gender and providing secure containment.

The various perspectives on competent supervision point to personal characteristics, the capacity to form a good working alliance with the supervisee, making links between supervision and therapeutic work, contextual or cultural issues that impact on supervision and the supervisor, theoretical orientation and the knowledge base of the supervisor, as well as issues such as age, gender and experience. Weaks (2002), a UK-based researcher, investigated what supervisees think makes for good supervision. The most important factor to emerge was the relationship between supervisor and supervisee and three key constituents were identified as 'core conditions' necessary for an effective supervision relationship to become established: equality, safety and challenge. Shanfield et al. (1992) assessed the behaviour of supervisors and found a high level of agreement about the use of empathy, focus on the supervisees' immediate experiences and making in-depth comments that facilitate understanding of the client. In a study involving the supervision of nurses who were asked what they found most helpful about their supervisors, it was the ability to form supportive relationships that was most important.

Having relevant knowledge/clinical skills, expressing a commitment to providing supervision and having good listening skills were also important characteristics of their supervisor. They viewed their supervisor as a role model, someone they felt inspired them, whom they looked up to and had a high regard for their clinical practice and knowledge base (Sloan, 1999). A British study carried out by Cushway and Knibbs (2004) explored trainees' and supervisors' perceptions of helpful and unhelpful aspects of supervision. Their analysis of two sets of data indicated broad agreement with the American studies, particularly in respect of helpful factors in supervision. Broadly these fall into person-oriented aspects and task-oriented aspects. Following factor analysis of their survey data, Cushway and Knibbs proposed two bi-polar dimensions of supervisory practice: the first described the relationship running from 'establishes good rapport' through to 'disinterested and remote'; the second is more task oriented and is described as running from 'competent and skilled' through to 'incompetent'.

In 2008, in response to the investment in supervision advocated through the IAPT programme, Roth and Pilling were commissioned to produce a document that summarised the competences needed to supervise psychological therapies. This resulted in a competence framework for the supervision of psychological therapies (Roth and Pilling, 2008a).

The competence framework for supervision was developed based on the principles that had been applied to the development of a competence framework for cognitive behavioural therapy (DH, 2007a). The guiding principle was to derive a list of competences from empirical research and manuals used in randomised controlled trials. Given the dearth of manualised supervision studies, review articles, text books such as that produced by Falender and Shafranske (2004) and other discursive literature were also consulted. An expert reference group of practitioners, many of whom were clinical psychologists, with substantial experience of providing supervision and supervisor training were recruited and met to debate both the structure of the competence framework and its content. The rigour with which the exercise was conducted has resulted in a comprehensive document that has gained considerable respect and credibility.

Falender and Shafranske (2004) underpin their competence framework with four superordinate values that they regard as essential to the supervision process: integrity-in-relationship, ethical values-based practice, appreciation of diversity and science-informed practice. In contrast the Roth and Pilling framework has four overarching domains: generic supervision competences, specific supervision competences, applications of supervision to specific models/contexts and metacompetences (Figure 2.1). The first domain includes the generic skills that would be necessary to be an effective supervisor in any setting and with any group of therapists. The specific competences domain includes the ability to help the supervisee practise specific skills, to directly observe the supervisee, apply standards of

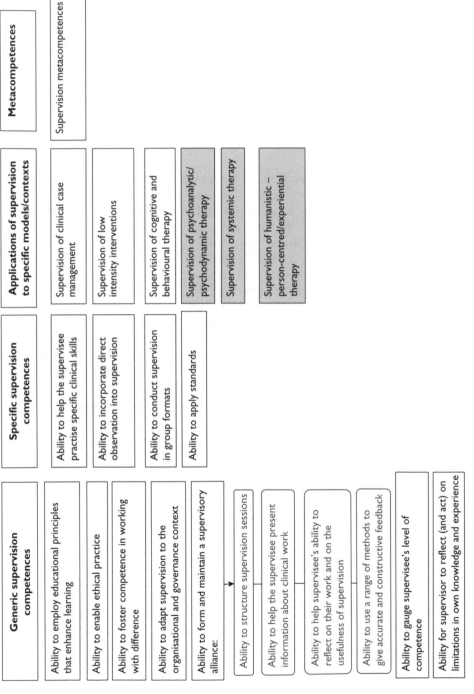

Generic supervision competences

Ability to employ educational principles that enhance learning

Ability to enable ethical practice

Ability to foster competence in working with difference

Ability to adapt supervision to the organisational and governance context

Ability to form and maintain a supervisory alliance:

Ability to structure supervision sessions

Ability to help the supervisee present information about clinical work

Ability to help supervisee's ability to reflect on their work and on the usefulness of supervision

Ability to use a range of methods to give accurate and constructive feedback

Ability to gauge supervisee's level of competence

Ability for supervisor to reflect (and act) on limitations in own knowledge and experience

Specific supervision competences

Ability to help the supervisee practise specific clinical skills

Ability to incorporate direct observation into supervision

Ability to conduct supervision in group formats

Ability to apply standards

Applications of supervision to specific models/contexts

Supervision of clinical case management

Supervision of low intensity interventions

Supervision of cognitive and behavioural therapy

Supervision of psychoanalytic/psychodynamic therapy

Supervision of systemic therapy

Supervision of humanistic – person-centred/experiential therapy

Metacompetences

Supervision metacompetences

Figure 2.1 Supervision competences framework (from Roth and Pilling, 2008d).

practice and conduct supervision in a group setting. Applying supervision to specific models and contexts includes sections related specifically to the IAPT programme as well as supervision of specific theoretical orientations. The final domain, metacompetences, highlights the need to adapt to working with complex issues using experience and professional judgement. The supervision competences framework is a comprehensive document that can be adapted to provide the curriculum for a supervisor training programme and potentially as a means of assessing whether all the competences have been acquired.

Conclusion

Supervision has evolved and changed over the past century and is moulded to the needs of professions, services and clinicians, as well as being incorporated into ethical frameworks and clinical governance protocols. Fashions and professional requirements, as well as government legislation and managerialism, have shaped requirements and mode of delivery as well as dictating content and process in some extreme cases. Supervision has evolved from an ad hoc discussion of clients between sessions with clients to the existence of a competence framework for supervision that details every aspect of supervisory behaviour. Some might question whether this is progress or regression, depending on their therapeutic theories, values and beliefs. It begs the question of whether supervision, like therapy, can be manualised and controlled or whether such attempts rob it of its spontaneity and integrity. However we view it, supervision is now institutionalised and a requirement for all.

Summary

- Supervision has been adopted as good practice to ensure safe and ethical therapeutic work with clients by the clinical psychology profession and other professional groups offering psychological therapies.
- Supervision has become more accepted and integral to training and service delivery in the realm of clinical psychology as diverse approaches to psychological therapy have influenced and encouraged reflective practice.
- Supervision has been enshrined in government guidelines for services as essential.
- A scientifically derived supervision competence framework, informed by research evidence, is freely available that provides detailed guidance on how supervision should be practised.

Chapter 3

The impact of recent NHS policy on supervision in clinical psychology

Graham Turpin

Introduction

In 2002 Joyce Scaife, Pete Rajan and I completed our chapter on enhancing NHS training placements within clinical psychology for the first edition of this book. We started by reviewing what we considered to be significant changes both to the NHS and also to the profession in the preceding decade: the emergence of workforce planning for the professions other than just medicine both within the NHS and also within the profession itself, NHS contracting for education and training, the move to 3-year doctoral training based solely within universities and a succession of reviews conducted by both the British Psychological Society and the Department of Health about the future standing of the profession and the growing demand for psychological healthcare. These themes continued throughout the chapter, where we confidently asserted the ever-increasing demand for clinical psychology services and posed the major issues addressed then by our chapter: how training throughput on courses could be optimised and how the bottleneck to expansion posed by limited clinical placement capacity could be overcome.

We reported on a series of surveys that sought to measure placement capacity across different areas of clinical psychology and to identify what psychologists and managers perceived as the obstacles to increasing further capacity and the number of trainees supervised. Factors identified were staff shortages in various specialities, reluctance of some staff to supervise and associated negative attitudes to training and supervision, lack of supervisor training, lack of physical and administrative resources to support trainees, poor coordination of supervisory resources within services, etc. Possible solutions and recommendations were greater flexibility around defining placements and a shift from pre-defined speciality placements to assessing clinical competence across placements, formalising expectations for supervision through job descriptions, greater support for training from senior NHS management, better physical resources, better integration of the trainee's experience within placements and the university in order to enhance clinical learning, training psychologists from overseas and ways of quality assuring placements using an accreditation process.

It is interesting to reflect on where we had got to by October 2002 when the chapter was written and the future developments that have now taken place. As we will see, certain themes continue, such as meeting the growing demand for psychological healthcare, concerns about placement and supervision capacity, quality assurance, ensuring buy-in of qualified staff and senior managers, the trade-off between direct clinical activity and time out to supervise other staff, the provision of supervisor training, the pressure for better physical and administrative resources and a focus around competence. However, the context in which these issues have evolved is now dramatically different; both clinical psychology services and the training community are faced with a very different landscape at the end of this decade compared with that which existed at the beginning of this century.

What are these dramatic changes? Some quick examples would be the emergence of the applied psychologies (i.e. clinical, counselling, forensic and health psychology) within the NHS, designing services from the patient's or user's perspective and based around care pathways, an emphasis on multi-professional workforce development as opposed to uni-professional service delivery, the emergence of assistant practitioner grades within the NHS, etc. These have all been supported by a raft of policy initiatives – National Service Frameworks and NHS reforms, New Ways of Working, changes to the delivery of community-based healthcare and social care, the Darzi reforms – all of which will be reviewed and referenced later in this chapter.

The purpose of this chapter, therefore, will be to document the changes and policy developments that have happened since the first edition of this book and to examine their impacts on supervision. The impact will be evaluated by assessing the current status of supervision, requirements for supervisor training and accreditation and the relationship between super-vision, on the one hand, and both trainee and service development and performance, on the other. We will deal first with developments within the profession and then move on to look at the significant developments out-side of clinical psychology more generally within the NHS, and particularly with reference to mental health services and ultimately focusing on the Improving Access to Psychological Therapies (IAPT) programme and the pivotal role that supervision has in developing these services.

Developments within applied psychology and their impact on supervision

To a degree, the developments within the profession have been more con-sistent with the direction of travel navigated in the first edition of this book.

One challenge had been the emergence of the other applied psychologies, such as counselling and health psychology, within the NHS. Despite the obvious interdivisional rivalries, applied psychology has been accepted as an overarching construct both within and outwith the profession. Although by no means perfect, there has been a greater interchange between the applied psychologies and especially through the Standing Committee for Psychologists in Health and Social Care, which is a committee of the British Psychological Society (BPS). This resulted in a number of cross-disciplinary conferences (e.g. Wainwright, 2004) and also combined meetings both with the Department of Health/Care Services Improvement Partnership and also the Workforce Review Team responsible for workforce planning within the NHS. Indeed, workforce planning concerned itself with *all* the applied psychologies but unfortunately this focused attention did not result, other than some developments in Scotland (NHS Education for Scotland, 2009), in the desired outcome that the training of other applied psychologies might be funded and commissioned alongside clinical psychology by NHS/SHA training commissioners. Further discussions about cross-divisional training also took place within the context of New Ways of Working, which we will deal with later. Suggestions were mooted about a core applied psychology training model (Kinderman, 2005) that might then lay the foundations for more specialised training in clinical psychology, counselling, health psychology, etc. Agreements were also reached by the National Assessors for Consultant Psychology Posts within the NHS that applied psychology posts should be advertised according to the competences required, and that for some posts this might mean that suitable applicants might come from a variety of applied psychology backgrounds and be judged suitable for a single job role.

Although these developments have a trajectory heading towards some degree of merger across the traditional BPS Divisions of Applied Psychology (see Turpin, 2009), they have been stopped in their tracks for the time being by the government's decision to introduce the statutory regulation of practitioner or registered psychologists through the Health Professions Council (HPC). To a degree, this will inevitably slow down any impetus for BPS Divisions of Applied Psychology to merge, especially since the threshold standards of qualification have been set differently across the seven applied areas.

The HPC requires all approved training courses to offer supervision to ensure the safe practice of *students* but their definitions and requirements for supervision for both trainees and qualified staff are not at all well developed. Indeed, a recent membership enquiry as to whether ongoing clinical supervision of qualified staff was a requirement for HPC registrants resulted in the following response being posted on the Division of Clinical Psychology (DCP) Managers' website:

> We recognise that ongoing clinical supervision is important for practitioner psychologists but we cannot enforce it because it is not within the power of our legislation, and we must also ensure that the standards we set apply to all the professions we regulate.
>
> (Policy Officer, Policy & Standards Department, HPC, July 2009)

It is surprising at this time that the requirement to seek out, receive and use supervision appropriately is not within the generic standards of proficiency of HPC registrants. Access to good quality supervision is frequently identified as a critical requirement for safeguarding patient safety within medical, nursing and social care practice (Leape, Berwick and Bates, 2002; Shajanania, Fletcher and Saint, 2006) and appears to be a curious omission from the HPC's otherwise rigorous requirements.

In contrast, the BPS has recently issued cross-divisional *Generic Professional Practice Guidelines* (BPS, 2008a) and specific guidance within clinical psychology (BPS, 2005), and other divisions of applied psychology, around requirements for the supervision not only of qualified staff but also trainees and psychology assistants. These guidance documents distinguish between the different functions and models of supervision, the process of supervision, supervision contracts, confidentiality, dual relationships, aspects of record keeping and the legalities of the supervisory relationship, to name but a few of the important topics on offer. This guidance also refers to cross-divisional supervision between different applied psychologists and their trainees, which also mirrors some of the clinical and managerial supervision arrangements that exist in practice within the NHS. It stresses the importance of all qualified staff receiving regular clinical supervision and this *was* also reflected in the revised *Code of Ethics and Conduct* of the Society (BPS, 2006b), a document that now has less impact and meaning given that the regulation of practitioner psychologists is now through the HPC.

A topic that was discussed in the first edition was the importance of supervisor competence and the role of supervisor training courses and accreditation in building up a competent supervision workforce. As we will see later, competences have become increasingly more important since they were identified in the first edition mainly as a means to increase placement flexibility. Clinical psychology training has embraced the competence model across the board and it now helps to inform the design of the curriculum, the nature of placement experience and also the methods of monitoring progress and assessment. These changes are documented in the latest version of the BPS accreditation criteria for clinical psychology programmes (BPS, 2008b) and are also reflected in publications within the USA (Kenkel and Peterson, 2010). The importance of competence has also been extended to supervision both within the UK (Roth and Pilling, 2008a–d) and also in the USA (Falender and Shafranske, 2004, 2008), and there has been a specific move to identify competences underpinning good supervision and devising methods of training to achieve these. Although most healthcare professions stress the importance of training and competence, many have shied away from supervisor accreditation since it has the potential to alienate some supervisors and limit the supervisory capacity within the system. Nevertheless, the BPS has been moving towards standardising supervisor training, particularly for clinical psychologists, through the intervention of the work of the STAR group (Fleming and Green, 2007; http://www.leeds.ac.uk/lihs/psychiatry/courses/dclin/cpd/DROSS/drossproducts.htm) and has established a formal method of recognising supervision skills within clinical psychology (http://www.bps.org.uk/professional-development/directory-of-supervisors/directory-of-supervisors_home.cfm). In addition, the DCP has supported the development of evidence-based supervision training developed by Derek Milne (Milne, 2009). These topics are covered in greater detail in Chapter 9.

A further development from within the profession, which relates to supervision, is the complex subject of career frameworks and the role of assistant and associate psychologists. Ever since the Trethowan Report (Trethowan, 1977) that set out the structure of clinical psychology within the NHS, there has been recognition that the large numbers of high quality psychology graduates graduating each year might contribute to the delivery of psychological services alongside trained clinical psychologists. As a result of high vacancy rates in the 1980s and 1990s, many recent graduates were provided with 1-year psychology assistant contracts under the supervision of a qualified clinical psychologist. Indeed by 2004 it was estimated that the number of graduate psychology assistants exceeded the number of clinical psychologists in training (BPS, 2004). Although the BPS had offered good practice guidance about their employment and supervision (BPS, 2007a), generally speaking these young graduates had no formal or recognised training once in post as a psychology assistant. From various quarters from within and outside the profession, it was suggested that these 'assistant practitioner roles' ought to be more formally incorporated into the profession. It was also suggested that a more senior assistant or clinical associate role might also be developed, and several pilots took place in the North of England (Lavender and Hope, 2007) and in Scotland (NHS Education for Scotland, 2009).

The driver for these developments was the recognition that the demand for psychological healthcare would always outstrip the supply of trained clinical psychologists despite the level of investment. Practical limitations, such as the size of the current workforce and the availability of supervision, would always limit the numbers produced annually. Up until the end of the decade there had been major investments in clinical psychology training (Turpin and Llewelyn, 2009), which resulted essentially in a trebling of annual training places from around 200 to almost 600 trainees. Unfortunately, this momentum was lost in the last few years and in some regions of England there has been a reduction in places due to financial stringencies. Nevertheless, the Workforce Review Team (http://www.wrt. nhs.uk/) has forecast consistently and recommended to Strategic Health Authorities (SHAs) around a 15% increase in the numbers of trained clinical psychologists in order to keep up with demand. Such increases, however, have not been deemed affordable by many NHS/SHA commissioners, and this has led many to suggest alternative solutions such as assistants in the psychology profession. The full story again is related to New Ways of Working, which will be addressed later.

In summary, a view from *within* the profession is that clinical psychology is healthy (more than 8000 clinical psychologists working within the NHS), it is in demand, it is now regulated by HPC, models of education and training are well established and have adopted a competence model, training quality is high and benchmarked at the doctoral level, supervision has been earmarked as essential for continuing practice and the training and accreditation of supervisors has become a reality. There have also been some major challenges, such as the New Ways of Working (NWW) and the IAPT programmes.

General policy developments in the NHS

Before picking up the challenges described above, it is worth reflecting on some general changes and policy initiatives within the NHS. The first crucial point to note is that there are now several NHSs within the UK, given that each devolved nation has a responsibility for planning and implementing healthcare. This has resulted in some very different health-care policies emerging across the nations of the UK, different legislative frameworks, different staff being trained, different sets of clinical guidelines being implemented, etc. Indeed, within the field of supervision, NHS Education for Scotland has been leading developments around supervision training and education (http://www.nes.scot.nhs.uk/mentalhealth/work/ #psych). I shall focus mainly on England since it is the policies of the Department of Health implemented within England that I am most familiar with. Where there are differences in Scotland, Wales or Northern Ireland, I will attempt to highlight them in the discussion.

There are also a number of policy trends that are worth identifying since these have acted as major drivers for change. Many of these developments were highlighted in the NHS Reform paper (DH, 2005a). This identified four main drivers to enhance the quality of the patient experience, which was at the heart of the reforms:

1   'Value for money', which also included the notion of money following the patient and the costing of care packages and interventions as reflected by 'Payment by Results'.

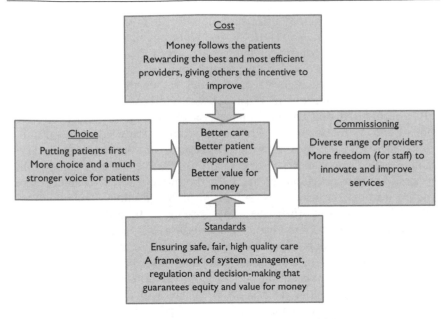

Figure 3.1 Organising principles of NHS reform (from DH, 2005a).

2   The development of commissioning and a separation from service commissioners and providers. The latter would include a greater diversity of providers from within the NHS but also the third and private sectors. Services would be contracted for and providers would need to prove their 'contestability'.

3   'User perspective and choice', which should inform commissioning decisions based on the needs and aspirations of local communities.

4   'Standards' to ensure that clinical governance and regulatory mechanisms were in place to ensure safe and effective practice.

These main drivers for reform are illustrated in Figure 3.1. Many of these drivers are still reflected by the new coalition government and the White Paper (DH, 2010a), which also emphasises developing a tariff for talking therapies, greater patient choice and involvement, greater diversity of provision and commissioning directly from GP consortia, amongst other policy developments.

There has also been a steady shift from centralised control by the Department of Health, as once represented by national plans, frameworks and targets, to more locally planned and commissioned health and local care. Local commissioning currently involves a collaborative of Primary Care Commissioners, Specialist Mental Health Commissioners and Local Authorities. This has led to the establishment of an internal market with a variety of potential providers (including private and third sector) chosen or contested on the basis of price and quality, and encapsulated through *World Class Commissioning* (DH, 2008a). Once again, the new White Paper (DH, 2010) will see continued involvement from local government, especially with regard to local public health policies, together with greater involvement of GPs and local communities rather than existing commissioners such as Primary Care Trusts (PCTs) or SHAs.

It is recognised that commissioning as a process is very much in development and many commissioners require greater knowledge and training around mental health. It is important, therefore, that they are informed and recognise the importance of supervision for delivering safe and quality services. Another development has been the move towards evidence-based practice through the widespread adoption of NICE clinical guidelines and technology appraisals (http://www.nice.org.uk/). Indeed, many of the standards of the new Care Quality Commission will be based upon NICE clinical guidance, which will place greater pressure on individual services to offer evidence-based interventions. This has also been coupled with a greater emphasis on measuring patient-recorded outcomes, as emphasised within the Darzi Report (Darzi, 2008). There will also be a continuing trajectory from hospital care to community provision (DH, 2006), with greater integration across health and social care, plus an emphasis on personalisation (DH, 2009a) and patients becoming responsible for making choices about their own packages of care and who might provide for them. Similarly, there is also the question of the cost and budgeting for packages of care and the proposed introduction of 'Payment by Results' into mental health services (DH, 2010b). These policy developments could continue to march off the page but I have highlighted those that seem particularly relevant now, although by the time of publication it may be that there is another government in place, and clinicians and civil servants will be eagerly awaiting the emergence of yet further new ideas and directions.

The developments described above set the context for the type of NHS that the profession of clinical psychology has inhabited over the last few years. They have clearly influenced the profession but perhaps have not had any direct impact on supervision per se. A summary of the relevance of psychology to the new NHS reform agenda was published with the summary guide to the NWW publication on IAPT (Lavender and Hope, 2007) and is reproduced as Figure 3.2. Governance and greater accountability is clearly a theme and links partly to some forms of supervision, but until recently the importance of supervision for improving the quality of service delivery had not been stressed.

Specific policy developments impacting on supervision

There have been several developments pertaining to the NHS in England, and these have an emphasis on mental health services.. The two main

POTENTIAL CONTRIBUTION OF APPLIED PSYCHOLOGISTS TO IMPLEMENTING NHS REFORM

Value for money
- Ability to assess and formulate complex problems
- Effective therapies and therapists
- Therapy innovations and service redesign
- Working through other staff (nurses, GPs, OTs, graduate workers, psychology assistants, etc.) to broaden delivery of therapies
- Leading and disseminating psychological knowledge within teams
- Education and training of psychologists and other staff through the organisation
- Offsetting costs of psychological burden and unexplained symptoms within medical and inpatient care
- Attending to the psychological needs of staff and organisations
- Advising on HR issues

User perspective and choice
- Knowledge of wide range of therapies and therapists
- Working with users to promote understanding of range of psychological approaches in order to achieve informed choice
- Promoting well-being, psycho-education and self-help
- Providing individually tailored psychological formulations
- Helping organisations to understand users' needs and their social context
- Championing a psychosocial understanding of both physical and mental health
- Supporting user agendas and promoting social inclusion

IMPROVED CLIENT EXPERIENCE
(Health, well-being and functioning of individuals, families and communities)

Commissioning
- Advising commissioners on needs assessments, effective interventions and outcomes
- Knowledge of a wide range of psychological interventions, not restricted to a single therapeutic modality
- Knowledge of psychological issues and disorders across the age range
- Integrating mental and physical health needs
- Providing a bio-psychosocial approach
- Helping to understand health issues and impacts within families
- Helping to understand health issues from a community perspective
- Addressing user perspectives, recovery and social inclusion

Standards
- Knowledge of wide range of interventions and competencies
- Knowledge of professional accreditation
- Expertise around clinical governance and risk
- Audit and service evaluation
- Promoting ethical practice
- Expertise around supervision and training supervisors
- Providing specialist supervision to other staff (e.g. psychiatrists, nurse specialists, counsellors, etc.)
- Critical thinkers and problem-solvers
- Flexibility in roles and working across care groups and health problems
- Ability to think organisationally and to support other staff
- Supporting Trust Boards in delivering business plans
- Ensuring that standards and knowledge are regularly updated through R&D

Figure 3.2 Potential contribution of applied psychologists to implementing NHS reform (from Lavender and Hope, 2007).

developments that we will focus on are the NWW and the IAPT pro-
grammes, both established under the guidance of the National Institute of
Mental Health England (NIMHE) and the Care Services Improvement
Partnership (CSIP).

New Ways of Working (NWW)

As discussed previously, the overall capacity for education and training
within clinical psychology is unlikely to keep up with the demand for
services. There have been a variety of recent responses within the NHS to
this challenge. Training more psychologists is one solution, which was
strongly advocated by the BPS and implemented during the last decade
(BPS, 1995a). The introduction of assistant practitioners has also been
suggested and this is linked to initiatives from within the NHS workforce to
examine 'skills mix solutions' whereby a tier of less extensively trained and
paid staff is included within the workforce.

The NWW's first challenge was to meet the workforce shortfalls within
psychiatry, which had resulted in, amongst other things: staff shortages,
poor recruitment into training and large numbers of expensive locum posts
upon which services were becoming increasingly dependent. The first NWW
Report was published in 2005, jointly with the Royal College of Psychiatrists (DH, 2005b). Although supervision was not directly touched on,
the report did break new ground by examining the assumed supervisory
and clinical responsibility position of psychiatrists over the work of other
professionals within the team. Indeed, the issue of medical/consultant
responsibility and accountability of other healthcare professionals
continues to be a difficult area (Pidd, 2009; Vize, 2009).

Following the success of NWW for Psychiatry, several other NWW
projects were established throughout mental health services, including the
allied health professions, pharmacy, social work, etc., but not specifically
nursing (DH, 2007b; www.newwaysofworking.org.uk/). Generally, these
project reports describe developing new roles and responsibilities, more
flexible working practices, new opportunities for training in order to
broaden therapeutic competences and an overarching career framework for
all staff who contribute to the delivery of mental health services.

The BPS also participated in a NWW for Applied Psychologists project,
which examined several important issues identified for the profession,
including education and training models, new roles including assistants
and associates, career frameworks, leadership and management, working
in teams, new mental health legislation and widening access to psychological therapies. All these reports, together with the overarching report,
are available on the BPS website (http://www.bps.org.uk/the-society/
organisation-and-governance/professional-practice-board/ppb-activities/
new_ways_of_working_for_applied_psychologists.cfm; http://www.bps.

org.uk/publications/publications_home.cfm). They identify some key issues and future developments shared across the applied psychologies, some aspects of which have been taken up following publication of the NWW Report, particularly around leadership, team working and IAPT. As Lavender (2009) comments, the NWW for Applied Psychologists happened at a time when some significant external factors impacted on the profession, and these included IAPT, the imminent regulation of practitioner psychologists by the HPC, the emergence of NHS Foundation Trusts in England and a more business-orientated NHS. It is likely that these issues also impacted on the take-up and implementation of the NWW for Applied Psychology reports. The introduction of a Stepped Care model through IAPT has picked up on many of the recommendations of the New Roles group about assistant practitioners and the utilisation of the large numbers of psychology graduates. It is likely that it will be some time into the future that the full impact of NWW for Applied Psychologists will be felt and evaluated. Finally, it should also be mentioned that the last NWW project concerned psychological therapies and has now been published at the time of writing (http://www.iapt.nhs.uk/wp-content/uploads/nww4pt-overarching-report-final.pdf). We will review the progress of this project when we refer to IAPT in the following section.

Improving Access to Psychological Therapies (IAPT)

Closely associated with NWW has been the IAPT programme. The origins of this programme lie with Lord Layard's hypotheses about the availability of psychological therapies (Layard, 2005b, 2006). The first of these concerned the limited availability of NICE-recommended psychological therapies to people consulting their GPs for anxiety and depression. The second was Layard's singular argument that many people with common mental health problems might also experience employment problems and eventually could become unemployed and dependent upon life-long disability benefits. Combining these two arguments, Layard persuaded the government to fund a major investment in improving access to psychological therapies. Essentially, it was argued that increasing access to effective psychological interventions would result in more people being adequately treated for common mental health problems, resulting in positive clinical outcomes, improvements in people's mental health and quality of life and a proportion of these people coming off benefits and returning to work. The IAPT programme has been described in detail via documentation from the Department of Health on the website (www.iapt.nhs.uk), such as *National Implementation Plan, Commissioning for all the Community, Curricula*, etc., or in reviews of the demonstration sites at Newham and Doncaster (Clark et al., 2009; Richards and Suckling, 2008). We have also discussed in detail the implications of the programme for workforce development generally within mental health

Table 3.1 NWW principles and IAPT

1 Ensuring that the skills and competences of ALL staff are being used to meet the needs of service users and carers in a more efficient and effective way
2 Approaching workforce development through service design and the development of care pathways
3 Ensuring that workers have the right competences consistent with evidence-based practice
4 Developing new roles, to bring new people and new competences into the mental health workforce
5 Developing the roles of existing staff to enable them to take on more or different tasks
6 Using senior staff to supervise and develop other staff
7 Ensuring the engagement of all stakeholders, from diverse professional groups to service users, in resolving *together* workforce development issues

services (Turpin et al., 2006, 2008, 2009). Accordingly, rather than describe the implementation of the programme in any great detail, I would like to focus on just two aspects of the programme. The first of these concerns the relationship between IAPT and NWW, and I will describe in more detail how the principles underlying NWW have influenced the workforce development aspects of the programme. The second aspect concerns the importance of supervision to the implementation of the programme.

Colleagues and I have recently reviewed the association between IAPT and NWW (Turpin et al., 2009) and illustrated the implementation of key NWW principles. These are listed in Table 3.1 and further discussed below in relation to IAPT.

Workforce design informed by users' needs

A fundamental principle that workforce design should be predicated on is that services are designed specifically, and collaboratively, with the needs of service users in mind. This is in contrast with the traditional top-down service planning model, whereby the availability and the contents of packages of care were decided largely by professions and the (in)adequacy of available resources. Moreover, it reflects the strongly held preference for talking therapies relative to medication advocated by many mental health charities and characterised by a recent report (*We Need to Talk*: http://www.weneedtotalk.org.uk/report.html) published by the Mental Health Foundation (2006).

Care pathways and service models

In order to design services that can adequately meet the demand to satisfy users' needs, it is important to identify care pathways that efficiently and effectively offer appropriate and timely care based on the assessment of individual need. The IAPT programme is an excellent example of these principles. The National Implementation Plan (DH, 2008b) identifies the psychological interventions that constitute the various care pathways for anxiety and depression according to clinical guidelines published by NICE, and then presents an overarching service framework based around the principles of Stepped Care (Bower and Gilbody, 2005).

Stepped Care is a model of service delivery whereby clients are offered an increasing choice of more intensive interventions. These interventions are usually delivered by more extensively trained and experienced therapists. The principles are to reduce the burden of care on the client, by offering interventions that require the least input or number of sessions. Regular progress reviews facilitate stepping the individual up to the next level of intervention. An essential part of this review process is case management supervision focused on clinical outcomes, and we will return to this later.

New and extended roles

The IAPT Stepped Care model, as mentioned above, essentially involves two kinds of practitioner: those who trained to deliver high intensity interventions and those who trained to offer low intensity interventions. High intensity practitioners are psychological therapists who are able to offer intensive psychological therapy, usually cognitive behavioural therapy (CBT) offered on a one-to-one basis and for around at least 12 sessions. These are staff who are already qualified practitioners but are extending their roles beyond their original scope of practice. Low intensity practitioners are now known nationally as 'Psychological Wellbeing Practitioners' (PWPs) who deliver low intensity interventions, including: guided self-help, computerised CBT, collaborative care and medications management, signposting to other services, etc., and may usually require as few as two to six sessions, the majority offered by telephone following an initial assessment (Richards and Suckling, 2008). These trainees are drawn from either graduates, usually but not exclusively in psychology, or people from local communities with extensive experience of mental health issues who may not have benefited from university education; this is a new, non-professionally affiliated role.

Evidence-based competences

In order to deliver a Stepped Care service, it is important to be able to identify the range of evidence-based interventions that needs to be available, the competences of therapists employed to deliver this range of interventions and the training required to engender these competences. Within

IAPT, the workforce team worked in collaboration with Skills for Health, in order to identify the competences necessary to deliver the IAPT programme. Initially this led to the scoping of competences underpinning the various different CBT interventions associated with research trials upon which NICE guidance had been based. This work has been widely published (Roth and Pilling, 2007, 2008b) and has now been extended into National Occupational Standards through Skills for Health (https://tools.skillsforhealth.org.uk/suite/show/id/81) and also encompasses other psychotherapeutic modalities, including psychoanalytic/psychodynamic, systemic and family and humanistic-person-centred/experiential therapies (http://www.ucl.ac.uk/clinical-psychology/CORE/competence_frameworks.htm). More importantly for this chapter, Roth and Pilling (2008a,c,d) have also established a set of competences for supervision that have helped to define the training for IAPT supervisors. The topic of IAPT supervision will be covered towards the end of this chapter.

The focus on competence and the development of new non-professionally aligned roles (see below) poses a challenge for supervision and training since it effectively dismantles traditional professional boundaries, the key issue being – who is eligible to supervise particular types of staff or trainees? Given the emphasis on competence and the essentially multi-professional outlook of NWW/IAPT, this is not easy to answer. Traditional supervision models were organised within professions whereas IAPT has required supervisors to be drawn from a range of relevant professions. Indeed, the eligibility of supervisors to supervise high intensity IAPT trainees has been a contentious issue. IAPT has required that supervisors be competent CBT practitioners and has relied on the only individually focused accreditation of CBT competence as offered by the BABCP (http://www.babcp.com/accredited-courses/babcp-accreditation-adding-value-to-cbt/). Other professional groups, particularly clinical and counselling psychologists, have claimed that CBT competence is part of their pre-registration training, and hence these professional groups should be able to offer IAPT supervision. This is not a trivial question of interprofessional rivalry, given that many BABCP-accredited therapists are nurse practitioners and not psychologists, but it might negatively impact on the implementation of the programme. Supervisor capacity, just as it was a decade ago for clinical psychology, is the most critical limiting factor in rolling out the programme. Hence, how one decides on supervisor eligibility is key. It is likely that the professional bodies associated with the IAPT programme will offer supervisor accreditation to their own members using a common set of IAPT competence-based standards. Indeed, accreditation of PWPs is likely to be organised across professional bodies, including both the BABCP and BPS. The BPS is also currently looking at how psychologists with specific competences within CBT might be registered at a post-qualification level.

Education and training of new roles

The IAPT workforce team used the above competences to define the nature of the IAPT workforce. It also surveyed the availability of psychological therapy training courses and the range and skills mix of existing staff within services. It became apparent that the existing training courses either within CBT or for graduate workers would require significant modifications to deliver these newly identified competences. Two nationally agreed curricula were also developed and published to support the training of these two new roles (http://www.dh.gov.uk/en/Publicationsandstatistics/Publications/PublicationsPolicyAndGuidance/DH_083150), and training courses have been established and commissioned by the SHAs.

Enhancing and extending the competences and roles of the existing qualified workforce

Should we assume that our existing qualified workforce is competent and fit for purpose? How do we tell? Is it via people's membership of professions, through educational qualifications, through accredited training courses and workshops? This has been a key issue for IAPT since the monies for new implementer sites have been targeted at those existing services where a third of the staff already have the competences to deliver high intensity interventions and hence will be able to supervise the high numbers of trainees who will be working within the service. However, many people trained in CBT some years ago and, without the recent requirements for ongoing continuing professional development (CPD) from either regulators or professional bodies, are likely to require further training and updating if they are to match the competences of the new IAPT trainees. There will also be staff working in existing services who may wish to upskill and extend their existing roles (e.g. community psychiatric nurses, social workers, etc.) or therapists who have trained in one modality and wish to offer therapy in another modality (e.g. psychodynamic counsellors wishing to train in either interpersonal psychotherapy or CBT). Continuing professional development, therefore, has a critical role in ensuring that the existing workforce is fit for purpose and competent, but also promoting flexibility so that existing staff can be trained in new and perhaps more appropriate competences and skills.

Using senior staff to supervise and develop others

Until the implementation of Agenda for Change, career frameworks and progression tended to be determined by qualifications and the time served in post. This has often resulted in senior clinicians performing job roles such as offering regular and routine outpatient psychotherapy sessions in ways that may not differ from their more junior colleagues. New Ways of Working, together with Agenda for Change, has shifted the focus from the individual to the job and its requirements. This has challenged many professional groups, since it has required senior or consultant members of the profession to measure up their contribution and cost to the service against their own job role. Within IAPT this has required senior clinicians, often from psychology, to become more involved with clinical leadership and service development issues, as previously illustrated in Table 3.1. In addition, an important aspect of the IAPT service model is that all staff receive ongoing expert supervision around clinical outcomes (http://www.iapt.nhs.uk/2008/12/iapt-supervision-guidance/). Indeed, we have argued elsewhere that a quality psychological therapy service is not just dependent upon the competence of its therapists but also individuals who can offer clinical leadership, provide aspects of clinical governance, service development and R&D and also link to user advocacy, social inclusion, diversity/equality issues, employment/work and medicines/physical conditions management (Turpin, 2009; Turpin et al., 2008). These are illustrated in Figure 3.3.

Many of these roles are ones that clinical psychologists, in particular, have been trained in and have demonstrated competences (see NWW for

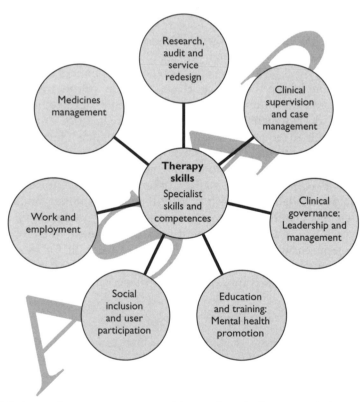

Figure 3.3 Areas of competences required for a safe and effective psychological therapies service (from Turpin, 2009).

Applied Psychologists: Good Practice Guide on the Contribution of Applied Psychologists to Improving Access for Psychological Therapies, http://www.bps.org.uk/document-download-area/document-download$.cfm?file_uuid=12EED74A-1143-DFD0-7E99-61A38B0BCA17&ext=pdf), especially when compared to other psychological therapists who may have received a more therapy-focused and specific training.

Ensuring the engagement of all stakeholders

Given the NWW focus on creating a new competence-based workforce, the vision of the service is no longer the province of any one profession or professional advisory body but has to be jointly owned across a variety of stakeholders, including different professions, users and carers and the voluntary sector to name but a few. IAPT has been a multi-professionally led project and has a wide range of associated stakeholders, as represented by the New Savoy Partnership and the 'Statement of Intent' (http://www.iapt.nhs.uk/2008/12/statement-of-intent-november-2008/). Currently, the IAPT National Team are in the process of rolling out continuing professional development trainings for experienced therapists and counsellors in the following modalities: Counselling for Depression; Couple Therapy for Depression, Dynamic Interpersonal Therapy and Interpersonal Therapy for Depression.

The central role of supervision and IAPT

Both the IAPT National Implementation Plan and the IAPT Commissioning Toolkit stressed the importance of providing high quality supervision to therapists delivering both low and high intensity interventions. Indeed, supervision competences were commissioned from Roth and Pilling (2008a–d) and SHAs were required to commission IAPT supervisor training courses that usually consisted of 5 days of training for qualified staff. Recent further guidance on the nature of supervisor training has been produced (http://www.iapt.nhs.uk/2009/12/17/guidance-for-commissioning-superviser-iapt-training-published/). In the autumn of the first year of implementing the programme, minimum standards for supervision within IAPT services, together with a Good Practice Guide (http://www.iapt.nhs.uk/2008/12/17/iapt-supervision-guidance/), were made available. The amount and quality of supervision received by IAPT trainees were built into the course accreditation process for both High and Low Intensity Intervention Courses and supervision for high and low intensity interventions was distinguished with the latter being more like case management supervision. Case management supervision, together with the supervision of high intensity interventions, requires the availability of routine clinical outcomes data to be monitored (e.g. IAPT Minimum Data Set, http://

www.iapt.nhs.uk/2009/09/15/improving-access-to-psychological-therapies-key-performance-indicators-and-technical-guidance-2009/), which also provides an opportunity to link supervision with therapist performance as judged by the outcomes achieved. In order to further emphasise this distinction to services and educators, a specific PWP supervision manual has been produced (http://www.iapt.nhs.uk/2010/03/16/reach-out-national-programme-supervisor-materials-to-support-the-delivery-of-training-for-psychological-wellbeing-practitioners-delivering-low-intensity-interventions/). We would argue, therefore, that IAPT services are uniquely distinctive within the UK and also internationally, with respect to the importance attached to all of the following service components: evidence-based therapeutic competence and training, routine clinical outcomes monitoring and the provision of supervision for all therapists and clients within the service.

The IAPT Good Practice Guide identifies several reasons why IAPT services should strive for quality in the supervision that they provide, the first priority of which is to enhance and safeguard the delivery of effective therapy for the client. Within the context of IAPT, supervision has a critical role for the implementation of quality psychological therapy services and optimising outcomes for clients for the following reasons.

Fidelity to the evidence base

Therapists in the IAPT programme should be able to carry out the same interventions and to the same level of competence as therapists in controlled trials (which demonstrate the efficacy of these approaches, and hence form the basis for NICE guidelines). These trials usually select therapists carefully, provide additional training and offer close supervision of individual cases (Roth, Pilling and Turner, 2010).

Although the research evidence to support the added value of supervision to better client outcomes is modest and only in its infancy (see Chapter 9; Milne and James, 2000; Roth and Pilling, 2008b; Wheeler and Richards, 2007), there is an emerging literature particularly within the USA about the impact of routine outcomes monitoring and feedback on obtaining effective clinical outcomes (e.g. Miller et al., 2007; Okiishi et al., 2003; Wampold and Brown, 2005; Worthen and Lambert, 2007). This may be equally important for both therapists in training and for qualified staff. For example, Mannix et al. (2006) have shown that ongoing supervision is critical for continuing skills and competency development in trainees.

Moreover, within IAPT services clinical supervision should be tailored to the needs of the client and focused on the individual clinical outcomes that must be assessed routinely within any IAPT service. The minimum standards for IAPT supervision require that it should be regular, at least 1 hour weekly, and should include all clients within the caseload over a 2–4 week period, discussed in priority of clinical need. It should be focused around measured outcomes and provided by an appropriately experienced and trained supervisor.

Effective case management and collaborative care

The above arguments about the importance of supervision do not just apply to high intensity therapies, as represented in the NICE guidelines, but also to Stepped and Collaborative Care as delivered particularly within the Doncaster demonstration site. Here, case managers received regular supervision of their caseload, each client being reviewed at least once every 4 weeks, and outcomes and decisions to step up or down were also subject to review. This process is necessary to ensure that clients are not overlooked in a high volume/high caseload system and relies heavily on an automated IT-based case management system. Within collaborative care, supervision has been demonstrated to impact positively on clinical outcomes. For example, Bower et al. (2006) found in a systematic review that the effectiveness of collaborative care could be optimised by the employment of case managers who had received specific mental health training and who also received regular expert supervision.

Dealing with individual cases and ensuring safe practice for clients

Many therapists receive individual clinical supervision where cases that are seen as challenging, 'stuck' or risky may be discussed in detail with a colleague or more experienced/senior member of staff. It is also important to ensure that all cases within IAPT services are subject to scrutiny and advice by the supervisor. Some clients may appear straightforward but it is always possible to miss something that supervision might appropriately address. Such supervision is important for risk management and governance, especially when less experienced staff such as low intensity practitioners or graduate mental health workers are dealing with specific risk areas (e.g. medication or self-harm issues) and will require regular supervision from more experienced mental health staff or GPs. Within this context, it is important in order to ensure client safety that all cases are regularly reviewed and not just those that a therapist or supervisor selects for discussion. Ladany (2004) has reported the failure of some therapists to disclose ongoing difficulties within their clinical work in supervision, which might reflect poorly on their own competence and performance as therapists. Outcomes tracking where the focus of supervision is on clients' progress – both positive and negative – may also ameliorate the effects of a supervisee being reluctant to disclose ongoing difficulties with particular clients.

Skills development and training

A common model of psychotherapy training within the workplace is for trainees to be on placement within a clinical service and for there to be a named supervisor who is responsible for their clinical work. The supervisor should be available to discuss progress of cases and facilitate skills development through case review, feeding back on audio/videotapes, being present in situ for therapy sessions/joint sessions and even formal involvement in the assessment of the trainee's competences.

Supervision is integral to both low and high intensity training courses and will supplement workplace supervision by providing intensive weekly supervision of selected cases by course staff and highly experienced supervisors during teaching days. The use of tape-recorded sessions with the client's permission, together with standardised measures of clinical competence (i.e. Cognitive Therapy Rating Scale: Young and Beck, 1980), will also characterise IAPT supervision. It is important that training courses and services have a clear understanding as to the relationship between these different types of supervision and that appropriate clinical governance arrangements are in place.

Staff support and the prevention of burnout

The availability of supervision has been shown to prevent burnout and to ameliorate the negative impacts of therapeutic work (e.g. secondary or vicarious traumatisation) on the health and well-being of therapeutic staff, as well as providing positive effects on staff well-being and performance within organisations (see Sabin-Farrell and Turpin, 2003). This may be particularly relevant for staff with high caseloads offering low intensity interventions.

Supervision may also enhance patient safety by addressing personal issues of the supervised therapist, who themselves may be experiencing psychological distress or an inability to cope with particular situations or challenging organisations, which may be addressed within supervision (Wheeler, 2007). Ultimately the supervisor should ensure that the supervisee is fit to practise and to take appropriate action if this is not the case. If the therapist is unfit to practise it is the supervisor's responsibility to take steps either to ensure that the therapist improves practice or that he/she ceases to practise until such improvements can be made.

Following publication of the Good Practice Guide, several important issues have emerged and are currently subject to ongoing development work within the IAPT programme. First, how should supervisor competences be assessed in the context of supervisor training? Currently, there are no reliable tools for assessing the competences of supervisors. Claimed competence within therapy may not be related to objective competence as measured independently from therapy tapes (e.g. Brosan, Reynolds and Moore, 2007, 2008). The Supervision Competence Framework may help in the development of rating scales that could be applied to taped supervision sessions in order to assess supervisors' competence. Until these competences can be assessed, it is important to ensure that the requirement to provide supervision is specified in IAPT person and job specifications. Not all therapists may wish or be available to provide supervision. Caseloads and activity levels for supervisors will need to be adjusted to ensure that they have sufficient time to provide supervision. Similarly, supervisors will also require time for their own supervision and continuing professional development and support. A weekly or fortnightly supervision group for supervisors could meet this requirement.

A second major issue is the distinction between high and low intensity supervising and whether supervisors are interchangeable. The Supervision Competences Framework, described above, identifies a series of specific competences to support low intensity interventions. Supervisors of low intensity trainees *must* have knowledge of low intensity interventions, and ideally have practised or have familiarity with their service delivery. Familiarity and understanding of the relevant information technology system used within the low intensity service will also be essential. Similarly, all supervisors should have received training in supervision, including, where appropriate, specific supervision training tailored for low intensity interventions. Furthermore, given that low intensity workers may be performing roles unfamiliar to their supervisors (i.e. medication management, telephone counselling, etc.), supervisors will require *additional* training both in low intensity working and supervision. It is also important that both supervisors and supervisees for both low and high intensity interventions are familiar with the content and limitations of each other's work. Arrangements might be considered to provide supervisors from more traditional psychotherapy backgrounds with an opportunity to experience and familiarise themselves by working within a low intensity service. Further guidance on the nature of case management supervision for low intensity therapists and a helpful supervision checklist is provided in the training materials provided by IAPT (http://www.iapt.nhs.uk/2008/08/training-resources-for-low-intensity-therapy-workers/). As mentioned earlier, a Supervisor's Manual for PWPs has now been made available.

Supervisors of low intensity therapists will also need to be clear about the clinical governance arrangements around autonomy and scope of practice. Different services allow different degrees of autonomy for these practitioners, including the extent to which activities such as assessment and risk issues are overseen by a more experienced practitioner. In particular, issues of safeguarding both adults and children, and self-harm and risk assessment protocols for PWPs, have recently come to the fore. The governance arrangements around clinical responsibility for both low and high intensity practitioners require careful consideration. Clear governance arrangements need to be in place describing the responsibilities of supervisors for trainees working within the service and those located within training providers and universities.

Within IAPT services, it is important that supervision is integrated with data collection and the monitoring of outcomes. The use of routine outcome measurement using the CORE system in the UK has provided useful indicators as to how outcomes and service monitoring can be communicated to staff in constructive and meaningful ways (Lucock and Lutz, 2009; Lucock et al., 2003).

Currently, low intensity workers tend to be supervised by nurse therapists, counsellors, gateway workers and psychologists. However, there is recognition that this might not always be appropriate or a good use of therapists' time. Indeed, IAPT is developing guidance for eligibility to be a PWP supervisor along the lines of the accreditation processes employed on high intensity courses. It is intended that there should be career progression and sustainability for low intensity workers, and it may be feasible for experienced low intensity workers to take on supervisory roles, given sufficient experience and training in supervision. Nevertheless, given the relatively brief duration of training for low intensity workers, and for some their relative lack of clinical experience, it will be important to consider carefully such a development. Levels of experience and additional training should be assessed for low intensity workers intending to take on a more responsible and supervisory role.

Nevertheless, some principles will be common to both sets of supervisors, such as the regular review of client's outcomes, risk status, levels of engagement, etc. All supervisors should also be familiar with issues of equality and diversity in therapy and supervision, and be sensitive to the cultural needs of particular client groups and therapists. Supervisors should be familiar with the work of the IAPT Special Interest Groups and 'Commissioning for the whole community' (http://www.iapt.nhs.uk/2008/10/commissioning-for-whole-community/).

Conclusion

Reflecting on recent developments, it is clear that supervision has come of age. Within the profession there is a better recognition of the importance of supervision both within education and training and in routine clinical practice. The emergence of the HPC as the regulator of practitioner psychologists ought to require that supervision becomes a key aspect of ongoing registration, so as to further enhance public protection and patient safety. With respect to training, further development is required around supervisor training, assessing supervisory competences and the accreditation of supervisors.

Perhaps the most important future challenges lie beyond the profession. It will be important that developments within the profession around supervision are competence based, can extend to a multi-professional context and incorporate workforce flexibility around new roles such as assistant practitioners. Notwithstanding these challenges, it should be recognised that many of the developments within Skills for Health, NWW and IAPT have been led by psychologists. Accordingly, we believe that psychologists should be recognised as being able to offer almost unique contributions to the development of supervision within services. In particular, we would expect to see future developments especially around clinical governance and the integration of routine clinical outcomes, supervision and enhanced outcomes for clients.

With respect to IAPT, the organisation and provision of quality supervision to IAPT therapists will be one of the factors that will determine the success, or otherwise, of the IAPT programme. If the IAPT programme is to return clinical outcomes equivalent to those obtained from the controlled trials upon which NICE guidance is based, it will be essential that IAPT therapists are appropriately selected, trained and supervised. IAPT has offered to service users the promise of clinical improvement and recovery, and services must prioritise the delivery of high quality supervision to their staff in order to ensure that this promise is kept.

Summary

Developments in clinical psychology supervision over the past decade are reviewed from the policy perspective but with an emphasis on mental health services. Within the profession, there is a continuing need to support and expand the supervisory resource, so as to optimise the capacity of the clinical psychology training system. However, many of the developments have been around supervisor training and the introduction of various systems of accreditation for supervisors, together with good practice guidelines.

A major challenge for the profession during this time has been the development of more multi-professional approaches to education and training, workforce planning and service delivery. Psychology as a profession was involved in a New Ways of Working Project that has emphasised the importance of supervision through working with assistants or associates, team working or leading and innovating within services. Similarly, the Improving Access to Psychological Therapies programme in England has placed great emphasis on the importance of supervision and has commissioned work on defining supervision competences to inform training curricula and programmes.

In conclusion, supervision has come of age and has been at the forefront of several major national initiatives to improve services. Psychologists have been very much involved in these initiatives both within and outside of the profession.

Acknowledgements

Much of the thinking within this chapter has emerged from a series of workforce design projects surrounding New Ways of Working and Improving Access to Psychological Therapies. Colleagues within those projects, such as David Clark, Roslyn Hope, Tony Lavender, Steve Pilling, Dave Richards, Tony Roth and Sue Wheeler, have helped to develop many of the ideas in this current chapter, together with present and former colleagues from the Clinical Psychology Unit at the University of Sheffield: Michael Barkham, Gillian Hardy, Jan Hughes and Joyce Scaife.

Chapter 4

Models of supervision and the supervisory relationship

Helen Beinart

In recent years there has been a growing interest in supervision and the supervisory relationship in the UK, demonstrated by a small but significant body of writing and research based on clinical psychology training and exemplified by the first edition of *Supervision and Clinical Psychology* (Fleming and Steen, 2004).

This chapter focuses primarily on models of supervision that are generic, that is, not based on psychotherapy models, but developed to aid our understanding of supervision, and the learning and training of supervision as a separate field of study. Selected models, including developmental, social role and some integrative supervision frameworks, are described. Our understanding of the supervisory relationship is then discussed, as the evidence points towards the overriding importance of the supervisory relationship in understanding supervision. The complexity of the developing evidence base for supervision and methodological issues that have beset this field is discussed, followed by some suggestions for methodologically competent studies. Recent research, conducted in Oxford, on the supervisory relationship is discussed in some detail. The chapter concludes with a summary about what supervisors and supervisees can do to enhance the effectiveness of their supervisory relationships.

Models of supervision can be divided into two broad areas: those developed from psychotherapy theories and those developed to explain supervision itself. Originally, supervision models were direct extensions of psychotherapy theories, for example, Ekstein and Wallerstein (1972) wrote about supervision models based on psychodynamic theories. More recently, these models have been developed and updated by authors such us Frawley-O'Dea and Sarnat (2001), whose work is based on the relational school of psychotherapy such as attachment theory. Cognitive behavioural models of supervision, described by Liese and Beck (1997) and Ricketts and Donohoe (2000), may focus on the structure of supervision sessions, for example, agenda setting and review or the development of specific techniques such as Socratic questioning. Systemic supervision emphasises a multi-dimensional, family life-cycle approach (e.g. Liddle, Becker and

Diamond, 1997) embedded within live supervision or reflecting teams (Andersen, 1991). A more detailed discussion of supervision models developed from specific therapeutic schools can be found in Watkins (1997) and is also considered in Chapter 5 of this book.

Whilst supervision models grounded in psychotherapy models have much to offer, it is important to recognise the differences between supervision and therapy. Bernard and Goodyear (2004) argue that whilst there are clear influences between supervision and therapy, there are substantial drawbacks to using therapy models for conceptualising supervision. Therapeutic models have proved too narrow to explain the complexity of supervision and have possibly restricted the evidence base by offering few directions for research and practice in supervision (Bernard and Goodyear, 2004). Supervision is predominantly an educative process (Holloway and Poulin, 1995) that supports supervisees in learning a range of professional roles (one of which is a therapeutic role). Thus, models of adult learning (e.g. Kolb, 1984) or reflective practice (e.g. Schon, 1983) may be helpful in understanding the processes that facilitate and support the learning of a professional role (Milne and James, 2002). Schon (1983) suggests that professional training draws on two different realms of knowledge: theory and research that form the basis of an academic programme, and knowledge derived from practitioner experience. Rapid expansion of therapy professions and the consequent growth in training numbers, and the need for competent supervisors to support them, has led to an increasing emphasis on practitioner-led supervisor training and much of the writing on supervision, particularly in the UK, reflects the realm of knowledge based on practitioner experience (e.g. Proctor, 1997; Scaife, 2001, 2009). The need for a framework for training beginning supervisors, as opposed to therapists, has led to a shift from therapy-based models to generic or supervision-specific models.

The focus in the next section is on the main generic models that have been specifically developed to explain the complex phenomenon of supervision. Although the majority of supervision models have some elements of overlap, for convenience the models can be broadly divided into the developmental models, (e.g. Stoltenberg, McNeill and Delworth, 1998), social role models (e.g. Bernard, 1979; Inskipp and Proctor, 1993; Scaife, 2009) and integrative models such as those of Holloway (1995) and Hawkins and Shohet (1989, 2000). Models that explore the supervisory relationship (Bordin, 1983; Holloway, 1995) will also be discussed.

Developmental models

The majority of developmental models attempt to explain the complex transition from inexperienced supervisee to competent clinician (Whiting, Bradley and Planny, 2001). Developmental models share the fundamental assumption that supervisees develop through a series of different stages on their journey towards competence and that supervisors need to adjust their supervisory focus and approach to match the individual supervisee's development needs. Developmental models differ in emphasis, with some mainly addressing the supervision of the developing supervisee, for example Loganbill et al. (1982), and others addressing the development of the supervisor, for example Hess (1986). The Integrated Developmental Model (IDM) of supervision (Stoltenberg, McNeill and Delworth, 1998) addresses both sides of the supervisory dyad and is discussed in more detail here.

The IDM (Stoltenberg et al., 1998) proposes three structures (awareness of self and others, motivation and autonomy) to monitor the development of supervisee competence in a range of areas (intervention, assessment, client conceptualisation, individual differences, theoretical orientation, treatment goals and plans, professional ethics). Each phase of development is characterised by particular learning needs. Supervisees at Level 1 are described as anxious, highly motivated and dependent on their supervisors for advice and guidance. Supervisees tend to be self-focused while dealing with anxiety about performance and evaluation. At Level 2, supervisees have developed sufficient skills and knowledge to become less internally focused and to increase their focus on the client – however, motivation and autonomy may vary. Level 3 supervisees develop the ability to appropriately balance the client's perspective whilst maintaining self-awareness, stabilising motivation and increasing autonomy.

In addition to addressing supervisee developmental needs, the IDM also identifies different tasks for supervisors at each development level. At Level 1 the supervisor provides structure and encourages the early development of autonomy. The supervisor's tasks include containing anxiety and providing a role model. At Level 2 the supervisor provides less structure and encourages more autonomy and appropriate risk-taking. Tasks include clarifying trainee ambivalence, modelling and providing a more facilitative and less didactic focus. At Level 3 the supervisor focuses more on supervisee personal/professional integration and tasks include monitoring consistency in performance, identifying deficits and working towards integration and refining a professional identity. Developmental models, such as the IDM outlined above, are attractive as they appeal intuitively, however there has been little longitudinal research to test their veracity. Nonetheless there is some sound evidence for the need for direction and structure at an early phase of learning (Ellis and Ladany, 1997) and the development of increasing autonomy as supervisees mature (Borders, 1990). However, the need for clear structure appears important across all levels of experience if dealing with a clinical crisis (Tracey, Ellickson and Sherry, 1989) or in new supervisory relationships (Rabinowitz, Heppner and Roehlke, 1986).

Social role models

Social role models assume that the supervisor undertakes a set of roles that establish expectations, beliefs and attitudes about what tasks and functions the supervisor will perform during supervision. Several models of supervision incorporate the tasks and functions (role) of the supervisor, for example those of Bernard (1979, 1997), Inskipp and Proctor (1993) and Scaife (2009). These models will be summarised briefly in this section.

Bernard (1979) developed the Discrimination Model as a teaching tool in order to provide a map for supervisor training. The Discrimination Model assumes flexibility on the part of the supervisor to respond to specific supervisee needs. There are two axes (roles and foci) within the model, consisting of three main supervisor roles (therapist, teacher and consultant) and three main foci of supervision (process, conceptualisation and personalisation). There is thus a matrix of nine choices for supervisor intervention. Bernard (1997) describes the Discrimination Model as atheoretical in that it can be used across any model of psychotherapy. The roles of therapist, teacher and consultant are relatively self-evident and will not be described in detail here. The three foci or learning dimensions are described as the primary functions of a competent therapist. Process skills refer to basic psychotherapy techniques and strategy, such as engagement and interviewing skills. Personalisation refers to the personal or emotional elements of the supervisee's experience, such as the ability to manage the client's feelings as well as their own within a therapy session.

Conceptualisation involves the tasks of thinking, analysis and theory–practice links often involved in formulation. The focus of supervision is likely to vary according to the theoretical orientation of the supervisor and the supervisee's level of development. For example, supervisors of beginning supervisees are likely to focus more on specific process skills such as interviewing, whereas supervisors of more experienced supervisees are more likely to focus on self-reflection (personalisation) and formulation (conceptualisation). One of the strengths of the Discrimination Model is that it provides a framework for training flexible and responsive supervisors, but it fails to address important issues in supervision such as evaluation and the supervisory relationship. The Discrimination Model is thus a testable model in which to conceptualise supervisor roles in relation to supervisee needs. There has not been a great deal of research to test the model but there is some evidence to support a shared understanding between supervisors and supervisees that these roles occur during supervision (Ellis, Dell and Good, 1988).

Inskipp and Proctor (1993) proposed three main functions of supervision: formative, normative and restorative. The formative function is to support a supervisee's learning and development through, for example, informing or instructing. The normative function includes the ethical and managerial responsibilities of the supervisor, which are likely to vary depending on the level of training and experience of the supervisee and the nature of the supervision contract. The restorative function includes the support function of supervision and acknowledges the emotional effects of working with people experiencing psychological distress. A safe and trusting supervisory relationship is essential for the supervisee to be able to honestly disclose the emotional impact of the work. Inskipp and Proctor (1993) suggest that most supervision sessions will incorporate all three functions but that the focus may change according to supervisee need. To the best of my knowledge, this model has not been explicitly tested but related research, for example in the area of supervisee non-disclosure (Ladany et al., 1996), may offer indirect support for the importance of the restorative function of supervision.

Scaife (2001, 2009) presents a General Supervision Framework (GSF) that builds on and develops the previous frameworks discussed. The three dimensions of supervisor role, supervision focus and supervision medium or mode make up the GSF. The supervisor role includes three roles that the supervisor may adopt in supervision: inform–assess (e.g. when teaching or evaluating), enquire and listen–reflect. Scaife suggests that the supervisor role will vary according to the task to be achieved but that the enquire and listen–reflect roles tend to support a more collegial or collaborative supervisory style. The supervision focus may be on actions and events (e.g. discussing what happened in a clinical session), knowledge, thinking and planning (e.g. developing a formulation) or feelings and personal qualities (e.g. discussing the personal impact of the work). The third dimension of the GSF concerns how the supervision takes place or the medium of supervision, for example, through live supervision, audio or video recordings, reported events and role-play or telephone and video-conferencing. Scaife presents the GSF as a testable model that can helpfully be used in contracting for supervision to aid the discussion about what may be possible in supervision and the supervisor and supervisee preferences.

Integrative approaches to supervision

Two integrative models will be discussed in this section: the Systems Approach to Supervision (Holloway, 1995) and the Process Model of Supervision (Hawkins and Shohet, 1989, 2000).

The Systems Approach to Supervision (SAS) was developed to assist supervisors in the systematic assessment of supervisee learning needs and supervision teaching interventions (Holloway and Neufeldt, 1995). Holloway's (1995) model builds on social role models (by describing tasks and functions of supervision) but sees the supervisory relationship as

central and takes into account a range of contextual factors. These contextual factors include the client, the trainee, the supervisor and the
institution. It is proposed that these seven dimensions or components of the
model (relationship, client, trainee, supervisor, institution, tasks and function) are part of a dynamic process in that they mutually influence one
another (hence, the systems approach). Each factor can also be examined
independently.

The SAS model addresses the complexity of the process of supervision
and provides a map for analysing a particular episode of supervision in
terms of the nature of the task, the function the supervisor is performing,
the nature of the relationship and the relevant contextual factors.

Holloway (1995) identified three elements within the relationship: (a) the
interpersonal structure of the relationship, including the dimensions of
power and involvement; (b) the phase of the relationship, referring to the
development of the relationship over time; and (c) the supervisory contract,
which includes establishing a set of expectations regarding the tasks, functions and process of supervision (discussed in more detail in the next
section). The tasks of supervision include development of therapeutic skills,
case conceptualisation, professional role, emotional awareness and self-
evaluation. The five main functions that the supervisor carries out during
supervision are monitoring/evaluating, instructing/advising, modelling,
consulting and supporting/sharing. Similar to the Discrimination Model,
Holloway depicts the tasks and functions of supervision as a grid. She
describes the interaction of deciding what to teach (task) with how to teach
it (function) as the process of supervision.

This model suggests that the supervisory relationship and the tasks and
functions of supervision are influenced by contextual factors related to
the supervisor (experience, expectations, theoretical orientation, culture),
the client (personal/cultural characteristics, identified problem, relationship), the supervisee (experience, theoretical orientation, learning style/
needs, culture), and the institution (organisational structure and climate,
professional ethics and standards). Much of this model is grounded in
social influence theory, which has some evidence base, but the complete
model has not been fully tested partly due to a lack of appropriate measures
and complexity.

The Process Model of Supervision developed by Hawkins and Shohet
(1989, 2000) is a popular model in the UK and is often used for multi-
professional supervisor training. It is an integrative model that combines
relational and contextual factors as well as the tasks and functions of
supervision. The model proposes seven elements and is sometimes known as
the seven-eyed supervisor because it presents seven possible foci during
supervision: the client or content of a therapy session; therapeutic strategies
or interventions; the therapeutic relationship or process; the therapist's
emotional reactions or counter-transference; the supervisory relationship

and any parallels with the therapeutic relationship (parallel process); the impact on the supervisor of the supervisor's counter-transference; and the overall organisational and social context (which may include professional ethics and codes). Hawkins and Shohet also emphasise contracting and educational, supportive and managerial tasks of the supervisor.

Models of supervision: Summary of theory and research

The previous section has reviewed selected models of supervision categorised for convenience into developmental, social role and integrated models, and where possible the available supporting evidence has been discussed. There is some evidence to suggest that the structure of the relationship is predictable (Holloway, 1982), that social influence factors may have some impact on supervisor perceptions of supervisee performance (Carey, Williams and Wells, 1988) and that supervisees expect supervisors to be trustworthy, expert and attractive (Friedlander and Snyder, 1983). In a study of clinical psychology trainees in the UK, Green (1998), using a qualitative research methodology, found that special knowledge, credibility and integrity were terms used by trainees to describe influential supervisors. He argues that these combined characteristics of Sapiential Authority are similar to the construct of trustworthiness.

A series of microanalytic studies on the content of supervision sessions draw the following conclusions: (a) supervision and counselling/therapy processes are distinct; (b) there are significant changes in discourse across the relationship; (c) there is a predominant pattern of verbal behaviours that resembles teacher/student interactions; (d) and the structure of the supervisory relationship has hierarchical characteristics (Holloway and Poulin, 1995). Milne and James (2000) suggest that goal-setting and providing specific instructions are associated with benefits to supervisees. The above findings provide some support for the hierarchical nature of the supervisory relationship, the role of social influence and the importance of a supervisory contract.

However, there is mounting evidence to suggest that the supervisory relationship is key to supervisee experience of supervision, and possibly to performance in the workplace (Olk and Friedlander, 1992). The next section will explore models of the supervisory relationship, and their evidence base, in more detail.

Models of the supervisory relationship

The supervisory relationship is unique in that it comprises at least three people: client(s), therapist (supervisee) and supervisor (and, for supervisees in training, the training programme). This has led to the concept of parallel process, which has its roots in psychodynamic supervision in the concepts of transference and counter-transference. Parallel process refers to the process or dynamics in the supervisory relationship replicating or mirroring those in the therapeutic relationship (Hawkins and Shohet, 1989). The concept of parallel process has been developed and expanded by systemic family therapists into the concept of isomorphism, which refers to relational and structural similarities between therapy and supervision rather than intra-psychic parallels. Although these concepts have been widely adopted in the practice of supervision within their respective psychotherapeutic traditions, there is sparse empirical support for them (Bernard and Goodyear, 2004). Selected models of the supervisory relationship discussed in more detail below consider supervision specifically and are generic with regard to psy-chotherapeutic model.

Bordin's model of the supervisory working alliance

Bordin (1983) defines the supervisory working alliance as 'collaboration for change' consisting of three aspects: mutual agreements and understanding of the goals; the tasks of each of the partners; and the bonds between the partners. Bordin suggests that clarity and mutuality of the agreement contribute to the strength of the working alliance. In addition to agreeing goals, the tasks by which each of the participants may achieve those goals also need to be negotiated. Bonds are developed through common enter-prise; indeed, Bordin suggests that time spent together, mutual liking, caring and trusting and the public/private dimension of the relationship influence the development of bonds. Bordin (1983) includes the following goals of the supervisory working alliance: development of specific clinical competences; developing understanding of clients and process issues; increasing awareness of self and the impact on process (therapy and super-vision); overcoming personal and intellectual obstacles towards learning; deepening understanding of concept and theory; providing a stimulus to research; and maintaining the standards of service.

Additionally, Bordin identifies three main tasks for the supervisee: preparation of oral or written reports of their work, objective observation of therapeutic work (either direct or recorded) and selection of problems and issues for presentation. The supervisor's tasks include coaching, giving feedback, focusing on areas of difficulty or gaps for the supervisee and deepening theoretical or personal understanding. The supervisory process is managed through establishing the contract and providing mutual ongoing feedback and evaluation. The supervisory working alliance was operatio-nalised by Ladany and Friedlander (1995) as mutual agreement on the goals and tasks of supervision and the emotional bond between supervisor and supervisee. Efstation, Patton and Kardash (1990) found that supervisory working alliance was related to supervisor style (attractiveness, interpersonal sensitivity and task orientation) and supervisee self-efficacy. Ladany and Friedlander (1995) found that working alliance was related to supervisee role-conflict and ambiguity, that is, the supervisee experiencing competing or unclear role expectations. Ladany et al. (1996) found that working alliance was also related to satisfaction with supervision.

Holloway's model of the supervisory relationship

> In the systems approach to supervision, relationship is the container of a dynamic process in which the supervisor and supervisee negotiate a personal way of using a structure of power and involvement that accommodates the supervisee's progression of learning.
>
> (Holloway, 1995: 41–42)

Hollway identifies three essential elements of the supervisory relationship: interpersonal structure (the dimensions of power and involvement); phases of the relationship; and supervisory contracts (the establishment of a set of expectations for the tasks and functions of supervision, and the supervisory relationship).

The interpersonal structure of the supervisory relationship is hierarchical and is described as 'power through involvement'. Each individual brings to the relationship their interpersonal histories that influence the level of involvement or attachment within the supervisory relationship. Both supervisor and supervisee influence the distribution of power or the degree of attachment to one another. Holloway argues that supervisory relationships develop over time from formal to informal interpersonal relationships. In the early phase participants rely on general socio-cultural information about roles. However, as more information is gathered the relationship becomes more individualised and predictable. As the supervisory relationship evolves to a more interpersonal one there is reduced uncertainty and participants become more open and vulnerable and more likely to self-disclose. Holloway proposes beginning, mature and terminating phases of the supervisory relationship. The beginning phase consists of clarifying the relationship, establishing a supervision contract and working on specific competences and treatment plans. During the mature phase the relationship becomes more individualised and less role-bound, which allows greater social bonding and influence. It also deals with developing formulation skills, working on self-confidence and exploring the personal/professional interface. The terminating phase allows for increased autonomy and the need for less direction from the supervisor. The supervisory contract is seen as important as a way of negotiating both goals and tasks but also parameters of the relationship. This clarifies both content and relational characteristics and establishes mutual expectations of the supervisory relationship.

Evidence base for the effectiveness of supervision

The research literature on supervision is extensive, but has been criticised on methodological grounds (e.g. Ellis et al., 1996). The reader is referred to reviews of the supervision literature for a full discussion of these issues (e.g. Ellis et al., 1996; Holloway and Neufeldt, 1995; Spence et al., 2001; Wheeler and Richards, 2007). In summary, these criticisms include small sample sizes, inadequate statistical power, lack of comparison groups, lack of theory (Ellis et al., 1996), use of analogue situations, use of measures with poor reliability and validity and reliance on single sources of outcome information (Spence et al., 2001).

Ellis et al. (1996) suggest that methodologically sound studies should aim to test specific theories or models of supervision and develop clear research questions and hypotheses informed by these theories or models. Methodologies should attend to the representativeness of the sample, use longitudinal designs to test developmental models, use psychometrically sound measures appropriate to the supervision context and attend to statistical power. They should also stress the importance of internal consistency of aims, hypotheses, method and analyses. The interpretation of results should attend to the strengths as well as the weaknesses of the study, explore alternative explanations and discuss the generalisability of the results. Similarly, qualitative research methodologies should be rigorous, provide appropriate quality checks, use known methodologies, show transparency and reflexivity and provide clear audit trails.

Lambert and Ogles (1997), in their comprehensive review of the effectiveness of psychotherapy supervision, conclude that it is tempting to assume on the basis of psychotherapy research that training and supervision are effective. They warn that there are no good outcome studies that make a clear connection between training and therapy outcome. In particular, it is not known how elements of training programmes such as teaching, supervision or practice contribute to the development of effective practitioners. The methodological issues inherent in this field of research are complex. Ellis and Ladany (1997) conclude that the overall quality of research has been 'sub-standard'. Although there are many theories and studies, much of the research is atheoretical: there is an absence of replication studies and a lack of viable measures specific to clinical supervision.

Much of the theory and research discussed above stems from the USA and is based on the psychotherapy, counselling and counselling psychology literature. It is unclear how applicable findings from counselling and psychotherapy are to clinical psychology: for example, Lawton and Feltham

(2000) suggest that supervision in counselling is more process-focused than supervision in clinical psychology, which tends to be more goal-oriented. Similarly, training methods and routes in the USA (Cherry, Messenger and Jacoby, 2000) are dissimilar to those in the UK, particularly with regard to the way clinical placements are structured, supervised and monitored. Until recently, for example Green (1998) and Milne and James (1999, 2000), there has been very little research exploring clinical supervision for clinical psychology in the UK. The general dearth of research into clinical psychology training and supervision in the UK, together with the finding that, regardless of the model adhered to, the supervisory relationship (SR) is one of the crucial factors in ensuring effectiveness of supervision (Ladany, Ellis and Friedlander, 1999), has led to the development of a series of studies, conducted in Oxford by the author and colleagues, exploring the supervisory relationship. These studies will be discussed in more detail in the next section.

Research into the supervisory relationship

Beinart (2002) explored factors that predict the quality of the supervisory relationship. The study used both quantitative and qualitative methodologies to test aspects of the two models of the supervisory relationship described earlier (Bordin, 1983; Holloway, 1995). Supervisees were asked to rate and describe the characteristics and qualities of the supervisory relationships that had contributed most and least to their effectiveness as a clinical psychologist. A sample of clinical psychology trainees and newly qualified (up to 2 years post-qualification) clinical psychologists from the South of England was used. Data were collected on just under 100 supervisory relationships.

The quantitative study found that satisfaction with supervision, rapport between supervisee and supervisor and the supervisee feeling supported by the supervisor were the main qualities of supervisory relationships considered most effective by supervisees.

A grounded theory analysis of the qualitative data, derived from written answers to open-ended questions about the quality of the supervisory relationship, suggested that there were nine categories that described the supervisory relationship. These were: boundaried, supportive, respectful, open relationship, committed, sensitive to needs, collaborative, educative and evaluative.

A grounded theory was developed that proposed that a framework for the supervisory relationship needed to be in place for the process or work of supervision to occur. The main aspect of the framework was the development of a boundaried relationship. This included both structural boundaries, such as time, place and frequency of supervision, and personal/professional boundaries that enabled the supervisee to feel emotionally contained within the supervisory relationship. The other aspects of the framework were the development of mutually respectful, supportive and open relationships where the supervisee felt that the supervisor was committed to the supervision and regular two-way feedback took place. It was proposed that in supervision certain optimal relationship conditions seem necessary for the more formal activities of supervision (such as education and evaluation) to take place effectively.

Clinical psychology supervisees described a strong preference for collaborative supervisory relationships where both parties were involved in setting the agenda and the goals of supervision. A certain amount of flexibility of approach and therapeutic model seemed to aid the collaboration. The two tasks of education and evaluation were helped if the supervisor was sensitive to the supervisee's needs, taking into account their previous experience, stage of training and the personal impact of the work. Unlike previous studies (e.g. Green, 1998) the wisdom and experience of the supervisor seemed less important than opportunities to observe the supervisor's work and have curious and stimulating discussions, which included making theory–practice links and collaborative work on formulation. Again, flexibility was important to supervisees who found didactic supervision or inflexible adherence to models less helpful. Interestingly, the evaluative aspects of supervision were only presented as an issue in poorer quality supervisory relationships. Supervisees valued and appreciated formative feedback and challenge in good collaborative relationships and the formal elements of summative evaluation did not seem to impact when regular, mutual feedback was built into the supervisory relationships.

The qualitative themes developed by Beinart (2002) were used by Palomo (2004) to develop a psychometrically sound measure of the supervisory relationship from the supervisee perspective. Exploratory factor analysis was used, both to provide a summary of the relationships between the items chosen and to aid the development of theory. As the ultimate aim of supervision is to improve client outcome, as well as to enhance supervisee learning and development, measures of both of these constructs were included. The Supervisory Relationship Questionnaire (SRQ) developed is a valid and reliable measure of the SR from the supervisee perspective and supports previous research in this field. Factor analysis of the SRQ yielded six components: safe base, structure, commitment, reflective education, role model and formative feedback. The components reflect the distinct nature of the supervisory relationship, including its educative, involuntary and evaluative nature, as well as the central core component 'safe base' that reflects its more generic facilitative, relational characteristics. As well as contributing to a theoretical model of the SR this study provides a new and unique outcome measure in a field where empirical research is not well developed and provides a useful and practical tool for individual supervisors to invite feedback and review in supervisory relationships. It also provides an objective measure that may be helpful to future research, training programmes and supervisors (Palomo, Beinart and Cooper, 2009).

Frost (2004) contributed an interesting study exploring the dyadic nature of the supervisory relationship over time. This is one of the few longitudinal studies that explores developmental models and phases of the supervisory relationship from both supervisee and supervisor perspectives. Using qualitative methods (e.g. interpretative phenomenological analysis), Frost found that the process of forming the supervisory relationship is critical in the early phase (first month) and if good beginnings are established the relationship continues to grow in warmth, collaboration and openness. However, the converse was also suggested by this study, where unmet expectations that were not voiced could lead to difficulties that may not resolve. Frost also found that the themes generated for supervisees and supervisors at each phase (beginning, middle and end) of the relationship were somewhat different, suggesting that supervisees and supervisors have different experiences of the supervisory relationship.

Clohessy (2008) used a qualitative methodology to explore supervisors' perspectives of their supervisory relationships with trainee clinical psychologists. Using Grounded Theory methodology, three categories were identified as important in the quality of the relationship from a supervisor's perspective. These were: contextual influences, the flow of supervision and core relational factors. Contextual influences on the development of the supervisory relationship included the team/service, the presence of the training course and the individual factors that the supervisor and trainee bring to the relationship (e.g. gender, ethnicity, prior experience of supervision). The flow of supervision reflects supervisor and trainee contributions to the process of supervision. Supervisor contributions were summarised as 'investing in the SR', and included ensuring a good beginning to the SR by planning ahead for the trainee, spending time together, establishing boundaries and expectations, encouraging learning and responding to individual needs. Trainee contributions to the flow of supervision were summarised as 'being open to learning' and included being enthusiastic and committed, adopting a proactive stance and being productive by making a contribution to the service. The more open to learning the trainee appeared to be, the more the supervisor invested in the relationship, creating a virtuous cycle that supported the development of positive core relational factors.

The core relational factors found in this study were the interpersonal connection between the supervisor and trainee, the emotional tone or atmosphere of the relationship and the degree of safety, trust, openness and honesty within the relationship. The findings suggest a reciprocal relationship between core relational factors and the flow of supervision. Although the most successful relationship seemed to be characterised by positive characteristics in all the three core areas identified, it seemed that SRs only needed to be 'good enough' to work effectively. A quantitative measure of the supervisory relationship based on the qualitative findings of Clohessy (2008) is currently under development.

The research discussed above supports other findings in the field. Falender and Shafranske (2004), in their summary of the literature in this area, suggest that a good SR consists of facilitating attitudes, behaviours and practices, including: a sense of teamwork (Henderson et al., 1999), empathy (Worthen and McNeill, 1996), approachability and attentiveness (Henderson et al., 1999), encouragement of disclosures by supervisees (Ladany et al., 1996) and supervisors' sensitivity to the developmental level of the supervisee (e.g. Magnuson, Wilcoxon and Norem, 2000).

Pointers for good practice

We are beginning to see a confluence of practitioner knowledge and experience with a growing evidence base in the UK, to the extent that we can begin to make recommendations for best practice. Primarily, the establishment of a safe supervisory relationship seems to be paramount and has been described by various authors as a safe base (Palomo, 2004) or a boundaried space. Both Frost and Clohessy's research suggest that invest-ment of time at the beginning is helpful in establishing a safe supervisory relationship. Another way to achieve this is by careful and clear contracting to allow the development of a relationship that supports 'collaboration for change' (Bordin, 1983), as discussed in Chapter 11 of this book. Con-tracting may include a discussion about mutual expectations and responsi-bilities in supervision, as well as the content of learning, the expected outcomes or competencies and how these will be evaluated. In the early phase of the relationship, providing the opportunity to contract for the supervisory relationship itself by exploring issues such as supervisee and supervisor learning styles and preferences, managing differences, feedback and review and acknowledging the power differential can be helpful. Setting clear boundaries both in terms of structure (regular, uninterrupted super-vision sessions, clear focus) and what can be brought to supervision is helpful. The supervisor maintaining interest and curiosity and showing some commitment to making the process work seems necessary for good relationships to develop. Conversely, it is not helpful to display a lack of interest or commitment to supervision, often displayed by turning up late and not maintaining the structural boundaries that might be expected. One of the ways of establishing and maintaining a strong SR is through overall modelling of ethical and respectful relationships with supervisee, clients and colleagues, which is greatly enhanced by mutual observation. The reader is referred to Scaife (2009) for a comprehensive discussion of contracting in supervision.

Establishing opportunities for mutual, regular, honest, open feedback and constructive criticism also aids the process of supervision. Given the potential power dynamic in the SR, it may be helpful for the supervisor to regularly invite and encourage feedback from the supervisee to ensure that their needs are being met and that they are engaged in the supervision process. This is particularly pertinent in situations where cultural or gender issues may lead to different views or assumptions being held regarding the supervisory relationship. The supervisor also has a quality control function and has a responsibility to observe, directly or via recording, the supervisee's work and to provide detailed feedback, often best done through encouraging self-assessment and reflection (Falender and Shafranske, 2004). It is generally helpful to include a discussion of the evaluation element of supervision during contracting so that feedback can be tailored to individual supervisee and supervisor preferences and learning styles. Providing support that encourages supervisee confidence and autonomy is important and needs to be tailored to the supervisee's learning needs. Ideally, supervisors should aim to be available, adaptable and flexible in their supervision style, focus, approach and model used.

The educative role in supervision is important and the relationship seems to be strengthened by collaborative thinking and building joint formulations that value the supervisee's and supervisor's knowledge and insights. Both sides of the dyad appear to value some playfulness, humour and creativity (Beinart, 2004), and practical and creative aspects of supervision are discussed further in Chapter 11. Comfort with raising and discussing difficult issues, in a way that is safe and containing, allows both parties to learn from mistakes and work together to resolve conflicts or miscommunications, which inevitably occur in the majority of relationships. It is helpful for supervisees to take an active part in supervision. This involves playing an active part in a collaborative relationship, showing interest and enthusiasm, identifying needs clearly, preparing for supervision by thinking about priorities and being open and receptive to learning and feedback. Although more difficult, supervisees who give clear and honest feedback to their supervisor can help to shape and develop the relationship. It is not helpful when supervisees fail to raise issues that they are struggling with, get defensive when offered feedback or do not take the advice of their supervisor without good reason or discussion.

Overall, an atmosphere where both supervisor and supervisee are committed to and invested in the process of supervision and communicate this to one another is helpful. This can be achieved by investing time at the beginning and by supervisees demonstrating openness to learning. If this occurs it appears that a virtual cycle of investment and openness can contribute to the building of strong supervisory relationships (Clohessy, 2008).

Summary

This chapter has described a selection of generic models of supervision (developmental, social role and integrative) and of the supervisory relationship (Holloway, Bordin) in some detail. It has discussed the complexity and difficulties of supervision research and some of the methodological issues involved. Some findings that support aspects of the theory have been presented, although as yet there is no fully evidence-based model of supervision. One of the reasons for this is the contention that the supervisory relationship is central to supervision and that we need to know more about this to build better theories. A discussion of recent research conducted in Oxford aimed at exploring the unique qualities of the supervisory relationship presented. This is followed by some points of good practice based on both theory and evidence.

Chapter 5

Generic or model-specific supervision?

David Green

There is a debate within the field of clinical supervision that roughly parallels a longer-standing argument in the world of outcome research in psychotherapy, which can be summed up thus:

> Is the essence of good supervision the same whatever the theoretical affiliation of the supervisor or do supervisees benefit more from being supervised in a manner that is consistent with, and specific to, the therapeutic model they intend employing to help their clients?

For the purposes of rhetorical clarity, it may be helpful to put a case for and against these alternative positions. However, in the real world I suspect that a 'both/and' stance will prove more helpful than 'either/or' simplicity, so that will be the likely take-home message of this chapter. But let us start off with a spot of muscular debate and leave the wimpish balanced conclusions for later.

In praise of model-specific supervision

Reflexivity

If therapists genuinely believe that the ideas and techniques that their discipline has developed are effective ways of understanding and promoting psychological growth, it would seem somewhat strange if they were unprepared to apply these same principles to help themselves – strange but not all that unusual.

In the heyday of behaviour modification the everyday environments of classrooms, prisons and long-stay wards were run according to carefully designed reinforcement schedules. I knew of no clinical psychology department that re-organised its own regime along the same lines. In a similar vein I have heard trainee clinical psychologists complain that their supervisor is treating them 'like one of their patients', when for example there has been some misunderstanding about where the personal/professional boundary might best be set in supervision discussions. While there is an important contractual point to be resolved here, it still sounds to me as if the trainees are expressing an implicit expectation that psychologists treat their colleagues and their clients differently – and they know to which category they would rather belong.

The principle of reflexivity argues that decent psychological theories should be capable of explaining the behaviour of psychologists as well as those they presume to help. If the models of change we use to inform our clinical work should be good enough for us too, then the same principle applies to the techniques we employ. If a cognitive behavioural therapist is prepared to ask her clients to keep thought diaries to help them become aware of recurrent patterns in their thinking, why wouldn't that be a helpful task for her supervisee to undertake? If a systemic practitioner regularly invites families with whom he works to complete a genogram as part of their collective exploration about where their expectations of how children ought to behave might have originated, wouldn't that be a relevant reflexive exercise for a trainee therapist to undertake?

It is an undiluted strength of model-specific supervisors that they stick by their principles – whoever they are trying to help.

Modelling

There are several advantages in having a supervisor who practises what they preach. Hypocrites rarely make credible role models. By contrast, supervisors who combine consistent adherence to their favoured theoretical model along with demonstrable therapeutic competence are well placed to exert a powerful influence on their supervisees' professional development. If the model they provide is less than perfect, so much the better (Bandura, 2006)! It is a well established axiom of the social learning literature that we all find it easier to emulate heroes with feet of clay as opposed to the flawless experts who never appear to get anything wrong.

In the musical *My Fair Lady*, Eliza Doolittle gets so frustrated by the verbosity of Professor Higgins and her younger admirer Freddy Eynsford-Hill that she bursts into exasperated song:

Sing me no song! Read me no rhyme!
Don't waste my time, Show me!

The particular words that Eliza wants to be translated into effective action are romantic, which is not generally a script to be encouraged in super-visory relationships but, switching contexts somewhat, many trainees will share her longing for some straightforward demonstration to complement the usual reflective conversations that are the staple diet of most supervision sessions. When supervisors use the same approach in supervision that the supervisee is using in therapy, they can model therapeutic technique in a safe yet convincing manner that allows trainees to *see* what is meant by, for example, 'circular questioning' or 'the downward arrow technique'.

Competent demonstrations of model-specific interventions serve two further educational purposes. First, they set a precedent for role-play and rehearsal in supervision, so the supervisee will be more likely to follow the supervisor's lead by conducting further behavioural experiments that will both reinforce good practice and provide opportunity for focused feedback on performance. A second additional benefit for the trainee is that they will get a taste of what it feels like to be at 'the receiving end' of some limited psychological interventions.

Procedural Clarity

It is a recurrent beef of clinical psychology trainees that no one will tell them exactly what is expected of them, particularly in their psychotherapeutic role. Left to their own devices, many develop an intuitive and informal way of responding sympathetically to their clients' needs. They keep their 'Sunday Best' psychology, in which theory and practice are seamlessly interweaved, for their essays and case presentations back at the university. As their clinical supervisors will often have little time (and, in some cases, little inclination) to directly sample the trainee's clinical work, opportunities for influencing this evolving therapeutic style by providing specific corrective feedback are likely to be distinctly limited.

However, model-specific supervision can offer a much less ambiguous alternative. The procedural clarity of cognitive behavioural therapy (CBT) training is a good example. The interventions to be employed in treating, say, social phobia are methodologically explicit. Furthermore, structured feedback on a trainee therapist's performance can be greatly assisted by the use of rating scales that allow the supervisor to assess how closely treatment guidelines have been followed (Keen and Freeston, 2008). This rigorous approach follows the framework developed by psychotherapy outcome researchers, who need to ensure that all the therapists participating in large-scale treatment trials are singing from the same proverbial hymnbook. The logic is simple. Where efficacy research has indicated that a particular approach to treating a problem has delivered encouraging results, the more closely a trainee adheres to the prescriptions of the specified intervention, the more likely their patient is to benefit. 'Getting it right' is the fundamental principle of quality control.

Of course the attractions of knowing what is expected of you as a novice therapist can be somewhat offset by an enhanced awareness of how frequently you miss the mark. A droll paper penned by I. M. Worthless (a pseudonym I suspect) and colleagues in 2002 described the symptoms of Cognitive Therapy Training Stress Disorder (or CTTD), from which many would-be CBT practitioners apparently suffer. It seems there is just no pleasing some people!

Theoretical coherence

When supervision is conducted within the framework of a single therapeutic model the various 'bits' of psychotherapeutic practice will hang together more persuasively than would probably be the case in a more eclectic way of working. This will be reflected in consistent links between the broad therapeutic principles that underlie a particular model's approach, the general methods that are especially characteristic of its *modus operandi* and the specific intervention techniques that have been developed by its practitioners (Burnham, 1992). Where appropriate assessment tools have been developed, it is possible to use a set of theoretically coherent measures to track both ends of the therapeutic process from input to outcome. Adherence measures provide sound indicators of how closely the actual intervention matches theoretically derived intentions. Tailored outcome measures (assessing, say, family interactional styles or degree of depression) allow therapist and supervisor to gauge how well the treatment is working. It all makes sense.

There are good reasons to think that when all aspects of a psychological intervention convincingly cohere in this way it will suit both client and therapist. The psychotherapeutic journey can take so many unexpected turns that it helps considerably if the fellow travellers can at least set off with some common agreements about where they want to go and how they plan to get there.

Cementing the alliance

Bordin's (1979) pan-theoretical model of the therapeutic alliance is widely known and has stimulated a great deal of research on the influence of so-called 'non-specific' factors on the outcome of psychotherapeutic interventions (Horvath and Greenberg, 1994). In essence he identified three components of successful therapeutic alliances:

- The parties need to get on with each other – a question of interpersonal chemistry.
- All need to agree on what they hope to achieve from their joint work – a consensus on goals.
- Client(s) and therapist(s) need to negotiate how they intend going about that task – a consensus on method.

From the foregoing discussion it follows that the careful negotiation of a therapeutic contract will likely be aided by a common understanding of how the client's problems might have arisen and what might be an acceptable and effective way of trying to help resolve their difficulties. While this desired state of affairs can be achieved by a lengthy period of 'getting to know you' mutual exploration, the same point can be reached a lot more quickly if both parties sign up to the same theoretical model.

Returning to the principle of reflexivity, it follows that the same sense of shared purpose will prove as beneficial to the alliance between supervisor and supervisee as it does to the alliance between therapist and client – Bordin certainly thought so (Bordin, 1983). There is therefore a credible argument to be made that when a supervisee and supervisor agree to work together within the confines of a single specific theoretical model they increase the probability that their working relationship will profit from some of the non-specific factors described in the pan-theoretical alliance literature.

Taking supervisor training seriously

Writing in 1997 Watkins reflected in the concluding chapter of *Handbook of Psychotherapy Supervision* which he edited, that he felt an uncomfortable mismatch between the central position that supervision has historically held in the training of psychotherapists of all persuasions and the flimsy literature on how clinical supervisors might best be prepared for their pivotal educational role. Reading between the lines he thought that we had collectively not taken this responsibility anywhere near seriously enough. That is not a charge that can be easily lain against those who are currently organising model-specific supervisor training in the UK.

The example of systemic therapy illustrates the level of commitment required to meet contemporary training standards in supervisor training. In order to be recognised as a qualified systemic supervisor the Association for Family Therapy (AFT) expects supervisors to have successfully completed a demanding training schedule that comprises:

- Two years of part-time study – 1 day a week in the first year and then 1 day a fortnight in the second year.
- Ongoing live supervision of supervision of family therapy using a pyramid arrangement.
- Supervision and scrutiny of videotape records of individual and group supervision provided by trainee supervisors of work conducted in their own agency.
- Regular peer supervision system with a 'consulting partner'.
- Performance evaluated through systematic self-appraisal, supervisor assessment and completion of a thesis of 10,000 words on some key aspect of supervision.

This palpably represents a commitment to try to do the job properly. The design of the training course is consistent with research findings seeking to identify the characteristics of effective Continuing Professional Development (Davis et al., 1992).

Of course it is possible to organise a similarly thorough training schedule for supervisors following generic rather than model-specific principles. It just doesn't seem to happen so often.

On the other hand . . .

The several arguments presented thus far in favour of employing a model-specific approach to clinical supervision make a compelling case. However there is another side to this debate that needs a similarly comprehensive airing. Why might it be wise to take the claims of single-model enthusiasts with a wee pinch of salt?

The Dodo verdict

As long ago as 1936 Saul Rosenzveig (an undergraduate contemporary of B. F. Skinner at Yale) published a paper in which he reviewed the evidence available at the time that any one of the then fashionable schools of psychotherapy was evidently the 'brand leader' in terms of treatment outcome. He concluded that there was minimal evidence for differential effectiveness and memorably summarised his findings by quoting the Dodo bird from Lewis Carroll's *Alice in Wonderland*. The Dodo had initiated a pretty chaotic 'caucus race' to persuade the various characters in the book to run around vigorously and dry off after getting soaked by Alice's tears. When they had all run out of steam the Dodo was asked who had won this impromptu contest. In an admirable piece of diplomatic fudging he opined: 'All have won and must have prizes'.

The evidence on which Rosenzveig could draw in those pre-war days was a tiny fraction of the psychotherapy outcome research currently available, but there are a number of contemporary commentators such as Wampold (2001) who would contend that, in broad terms, the Dodo verdict on the relative merits of the range of psychotherapies that are currently in vogue still stands. It is important to acknowledge that not everyone shares this reading of the extant literature (Chambless, 2002; DeRubeis, Brotman and Gibbons, 2005).

In one sense this debate is not especially germane to the case for model-specific clinical supervision. Supervisors favouring the major psychotherapeutic schools can all cite convincing meta-analyses demonstrating the effectiveness of their preferred treatment over no treatment or placebo controls (CBT: Butler et al., 2006; systemic: Shadish et al., 1995; psychodynamic: Leichsenrig and Rabung, 2008). Furthermore nobody is nowadays arguing about whether or not psychotherapy works. The point at issue is: 'Are some therapies more effective than others for particular people with particular problems?'

So psychotherapy outcome research can be cited in support of model-specific clinical supervision by practitioners with a range of theoretical affiliations. But can we be certain that we understand the processes by which these positive results have been achieved? Probably not.

Mechanisms of change

The coherence of single-model approaches applauded in an earlier section of this chapter stems from the central theoretical premise first expressed by the free-thinking individuals who got the ball rolling in the first place. This might be the faith that therapeutic interpretation can help clients become more consciously aware of the motivations behind their behaviour, or that the constricting stories we habitually tell about ourselves are open to revision, or that all individuals have an untapped capacity to resolve their problems that they can access given the right psychological climate, and so on. These insights into potential change mechanisms lie at the core of all schools of psychotherapy and inform the treatment procedures developed by practitioners working within various theoretical traditions. We might therefore be tempted to conclude that when interventions developed in this fashion have been demonstrated to be clinically effective, they have worked in precisely the way anticipated by the models' originators – *quod erat demonstrandum.*

However, outcome research that classically compares pre- and post-treatment measures can demonstrate only that change has occurred but cannot answer questions about how that change has come about. This requires complex and sophisticated process research, which remains relatively thin on the ground. A few research findings suggest that the scientific investigation of mechanisms of change might well produce some unexpected results.

Two recent meta-analyses of studies relating to mechanism of change in psychotherapy (Johansson and Hoglend, 2007; Kazdin, 2008) have drawn similar conclusions about the state of current knowledge in this field. We don't know much for certain at all. Kazdin considered that only one mediating variable has as yet been convincingly demonstrated (de-conditioning of anxiety), while Johansson and Hoglend reported finding no compelling evidential support for any hypothesised change process in 61 studies of mediator analyses in psychotherapy. This form of research is time-consuming (in that it requires multiple data-collection points) and statistically complex (as simple correlational analyses cannot establish cause-and-effect relationships) but its importance is underlined by a series of intriguing papers that challenge our preconceptions about how psychotherapy works.

The first is a recurrent finding that those who are going to respond well to psychological interventions tend to make their most significant shifts at an early stage in their treatment. For example, the large Project Match study in the USA comparing three different standardised forms of psychological treatment for alcohol abuse demonstrated that most change (as measured by days abstinent) across all three conditions was achieved by the third session of therapy (Babor and Del Boca, 2003). Metaphorically speaking these dramatic improvements were made when the doctor had barely had time to open his medicine bag!

This is one of several concerns aired in an excellent critique of the assumption that cognitive therapy works through challenging faulty thought patterns (Longmore and Worrell, 2007). A second challenge stems from so-called 'dismantling' studies that sequentially deliver the separate components of complex therapy packages to examine their various contributions to treatment outcome. For example, a recent meta-analysis concluded that the cognitive element of CBT added nothing significant to the effectiveness of good old-fashioned behavioural activation in the treatment of moderate depression (Cuijpers, Van Straten and Warmedam, 2007).

Another way of testing whether devotees of particular therapeutic schools are correct in their beliefs about how their favoured approach achieves results is to ask their consumers what aspects of treatment *they* found most/least helpful. A good illustration of this approach is a UK study into the experiences of mothers of learning disabled children who had been part of a support project employing the principles of solution-focused therapy (SFT: Lloyd and Dallos, 2008). By and large their feedback was encouraging but participants expressed a near-universal distaste for the 'miracle question' that the founders of SFT considered a *sine qua non* of effective practice (Molnar and De Shazer, 2007). While we might argue that those who use mental health services have no more special insight into the factors that influence their behaviour than the rest of us (Humphreys and Wilbourne, 2006), this sort of finding should at the very least make us reconsider the level of confidence we have in our theories about how individual therapies work.

Intriguing stuff, but what implication does this have for clinical supervision, you may ask. You don't have to fully understand how an effective therapy works if it consistently delivers the goods. The Bell and Pad treatment of childhood enuresis first promoted by Mowrer and Mowrer in 1938 remains a popular and successful treatment for bed-wetting (Butler, 2004) and to this day no one understands the therapeutic mechanism at work. There is however a consensus that there is much more going on than the simple classical conditioning rationale that inspired the system's developers.

Why not use supervision to monitor trainees who are delivering effective protocol-driven interventions and let the search for therapeutic mediators carry on at its own pace?

Manualised therapy

The apogee of model-specific supervision involves direct sampling of therapists' behaviour to ensure that they are following the directions provided in an operationally defined treatment manual. Therapy manuals were initially developed as part of the machinery of randomly controlled outcome studies investigating the effectiveness of psychological treatments. Researchers needed to ensure that therapists participating in treatment trials delivered a standard 'pukka' product for the same reasons that drug companies need to exercise quality control over the medications prescribed in pharmaceutical trials. Once the criteria for proper delivery of, say, multi-family systemic therapy had been agreed and operationalised, researchers could analyse tapes of treatment sessions and gauge how closely participating therapists had adhered to the manual's specifications. Once a 'good enough' level of adherence had been agreed, only data from therapists whose sessions met that criterion were entered into the trial's analyses. Where interventions provided according to a specific treatment protocol have been proved to be beneficial in the stringent conditions of a randomly controlled efficacy trial, the logic of evidence-based practice (EBP) is compelling. If you want to get similar results for your patients, repeat the exercise – by the book.

Given the care and effort put into developing treatment manuals and evaluating the effectiveness of precisely described therapeutic interventions, we might expect that this method of delivering psychological care would have demonstrable advantages over the much derided 'treatment as usual (TAU)'.

Well, yes and no. Certainly some researchers (frequently those with an established affiliation to a particular theoretical position) have reported that adherence to treatment manuals is indeed related to improved outcomes in comparison with appropriate control groups, but this is by no means a universal finding (Miller and Binder, 2002). In a recent meta-analysis of the available published evidence, Perepletchikova and Kazdin (2005) concluded that there was not a compelling case that manualised treatments were more effective than matched non-manualised alternatives. Interestingly interventions where therapists apply the principles of motivational interviewing in their work with problem drinkers, as opposed to following a more prescriptive treatment manual, seem to be significantly *more* successful (Hettema, Steele and Miller, 2005). Furthermore, even where therapists in controlled trials all adhere to the same treatment protocol they tend to produce notably different outcomes. Huppert and colleagues reported treatment effect sizes ranging from 0 to 18% for the 14 different CBT therapists participating in a large randomised controlled trial (RCT) study into treatment of panic disorder, and none of this variance could be explained by the minor differences in how well individual therapists had followed the script (Huppert et al., 2001).

Preoccupation with technique

The points raised thus far amount to a concern that training supervisees to follow treatment manuals may lead them to establish patterns of practice, some elements of which may ultimately prove redundant or even qualify as superstitious behaviour. Traditional generic approaches to supervision could easily lead to the same outcome. While behaviour learned by rule-following is theoretically more resistant to change than that acquired as a result of naturally occurring environmental contingencies, it is doubtful whether any supervisee's developing treatment skills have been predominantly shaped by feedback from clients about what they have found helpful or, even more importantly, unhelpful. As a profession clinical psychology does not have much of a tradition of seeking out that information. What is more, the folk we would really like to hear from – the estimated 47% who drop out of psychotherapy prematurely (Barrett et al., 2008; Wierzbicki and Pekarik, 1993) – are unlikely to be available to ask.

However, a pre-occupation with correctly following prescribed treatment procedures can place other constraints on clinical psychology trainees' development and the quality of service they are able to provide for their clients.

Evidence-based practice represents a 'best guess' at what treatment tack is likely to be most useful for most clients with a particular presenting problem. It is a probabilistic assessment, not a guarantee of success. Some clients will not respond as hoped and a small minority may well deteriorate (Morley, Williams and Hussain, 2008). When a trainee brings a case that is not progressing smoothly to supervision, as of course they should, how might the supervisor best respond? In model-specific supervision it makes sense first to check whether the intervention is being delivered in accordance with the appropriate treatment protocol. If the supervisor is operating from a more generic perspective s/he might invite the trainee to engage in a spell of reflection on what might be happening in therapy and how this particular impasse might have arisen. These reflections might be followed by a more theoretically informed analysis as supervisor and supervisee seek to frame the difficulty in formal psychological terms. The pairing would then consider the practical implications of their deliberations and agree a plan of action that the supervisee would subsequently enact, so completing one round of the experiential learning cycle (Kolb, 1984).

Of course a similar process might well occur in a model-specific supervisory relationship. The trainee might be invited to use the framework of the shared theoretical model to develop a further understanding of their client's and indeed their own reactions in therapy. However, the EBP rationale does not give the same leeway to practitioners to experiment with different interventions even if they represent variations on the same theoretical theme. Assuredly some authors of therapy manuals allow more 'wriggle room' than others (Carroll and Nuro, 2002) but this built-in flexibility to adapt interventions to local conditions inevitably violates the basic assumptions behind the EBP stance on treatment integrity (Beutler, 2009).

Overall therefore I consider that model-specific supervision is more likely than generic supervision to value technical adherence over free-thinking reflection. Furthermore generically inclined supervisors will, almost by definition, encourage their supervisees to draw on a greater range of theoretical models in their clinical formulations. Their trainees will also probably have more room to manoeuvre in deciding how individual cases should be managed.

It is however important not to equate EBP in clinical supervision with model-specific approaches to supervision. They frequently overlap but logically need not. It is quite possible to take a particular theoretically informed stance in supervision that pays no heed to available outcome research findings, just as it is quite possible to use the results of research linking non-specific factors with psychotherapy outcome to direct a supervisee to follow specific evidence-based technical interventions (Norcross, 2002).

But isn't this basically an empirical question?

Surely it is not beyond the wit of some bright spark researcher to design an experiment that would put the apparently rival claims of technique- or process-focused clinical supervision to the practical test. Fortunately a recent Australian study has taken just such a hard-edged empirical approach to trying to resolve the issues thus far reviewed in this chapter (Bambling et al., 2006). The paper reports an investigation of the impact of alliance-focused supervision on the treatment of depressed adults using problem-solving therapy (PST). This is a structured and well-researched cognitive therapy popular in Australia. All therapists were trained to a demonstrated level of competence in PST and delivered a standardised eight-session intervention to their clients. Participating therapists were randomly allocated to one of three groups: no supervision, skill-focused supervision and process-focused supervision. Consistent supervisory practice was ensured by manualised training and monitoring to check adherence. The first supervision session served as an introduction, explaining to both groups of supervisees what they should expect of their supervisors, and then weekly supervision sessions continued as per the two supervision manuals.

The measures taken in this carefully designed study were as follows:

- The Working Alliance Inventory (WAI) measuring the client/therapist alliance was completed by clients at the end of sessions 1, 3 and 8.

- The Beck Depression Inventory (BDI) was completed at sessions 1 and 8.
- An assessment of client satisfaction was made at the end of therapy.
- Drop-out rates were recorded for each condition.

The results of this study proved both encouraging and somewhat confusing for clinicians interested in gaining a better understanding of the mechanisms of supervision, and are worth reviewing in detail:

- At the end of treatment both BDI and WAI scores were significantly better for clients who had been treated by therapists in the supervised than in the unsupervised groups, but there was no difference in outcome between the two supervised groups. Precisely the same pattern held for measures of client satisfaction and drop-out rates. Supervised therapists got significantly better results than unsupervised therapists but there was no difference between the two supervision groups.
- Adherence to the problem-solving therapy manual was similar across all three groups and, interestingly, proved unrelated to the final outcome of treatment. However, WAI and BDI scores were strongly correlated, as predicted by the therapeutic alliance literature.
- However, the difference between the alliance scores reported by clients seen by supervised as opposed to unsupervised therapists was firmly established at the end of the first therapy session and stayed relatively constant thereafter. The only supervision discussion to precede this opening therapy session was the initial contracting conversation in which the two parties agreed how they would operate once 'proper' supervision started!

The results of this experiment are reasonably clear-cut. It seems that supervision works, in that clients appear to have gained more benefit from seeing a supervised as opposed to an unsupervised therapist even though all therapists were following a treatment protocol in which they had received recent and thorough training. The specific style adopted by the supervisor conferred no advantage either way.

Quite how these results were achieved remains a complete mystery.

So what?

This somewhat idiosyncratic tour of the ill-mapped territory of generic or model-specific supervision must now come to an end. From the foregoing discussion the alert reader will already have anticipated that no clear winner will emerge from this particular contest – for the time being at least. Rather than simply bemoan the lack of convincing evidence on which to base their practice (Ellis and Ladany, 1997), the opportunist supervisor in this instance might look to take the best of both worlds.

From model-specific approaches s/he could: aspire to make explicit theory/ practice links; be prepared to model therapeutic technique in supervision; be explicit about what constitutes a 'good enough' intervention; and invest serious time and effort in developing their own competence as a supervisor.

Following the tenets of the generic tradition in supervision s/he could: encourage trainees to take the time to stop and think carefully and independently about their work; direct supervisees to draw on theoretical ideas and empirical evidence from all corners of the discipline of clinical psychology; and promote the development of formulations and interventions that are tailored to the unique circumstances of each individual client.

There are good reasons to think that this 'both/and' solution will benefit trainees and their clients. Current empirical research into the development of professional expertise (Ericsson, 2009) identifies training experiences that are required to achieve optimal levels of occupational performance. Some of these factors, such as intense and enduring domain-specific work experiences, fit well in a generic framework while others, such as deliberate technical practice, map better onto the tenets of model-specific supervision. A final factor – the overriding importance of timely and accurate feedback – applies equally easily to both traditions. Surprisingly the benefits of employing continuous client feedback in psychotherapy supervision have only recently been subjected to any serious scrutiny (Reese et al., 2009).

Sceptical readers may find themselves dissatisfied with what they consider to be 'wishy-washy' conclusions. However if hard-headed scientist-practitioners can find defensible ways of combining EBP-driven therapy with theoretically informed creative interventions (Scott and Dadds, 2009), then why can't supervisors manage something similar in their work?

For myself I wish to retain a proverbial foot in both camps and if that comes across as 'woolly minded' and intellectually unsatisfactory I will end by citing the Yorkshire wisdom of J. B. Priestley in my defence:

> It is the woolly mind that combines scepticism of everything with credulity about everything. Being woolly it has no hard edges. It is easy, pliant, yet it has its own toughness. Because it bends it does not break. . . . The woolly mind realises that we live in an unimaginable gigantic, complicated, mysterious universe. To try to stuff the vast bewildering creation into a few neat pigeon-holes is absurd. We don't know enough and to pretend we do is mere intellectual conceit. The best we can do is to keep looking out for clues, for anything that will light us a step or two into the dark.
>
> (Priestley, 1972: 30)[1]

So there. . . .

Summary

This chapter considers the case for, and against, model-specific supervision. Where supervisor and supervisee opt to operate within a single shared theoretical model they are likely to reap a number of benefits (such as improved technical specificity, greater coherence, commendable psychological reflexivity, and an enhanced supervisory alliance). The logic of the EBP movement also encourages supervisors to promote adherence to the prescriptions of treatment manuals tested in outcome research trials. However, some elements of the EBP case (such as the notorious Dodo bird verdict, the uncertain evidence regarding mechanisms of change and the absence of a strong empirical link between adherence to therapeutic protocols and client outcome) remain open to question. The chapter concludes with a detailed review of a recent trial comparing the effectiveness of skill as opposed to process-focused supervision and some tentative recommendations on how creative supervisors might draw on both model-specific and generic traditions in their work.

Note

1 Excerpt by J. B. Priestley from *Over the Long High Wall: Some Reflections and Speculations on Life, Death and Time* (© J. B. Priestley, 1972) is reproduced by permission of PFD (www.pfd.co.uk) on behalf of the Estate of J. B. Priestley.

Chapter 6

Developments in supervisor training

Ian Fleming

Introduction

It is self-obvious that training clinical psychologists in supervisory skills will be an essential contributor to the quality and availability of supervision. In this chapter I will describe developments in the training in supervisory skills available to clinical psychologists. In particular I will refer to the recent work of the Supervisor Training and Recognition (STAR) group – formerly the Development and Recognition of Supervisory Skills (DROSS) group – and describe the contribution that it has made to the development of an understanding of the importance of supervisor training and in the evaluation and accreditation of supervisory skills. The chapter will consider related developments in other professions and discuss some of the important ongoing issues concerning training.

Recent developments in supervisor training

Most clinical psychologists obtain training in supervisory skills from their local *pre-qualification* clinical psychology training programmes. This seems to be the preferred route (Fleming, 2004) although there are available alternative sources of training. Since the first edition of this book, there appears to have been an increase in the availability of training workshops in supervision skills, both one-off training events and also programmes of training. These would often be associated with Higher Education Institutions. Generally both sorts of events are aimed at people from broad, non-specific mental health or social care backgrounds. Apart from the clinical psychology training programmes there are very few resources aimed specifically at clinical psychologists. In this respect the Doctoral Clinical Psychology programmes are providing important Continuing Professional Development (CPD) for qualified practitioners.

For many years it has been a requirement for clinical psychology training programmes to provide training for supervisors, and this has been a constituent part of the British Psychological Society's (BPS) accreditation process for training programmes (BPS, 2008b). In recent years there has been an increase in the specification of this training, and the most recent accreditation requirements state that:

> Regular workshops on supervisory skills and other training events for supervisors must be organised by the programme to ensure effective supervision. Supervisors should be encouraged to attend workshops and training events periodically. Programmes must ensure that the training events offered meet the needs of both new supervisors and more experienced colleagues. Suggested learning objectives for introductory training are provided at Appendix 5.
>
> (BPS, 2008b, section 9.7)

(The statement about Appendix 5 refers to the adoption by the professional body of the learning objectives for supervisor training developed by the STAR group.)

Although over time the BPS has increased the requirements for the provision of supervisor training, this remains at the level of guidance and there is a resistance to stipulate, for example, that training is a necessity for supervision. Historically this has been defended by a reluctance to introduce requirements that might reduce the availability of supervisors in an era of the expansion of training places and thus an increased need for clinical placement supervisors.

The arrangements for the BPS to be solely responsible for the accreditation of training programmes changed in 2009 when clinical psychology became regulated by the Health Professions Council (HPC). As a result various responsibilities were transferred from the BPS to the HPC, including that of accrediting clinical psychology training programmes. At the time of writing (April 2010) there is in place an agreement for the BPS to continue to play a part in the accreditation process, and a new document congruent with the new procedures has been published: *Standards for Doctoral Programmes in Clinical Psychology* (BPS, 2010). It is pleasing to see that section 5, concerning supervision, is consistent with the previous BPS document in 2008 (mentioned above) and includes the learning objectives for supervisor training.

A survey described in the first edition of this book (Fleming, 2004) showed that in 2001 all of the responding clinical psychology training programmes organised training for qualified clinical psychologists in supervision skills, and that over 70% of these organised regular programmes of training. There was in general a high demand for supervisor training. There was some commonality in the content of this training, although exact details were not reported, and it was concluded that '. . . there is a shared view about the core issues for supervision training, and therefore by extension for what constitutes effective supervisory skills . . .' (Fleming,

2004: 83). This conclusion was very similar to that obtained in a survey of clinical psychology supervisors in Scotland carried out by the National Health Service Education for Scotland (NES). Resulting recommendations were for the development of new resources for supervisor training (Allen, Bagnall and Campbell, 2003).

Information gained in August 2009 from 26 of the 30 UK training programmes in clinical psychology confirmed that all except one provided regular training in supervisory skills. Almost all of the clinical psychology training programmes were 'STAR ready' in the sense that their training met the minimum standards for supervisor training advocated by the STAR group (see below).

Although there has been an increased emphasis on the training requirement, details of the content, form and extent of training remain unspecified. It is unclear how supervisor training will be affected by the replacement of the BPS by the HPC in the accreditation process. At the time of writing (April 2010) it is envisaged that the BPS will continue to be involved in this through a process called 'accreditation through partnership'.

Since 2005 the NES has been organising supervisor training specifically for clinical psychologists in Scotland (Bagnall, 2010). One of many important features of this training has been the requirement for participants to demonstrate the transfer of training into practice through the production of *portfolios*. Since data from the aforementioned 2009 survey indicate that currently there is limited experience of evaluating the experience of supervisor training, the use in Scotland of these portfolios, and their internal assessment and external review, is highly innovative.

Portfolios are completed that need to demonstrate evidence for the achievement and use of supervisory competences, and the writers also need to demonstrate an understanding of the theoretical basis for practice and ongoing reflection of their supervisory practice. The portfolios comprise 12 statements that had been mapped onto the Intended Learning Outcomes for the training. The experience of assessing portfolios has enabled the development of guidance to facilitate the most effective organisation of the content. For example, referencing sheets for each competence are used that help the participant structure their response in the categories: *experiential evidence, the rationale for selecting this evidence* (the theory–practice links) and the participant's *learning from the experience* (reflective learning). Participants are required to monitor their performance and progress against each of these statements and to submit evidence to support this from their current supervision (of a clinical psychology trainee). Participants provided evidence from different sources, including communications with the trainee and others, notes from supervision (both formal and informal/personal) and reflective content (e.g. from logs and journals). In 2009 it was decided that this training would be replaced by a more generic form of training suitable for a range of mental health professions, with an additional dedicated module for clinical psychologists. Again, there have been close links between DROSS/STAR members and the NES concerning this initiative.

Although clinical psychology training programmes within Higher Education Institutions (HEIs) provide the bulk of training for supervisors, other providers of supervisor training exist. These include a range of one-off training days and bespoke courses or programmes of training organised by other educational establishments and independent providers.

Because the training provided by clinical psychology training programmes is free to users (an element for this training is contained in the Strategic Health Authority contract for training), it seems unlikely that many clinical psychologists will choose an expensive alternative – and less likely that their employers will fund them to do so – although it is proposed in Scotland that employing Trusts will pay for their staff to utilise the NES training

What happens in other health professions?

In the first edition of this book it was stated that where supervision was concerned clinical psychology had some catching up to do with other mental health professions. Although such a statement may have seemed controversial to a profession that can be seen to portray itself as vanguard-ist, this has not been the case. Instead in the intervening years there has been an ongoing commitment to developing good practice in supervision. This has been timely in view of policies that have described changes to the professional role of clinical psychologists, for example: New Ways of Working (BPS, 2007b) and Improving Access to Psychological Therapies (BPS, 2007c). The impact of these policies is discussed more fully in Chapters 3 and 5 of this book. The projection within these documents for an increased role for psychologists in supervising others required two things: we needed to develop our own supervisory competence (the core of this book) and we needed to find out more about the supervisory practice of other health professions.

A number of health professions already have in existence a form of accreditation for suitably trained clinical supervisors – often called *clinical educators*. Commonly, a local HEI programme trains individual clinical educators and then recommends (but, in effect, awards) to their profes-sional body that the individual be placed on a register. This model – with its minimal administration – appeared to have a lot of value to the STAR group in its deliberations about the best means of awarding accreditation.

The following provides a brief, but not inclusive, overview of related developments in other professions in health and social care:

- As described in Chapter 2, in *counselling and psychotherapy* (UKCP, 2008) there has been a longstanding requirement for supervision and the different constituent bodies within the United Kingdom Council for Psychotherapy have requirements for supervision.

- *Psychiatrists* are benefitting from increased attention to supervision and the skills required of supervisors. Innovative practice can be found, including that of the London Deanery (London Deanery, 2010), which organises 'a unique programme of training in the conversational skills needed for effective supervision' that extends over 3 days.
- Within psychiatry there remains a distinction between *educational and clinical* supervision. Definitions for each have been altered by the Royal College of Psychiatrists in early 2009 to enhance their contribution to effective professional training. Both contain specific references to individuals being 'appropriately trained' in their respective responsibilities (Howard, 2009).
- Simultaneously with these developments the Royal College of Psychiatrists encourages consideration of *coaching* to aid personal and professional development. It is also involved with an online initiative, one module of which is entitled 'Giving feedback to trainees' and is aimed at Educational Supervisors who carry out the workplace-based assessments (WPBA) of trainee psychiatrists.
- Within general *medical education* there has been a growing emphasis on the importance of supervision. Kilminster, Jolly and van der Vieuten (2002) called for a framework for effective training for supervisors that was derived from empirical and theoretical work. In 2007 a guide was published into what was known about effective educational and clinical supervision practice (Kilminster et al., 2007). This contained a number of recommendations concerning the aims and practice of supervision and emphasised the importance of contracts, the supervisory relationship and training in supervisory skills.
- *Educational psychologists* have, through their division of the BPS, recently developed Quality Standards for their services. One section entitled Professional Supervision of Trainee Educational Psychologists includes the standard 'A commitment to attending supervisors training'. Another standard states that the process of supervision 'is carried out by peers and/or managers who . . . have been involved in training relating specifically to supervision' (DECP, 2006: 12).
- Recent research (Gaitskell and Morley, 2008) found that in a survey of *occupational therapists* in the UK 23% had no training in supervision and 61% had only basic training of around 1 day duration. Others have pointed to the general paucity of training in supervisory skills available to members of the profession.
- The *Royal College of Speech and Language Therapists* is currently introducing a process of annual certification for providers of training for speech and language therapy, to ensure that high standards are maintained. City University runs 2-day courses for Clinical Supervisors

in Speech and Language Therapy and University College Plymouth provides a training programme for Clinical Educators, with a basic and advanced course each of 1 day, and learners are required to complete reflective logs to embed learning.

- *Art therapists* have extensive guidance on the roles and tasks of placement supervisors (BAAT, 2009), although it is unclear whether there is training available for this role, and there is reference to it being important that all placement supervisors should understand the purpose of clinical supervision. Ideally, since all art psychotherapy training courses teach psychodynamic principles, the professional orientation of the placement supervisor should reflect this.
- In *drama therapy* also there is extensive guidance on the tasks of supervision, including statements concerning anti-discriminatory practice, modes of supervision, and so on. Supervisors are required ('must take all reasonable steps') to have supervision of their own supervision work (BADT, 2006).
- There is an extensive literature on the use of supervision in *nursing*. NHS Trusts include Clinical Supervision within Strategy Policies for Nursing and Midwifery. In 2007 the Nursing and Midwifery Council amended its rules to increase the requirements for training of supervisors. An example from the Dudley Group of Hospitals NHS Trust specifies that all supervisors will receive at least 2 days or the equivalent training at the outset of their supervisory role and that further updates in supervision will be essential in maintaining the role. This policy also discusses and distinguishes managerial and clinical supervision. A recent paper (Waskett, 2009) describes attempts to embed the supervision of nurses into organisational structures: the 4s model. Training emphasises a solution-focused approach that is simple, collaborative and respectful, and is reported to be transferable.
- However, another recent paper (Williams and Irvine, 2009) concluded that 'nurses who undertake the clinical supervisor role are rarely offered guidelines for fulfilling the role'. Also there is research to suggest that the potential of clinical supervision can fail to be delivered (Robinson, 2005).
- *Radiographers* have in place specific guidance for supervisors and a form of accreditation (Society of Radiographers, 2006). There is a specific requirement that 'appropriate supervisor training programmes need to be made available'.
- At the University of Leeds School of Healthcare (University of Leeds, 2008) there is a course entitled *Training the Trainers. A Course for Supervisors of Trainees in the Clinical Setting.* Although aimed primarily at *pharmacists*, the programme states that it is useful also 'in providing generic support for supervisors of other healthcare trainees in the clinical setting'. The course is at Master's level with two modules

of 9.5 days of teaching altogether, and is of particular interest because of its emphasis on multi-disciplinary supervision.

- Staff working for *NHS Direct* have a Clinical Supervision Policy written in 2008 that refers to a training package in clinical supervision and states that it 'will be nationally agreed . . . that clinical supervisors will receive training to enable them to carry out their extended role' (Haslam, 2008).

- The profession of *family therapy* acknowledges the importance of supervision and maintains a register of supervisors. Supervision skills are seen as distinctive from therapy skills and require further training. The Association for Family Therapy (AFT) has taken care over a number of years to develop training for supervisors. A recent document suggested that once the register becomes widely used 'the requirement for a registered supervisor in training and in CPD will become the norm' (Lask, 2009).

- Clinical Educators (supervisors) in *physiotherapy* benefit from extensive guidance (Chartered Society of Physiotherapy, 2004) about requirements for the role and for clinical placements. Accreditation is awarded by the Chartered Society of Physiotherapy (CSP) and underpinned by six learning outcomes, and Clinical Educators are able to achieve this through either a programme (training) or a grand-parenting route. For the former, training to meet the agreed learning outcomes is provided by local HEIs – alongside ongoing Continuing Professional Development (CPD) – and there is reference on both routes to the desirability of individuals maintaining portfolios to demonstrate competence. Within the guidance there is a clear reference to the importance of competence in the supervision of members of other professions, and not physiotherapists alone. Clinical psychologists were able to learn from the requirements of the CSP in developing their own accreditation process.

This overview suggests that other health professions (and especially those working in similar contexts to clinical psychologists) are also developing expertise in supervision, and attending to issues of training and quality assurance. There is quite a lot of common ground across professions and useful experience that can be learned and is transferable. These are important points to consider in the context of multi-disciplinary supervision.

Developments in supervisor training

In 2003 a shared interest in supervisor training led to the formation of an informal group mainly composed of staff from clinical psychology training programmes in the North of England and Scotland. The initial subjects for discussion included the status of training in supervisory skills, the content and form of supervisor training, evaluation processes and ongoing research into the effectiveness of supervisor training. From the outset one SHA recognised the importance of developing supervision and provided financial support.

Readers are reminded that the majority of supervisor training for qualified clinical psychologists in the UK was provided by pre-qualification training programmes. In addition to this training role, these staff (usually clinical tutors) had regular, close professional involvement with supervisors for trainee clinical psychologists from their programmes. These relationships extended to evaluative and supportive roles, although certainly not the managerial role that is the third part of the supervisory triad presented by Hawkins and Shohet (2006). The very absence of managerial responsibilities of supervisors, and the consequent reliance on the development of high quality trusting and facilitative relationships with individual supervisors, is an important strength of the relationship between clinical tutors and clinical psychologist supervisors, and will be discussed later on.

The group carried out an ambitious programme of work between 2003 and 2008: developing a list of intended learning outcomes for an *Introductory Course of Supervisor Training*; agreeing on some minimal standards to accompany this training; and developing an options appraisal for a form of accreditation. Further details are contained on the website (http://www.leeds.ac.uk/lihs/psychiatry/courses/dclin/cpd/DROSS/dross_welcome.htm); see also Fleming and Green (2007).

Whilst this work was carried out by clinical psychologists – and thus located within the Division of Clinical Psychology of the BPS – from the outset it was recognised that it would have relevance to the membership of other divisions: the basic themes of supervisor training and governance were very likely to be important to all applied psychologists. As the discussions about accreditation (see below) became focused on the role of the BPS as the relevant professional body, this provided an increased impetus to talk with other divisions.

Fortunately the expectations of common ground were confirmed in meetings with representatives of other BPS Divisions. From these meetings it became clear that the work of these clinical psychologists had more direct application for the memberships of some divisions than others.

Accreditation

One of the main aims of the STAR group was to seek accreditation for clinical psychologists with competent skills in supervision. This aim was consistent with developments in other health professions and their experience was scrutinised.

Historically, discussion of supervision has been limited to that of supervising *trainee* clinical psychologists; only more recently has consideration been given to supervising peers or members of other professions. Also, supervisory activity has been viewed as voluntary. More recently the conditions of service for NHS clinical psychologists within the Agenda for Change (DH, 2004) has stated that regular supervisory activity should be seen as a requirement for career progression, although it is unclear whether this is mandatory or remains essentially an activity of choice. Clinical tutors who organise training placements will recognise the shortfall in available placements for their trainees when compared with the potential number available. However, other factors (especially room space) confound the drawing of any clear conclusions.

Although specific requirements for supervision varied across the different divisions of the BPS, there was considerable agreement on the general value of supervisor training, on the learning outcomes for training and on the principle of accreditation for supervisors. Thus, although originating in the specific requirements of clinical psychologists, there was a lot of agreement on the general principles of improving supervision and supervisor training across the different divisional memberships within the Society. It was felt that developments could embrace different working arrangements for the supervision and training of supervisors (e.g. the varied role of HEIs in the training of supervisors and different processes of monitoring supervisory performance). This generic application fits with the recent and ongoing development towards *applied psychology* (and even the merger of the traditional Divisions of the BPS; Turpin, 2009) described in Chapter 3 of this volume.

The current situation

On 1 April 2010 the BPS opened the *Register of Applied Psychology Practice Supervisors* (RAPPS) and individuals are encouraged to join. Entry to the Register is dependent on undergoing a period of supervisor training that meets agreed minimal standards, currently emphasising content that is consistent with the learning objectives adopted by the BPS. For the first 3 years only there will be opportunities for gaining entry alternatively via a grand-parenting clause that will rely on the validation of previous and current supervisory practice. Details of the requirements for quinquennial renewal of membership are being finalised. These requirements are similar to those in other professions, such as the Chartered Society of Physiotherapy and the Association for Family Therapy (Lask, 2009).

Since the impetus for accreditation originated amongst clinical psychologists it was acknowledged that it was likely that clinical psychologists would form the bulk of the initial membership of the Register. It was expected that this situation would be short-lived and that the developments in all aspects of supervision in other divisions would stimulate interest across the membership.

Future directions

The developments in training for supervisors, and the impact of policies affecting the clinical psychology profession, suggest a number of issues that will be important in the future.

Introductory and further training

Clearly, an introductory programme of supervisor training is only the beginning. What will complement this?

A presumption underlying introductory training suggests that it is followed by *intermediate* or even *advanced* training. Experience suggests that there is a real demand for this, and it is professionally satisfying to see supervisors enthusiastic to extend and develop their supervisory skills. Currently, it is unclear who will have the resources to provide this. In the absence of funded alternatives, it would seem that clinical psychology training programmes will continue to provide introductory training, and this expectation may extend to the provision of advanced training in supervisory skills. In Manchester there are preparations to offer to supervisors who have completed the introductory training a number of advanced training days. This will also facilitate the requirements for CPD that are indicated as necessary for re-accreditation. It is also likely that the Division of Clinical Psychology in future will take on a more active role in the provision of CPD for its members; if so, there should be room within this for advanced supervisor training in supervisory skills.

The specific role ascribed to clinical psychology training programmes (with rare exceptions) is that of *pre-qualification* training. However, although a number of aspects of clinical training require the intimate observation, knowledge and discussion of the day-to-day practice of large numbers of local clinical colleagues, the *training of supervisors* emphasises this. Indeed training – if it is to hold value – implicitly involves evaluation. I am unaware of this issue being addressed directly, and find it interesting to consider to what degree there is acceptance and *legitimacy* for extending the activity of trainers into aspects of practice and post-qualification CPD. I like to think that trainers have good relationships of sufficient depth with local clinicians to allow for this development. An example of this issue is the introduction of a policy with which the three local training programmes in the North West of England will address issues of serious concern that arise on placements.

At Manchester this issue of the boundaries of the trainers' role has been discussed within supervisor training. In general there has been a favourable and positive response to possibilities of extending the work of trainers into areas that require some commentary on clinicians' practice – for example in relation to their supervisory skills and competencies. Perhaps any concerns about this extended role are exaggerated or unnecessary, but its continuation requires vigilance, care and clear communication between training programme staff and local clinicians. Furthermore, in Manchester we feel that this is helped by: the numbers of local clinicians who graduated from the training programme, are familiar with its processes and are great supporters; the excellent communication between the programme and the local NHS clinicians; the contribution by clinicians to committees and programme bodies; and the ongoing supervising practice of many programme staff in their clinical duties.

When should supervisor training begin?

The optimal timing for training in supervisory skills is important. The potential for further training in supervisory skills to constitute important CPD has already been discussed, but when should the initial training in supervisory skills commence? As has been discussed, traditionally supervision was considered as a post-qualification activity and focused on the professional gate-keeping role associated with the supervision of trainee clinical psychologists. Developments in clinical psychology training – to some degree themselves responses to different service requirements – suggest that exposure to training in supervisory skills and models should not be left until after qualification.

Perhaps it is more useful to see initial training for supervision lying within pre-qualification training, with a clear bridge across the qualification divide. This question was posed in 2004 in the first edition of this book, and there is evidence that increasingly training programmes are attending to competences in supervision *within* the 3 years of training.

There are three main reasons for this. The first is that it is important to provide the skills to trainees to enable them to play an active part in their own supervision. In my experience this ability is regularly discussed during supervisor training, and training in supervision skills and processes will inform and help trainees to enhance the effectiveness of the supervision they receive during training. A second factor originates in the competences that trainees need to acquire to become trained. Trainees on a range of clinical placements commonly will be required on placement to offer guidance, opinions and consultation to other staff, to work through other staff and to evaluate the practice. (In this way *New Ways of Working* are not so new, except perhaps to working with working-age adults with mental health problems.) In particular I am thinking of the ability to indirectly deliver psychological interventions and to work 'through others' (often non-psychology staff). Although this activity may not typically be called 'supervision', it includes many elements common to what we understand as supervision. Trainees are often sought out for their opinions and advice in clinical settings – sometimes in ways different to their own supervisors –

and a trainee may be asked to actively 'supervise' another worker in a specific situation. (This was a competence in the previous BPS Accreditation Criteria for training programmes and remains so: section 2.3.9.2 in the current BPS Standards for Doctoral Programmes in Clinical Psychology.) The closest that the HPC comes to this in the Standards of Proficiency for Practitioner Psychologists (HPC, 2009a: section 2b.4) is that of 'implementing interventions . . . through and with other professionals'. The recognition of this need has led to the development and expansion of space devoted to supervision within the curriculum.

Training programmes are increasingly preparing individuals for an active role in supervision. A survey (Youngson et al., 2005) found that training programmes were increasing the amount of teaching and training to trainees in preparation for their role as supervisees. The provision of *peer group supervision* during the 3 years of training was seen as a useful experiential route to gaining competence in supervisory (as well as supervisee) skills, with participants beginning to think of themselves as supervisors as well as supervisees (also see Akhurst and Kelly, 2006; and Chapter 10 of this book). Clarke (2006) confirmed that trainee clinical psychologists were enthusiastic about formal preparation for being supervisors, and in the first edition of this book Green (2004) reported on the successful experience of running supervisor training attended by both supervisors and supervisees in the form of final-year trainee clinical psychologists. It is expected that this development towards the provision of training in supervisory skills at an earlier stage of the professional career will continue.

Finally, there is utility in providing 'joined up' training in supervisory skills. In Manchester there is a high local retention of trainees, with around 80% obtaining a first post-qualification post in the region. It has been particularly pleasing to see cohorts of individuals complete their clinical psychology training and then, very soon after, qualify to go through our supervisor training before going on to enthusiastically and regularly provide supervision for future members of the profession. Within the supervisor training it is common to hear individuals reflecting on both their experience of being supervised and the training they receive for this, as they develop the aspects of the new professional role, such as that of being a gate-keeper for the profession (Hawkins and Shohet, 2006).

A development towards supervisor training that bridges pre- and post-qualification is consistent with the statements in policy documents that qualified clinical psychologists may be valued more for their managerial, leadership and supervisory roles than for their clinical skills per se (BPS, 2007b, d). Clinical psychologists need these skills to enable them to supervise the members of other professions and groups that are proposed in these papers. This development also requires us to consider the content of these skills and to consider the relative value of generic skills or those more closely linked to particular psychological models (e.g. as described in Chapters 3 and 5).

The content of supervisor training

In addition to reaching agreement on the competences that introductory training should include, minimal standards for supervisor training were developed, including the length (minimum 3 days) and an ongoing commitment to demonstrating resultant change in supervisory practice.

There was a reluctance to be too prescriptive about the content of training, although agreement was reached on the learning outcomes that introductory training should deliver (Table 6.1), and these were subsequently adopted by the BPS Committee on Training in Clinical Psychology (see above) and are a requirement for membership of the RAPPS.

It can be seen that this training has a broad canvas. It includes a model of learning that emphasises reflection and goes on to describe a number of different tasks within supervision. The supervisory relationship is given prominence, and suitable attention is devoted to considering and understanding the impact on supervision of issues of difference and diversity. Ethical issues are considered and different models and formats for supervision are explored. It does not conform to a single theoretical model or psychological model, and refrains from a prescriptive approach to the supervisee's learning.

It may be useful to briefly describe the introductory training module at Manchester. Supervisor training has been provided continuously for nearly 20 years, and a systematic organised programme was first developed in 1998 (for an earlier account, see Fleming and Steen, 2001). The programme is provided annually and has been amended in the light of feedback; a further revised programme commenced in February 2010. The training is provided within 5 full days across 20 months. There are regularly 20–25 participants and group work is emphasised. The content is as follows:

- Day 1: A 'preparation' day for supervising, including an introduction to the tasks involved in being a supervisor and the training programme requirements.
- Day 2: Identifying and developing the skills involved in supervising and relating supervision to models of learning.
- Day 3: The supervisory relationship and the difference and diversity in supervision.
- Day 4: Evaluating and managing difficulties in supervision, considering alternative formats and future needs, such as supervision of supervision.
- Day 5: Mentoring day – review of portfolios (see the discussion below of the transfer of training into practice).

Table 6.1 Learning objectives to be addressed by introductory supervisor training programmes

Understanding and application
1 Have knowledge of the context (including professional and legal) within which supervision is provided and an understanding of the inherent responsibility
2 Have an understanding of the importance of modelling the professional role (e.g. managing boundaries, confidentiality, accountability)
3 Have knowledge of developmental models of learning that may have an impact on supervision
4 Have knowledge of a number of supervision frameworks that could be used for understanding and managing the supervisory process
5 Have an understanding of the importance of a safe environment in facilitating learning and of the factors that affect the development of a supervisory relationship
6 Have skills and experience in developing and maintaining a supervisory alliance
7 Have knowledge of the structure of placements, including assessment procedures for disciplines at different levels of qualification up to doctorate level, and the expectations regarding the role of a supervisor
8 Have skills and experience in contracting and negotiating with supervisees
9 Have an understanding of the transferability of clinical skills into supervision and the similarities and differences
10 Have an understanding of the process of assessment and failure, and skills and experience, in evaluating trainees
11 Have skills and experience in the art of constructive criticism, ongoing positive feedback and negative feedback where necessary
12 Have knowledge of the various methods to gain information and give feedback (e.g. self-report, audio and videotapes, colleague and client reports)
13 Have skills and experience of using a range of supervisory approaches and methods
14 Have knowledge of ethical issues in supervision and an understanding of how this may affect the supervisory process, including power differentials
15 Have an understanding of the issues around difference and diversity in supervision
16 Have an awareness of the ongoing development of supervisory skills and the need for further reflection/supervision training
17 Have knowledge of techniques and processes to evaluate supervision, including eliciting feedback

Attitudes (value base)
1 Respects trainees
2 Sensitive to diversity
3 Committed to empowerment of supervisees
4 Values the ethical base guiding practice
5 Believes in balancing support and challenge
6 Committed to a psychological knowledge-based approach to supervision
7 Recognises the need to know own limitations
8 Supports the principle of life-long learning

Capabilities
1 The capability to generalise and synthesise supervisory knowledge, skills and values in order to apply them in different settings and novel situations

Generic or model-specific skills?

Discussion of the content of supervisor training raises the issue of whether there is a consistent and agreed model underlying the approach to introductory supervisor training. These issues are discussed at greater length in Chapter 5 of this book, and it does seem that there is the potential for supervisory developments to pull in different directions. A particular example concerns the developments associated (at the time of writing – April 2010) with *Improving Access to Psychological Therapies* (IAPT; BPS, 2007c), which are discussed further in Chapters 3 and 9 of this volume. Within the IAPT model, prominence was given to the role that supervision should play in the 'stepped' delivery of therapeutic interventions, based on particular psychological models. Consistent with this was a particular form of supervision centred on enabling participant adherence to evidence-based modularised therapy, based on cognitive behavioural therapy (CBT) models. To effect this, high intensity IAPT workers were required to be trained in supervision skills. These skills are arguably closer to those necessary for case management and might, for example, place less emphasis on the supervisory relationship and the power of reflection in achieving improved practice and knowledge.

Since many of these supervisors were likely to be clinical psychologists (with sufficient proficiency in CBT), the exact nature of supervision training came to the fore: Was there compatibility between different forms of supervisor training? This is crystallised in the question: Do individuals who have been trained in supervision skills that include the generic learning objectives (and which therefore are compatible with accreditation for the BPS Register – see above) need also to complete training in IAPT supervision skills? Similarly any requirement for the converse also seemed inappropriate.

In Sheffield, Jan Hughes (author of Chapter 11) has worked to resolve this issue. The University of Sheffield clinical psychology training programme obtained the contract to provide the training for all IAPT supervisors in the Yorkshire and Humber SHA. After a mapping exercise that identified a degree of overlap between the generic and IAPT learning objectives, there was also consideration of adapting the former to meet the latter's requirements, although certain competences remained specific to IAPT. An outcome was found in delivering a 3-day generic training programme for IAPT staff, with the addition of 2-day modules for either low or high intensity workers. The generic training was considered sufficient for future BPS accreditation.

Despite this example, the current picture seems a little confused and is not assisted by suggestions that suitability to join the RAPPS (based on a minimum of 3 days' supervisor training) would not enable an individual clinical psychologist to supervise an IAPT worker (see Chapter 3).

How do these developments in supervisor training relate to policy changes for clinical psychologists?

At this stage it would seem appropriate to consider the relationship between the recent developments and the wider policies impacting on clinical psychologists. The developments in supervisor training discussed in this chapter are consistent with efforts to demonstrate effective working, to utilise and contribute to NICE guidance (see Chapter 9) and to contribute to the future roles and tasks envisaged for clinical psychologists (Chapter 3).

For some time there have been strong recommendations for clinical psychologists to extend their expertise into clinical leadership, management and supervision of other staff (BPS, 2007d). Putting aside the comment that these terms can be used interchangeably, it is undoubtedly the case that clinicians have been involved in aspects of all three for some time; it is the emphasis that is new.

Thus any development in supervisory skills will clearly fit with an agenda that gives priority to the supervision of staff from other professions. This is acknowledged and has led to an emphasis on training supervisory competences within the pre-qualification training, as described above.

However, there are a couple of caveats. At times policy documents give the impression of a simplistic view of what is involved. Multi-disciplinary supervision, perhaps more than any other, requires an explicit agreement about the tasks and the processes involved. The absence of this can lead to ineffective outcomes, and is perhaps analogous to the notion of team-working that also needs understanding to be effectively developed. NHS Trusts have been prone to developing policies for supervision that confuse clinical and managerial supervision, and case management, with wider clinical supervision – although better examples exist (e.g. *Lincolnshire Community Services NHS Trust Clinical Supervision Framework 2008*). It is possible that different professions prioritise different features of supervision. If so, communication about what is agreed will be crucial.

Demonstrating efficacy: Transferring training into practice

There is little available research to demonstrate the direct transfer of skills from supervisory training into supervisory practice. (This is absent too from the literature of other health professions.) One well-developed exception to this is that required of participants on the NES training in Scotland (as mentioned above). The NES programme referred to above has had an inbuilt requirement for portfolios to be submitted and the experience of this is instructive (Bagnall, 2010).

In the development of the RAPPS, it was agreed that there would be only minimal requirements to demonstrate effective supervisory practice and that there was a transfer of training into practice. The necessity to demonstrate the link between training and practice was never doubted, and it is likely that such a requirement (although exceeding the generic requirements for the Register) may be consensually agreed locally between HEIs and supervisors and built into re-accreditation requirements.

The 2009 survey referred to earlier indicated that a growing number of training programmes (60%) are engaged in measuring/demanding/ evaluating evidence of the transfer of training into practice. Procedures varied, although a common core appeared to consist of a portfolio in which an individual would demonstrate and reflect on their supervisory practice. The value of this would need to be balanced against the available resources, especially if supervisor training remains the responsibility of clinical training programmes. There is further discussion of this in Chapter 9.

It will need to be decided whether these portfolios are used for formative or summative assessment. The former has the advantages of avoiding the necessity for an apparatus compatible with rigorous examination and appeals. It also implies an ongoing process in which feedback can be provided to improve practice. However, although the existing requirement for membership of the Register is based on having received training or existing supervisory practice, there remains a need to ensure that the Register considers quality standards.

Supervision of supervision: Different forms. What do people want? What is practical?

Just as it is important to demonstrate the effectiveness of supervisor training, it is also important to maintain these changes. The use of portfolios can be helpful (see above) and an alternative that should be considered involves providing *supervision* of supervision. The argument for this has prima facie validity, but there is little known about the practice, one exception being a paper by Yerushalmi (1999). The ongoing supervision of supervision features in a number of NHS Trust policies for supervision, although there is little accompanying detail. In South Staffordshire Primary Care Trust for example, Standard 12 in the Clinical Supervision policy states that 'All clinical supervisors will have access to a support group every 6 months' (South Staffordshire PCT, 2010: 4).

Group supervision has a number of practical advantages. Groups can meet fairly easily and there may be advantages in the use of an external facilitator. There is a potential role for supervision trainers here, and initial conversations with supervisors for trainees on the Manchester programme have indicated a favourable response.

One example of an attempt to develop regular ongoing supervision for qualified clinical psychologists was described by Fleming et al. (2007). It is likely that a number of similar forms exist of ongoing supervision of supervision, but there is no accurate account of these. Further discussion of different potential formats for such provision is provided in Chapter 10 of this volume.

The future role of the British Psychological Society

Some of this discussion has assumed that the BPS will continue to influence developments concerning supervision and supervisor training. At the time of writing (April 2010) it is unclear to what extent this will be the case in future. In 2009 the registration of clinical psychologists was made the responsibility of the HPC, and the BPS and the Division of Clinical Psychology are emphasising to clinical psychologists their 'added value' in professional issues, including CPD, and by implication supervision.

Although a large proportion of the standards written and published by the HPC would presume a level of high quality and continuing clinical supervision, there is little written in the HPC documentation specifically concerning supervision and supervisor training. This seems particularly pertinent since the HPC registers a number of health professions. Developments in supervision within some of these professions were reviewed earlier in this chapter. It would appear that these developments take place independently of procedures for registration and, if this is the case, there is optimism for a prospect that sees the BPS and Division of Clinical Psychology continuing to take a lead in further developments to do with supervision, and the recent BPS Standards (BPS, 2010) are an important contribution to this.

The HPC does require practitioner psychologists to 'understand models of supervision and their contribution to practice' (HPC, 2009a: section 2c.2) in the *Standards of Proficiency*. In addition, the *Standards of Education and Training* (HPC, 2009b) state that education providers need to ensure that Practice Educators (supervisors) 'must undertake appropriate practice placement educator training and development' (section 5.8) and 'must be appropriately registered, unless other arrangements are agreed' (section 5.9). Although lacking in detail, these statements might have implications for the training and accreditation of supervisory practice/supervisors.

Where supervision is mentioned (rather than discussed) it is within the description of CPD (HPC, 2009a), with supervision being identified as one of a number of activities that could be evidence of CPD. There does not appear to be any detailed discussion of training in supervision skills.

Conclusions

The last decade has witnessed a significant development in supervisor training within clinical psychology. It seems unlikely that alternative providers of training in supervisory skills will replace the trainers from clinical psychology doctoral training programmes. Trainers have worked collaboratively to identify the best forms of supervisor training and suitable content. Agreement has been sought on the competences that should result from introductory training, and the Society has agreed to hold a Register that identifies competent supervisors.

Training developments are consistent with best practice in other professions and in places exceed this.

Important issues for the immediate future include the development of advanced supervisor training, the relationship between model specific requirements and those for more generic training, the roles of clinical trainers in the transference of training into practice, and the continuing importance of evaluation and research.

Summary

Supervisor training for clinical psychologists has moved beyond its infancy. In recent years there has been an increase in the importance and resources devoted to supervisor training. Of major importance has been the attention given to the content of training that best provides participants with the skills to practise supervision. Lastly, there has been attention to research into the effectiveness of both training and supervision.

In moving forward, clinical psychology has been able to observe and learn from the practice in other health professions. In turn, it is hoped and expected that other branches of applied psychology will also be able to use the experience gained by clinical psychologists.

These developments have coincided with a proposal for the profession of clinical psychology that its members play a greater role in supervision and clinical leadership in their respective services.

It is satisfying as a trainer to report a cultural change as well. Clinical psychologists want to supervise and to do so effectively and be trained to do so. Not satisfied with introductory training, supervisors are keen to enhance and develop their practice through a variety of forms of CPD, including advanced training and supervision of their supervisory practice. In addition, they want these skills to be recognised. The development towards the accreditation of supervision skills by the professional body representing clinical psychologists is the culmination of this. It is unclear whether the registration role of the HPC will affect this.

In conclusion there have been major and effective developments in the training of clinical psychologists as supervisors, and there is every indication that this impetus will continue in the future.

Chapter 7

Difference and power in supervision:

The case of culture and racism

Nimisha Patel

The centrality of power relations in the supervisory process is the main theme within this chapter, focusing on the case of culture and racism and how they can be addressed to enhance the effectiveness of supervision and psychological practice.

This chapter attempts to address three questions:

1 Why address power and difference in supervision, specifically in relation to ethnicity, racism and culture?
2 What are the key issues with regard to culture and racism and how might they become salient in the different aspects of supervision and supervisory tasks?
3 How could supervisors in particular, and supervisees, enhance supervision by addressing power in relation to culture and racism?

Some of the implications for supervisors, supervisees, the profession of clinical psychology and psychological services are also considered.

Power and supervision

Supervision can be described as a collaborative process between the supervisor and the supervisee, with the explicit task of ensuring ethical and professional therapeutic practice aimed at improving the client's psychological and social quality of life. Taylor (1994) identifies three purposes in terms of the 'overseeing therapy' aspect of supervision: transmitting the values and ethics of the profession; controlling and protecting services provided by the supervisee; and helping the supervisee to develop a conceptual framework and intellectual and practical skills. The role of the supervisor combines responsibilities to the profession with those towards the client, and illustrates the centrality of power relations in the supervisory process, often neglected in practice. The neglect and invisibility of the role of power in supervision can inadvertently lead to a misuse of power and often give rise to a supervisory process characterised not by collaboration but by coercion, however subtle and unintentional. Arguably, collaboration is key to a supervisory relationship where both the supervisor and the supervisee are engaged in a learning process and where responsibility and accountability are more equally shared (Orlans and Edwards, 2001).

The notion of collaboration necessitates some exploration of different ways in which power has been understood in the supervisory context. Taylor (1994) suggests that a feminist emphasis in both counselling and supervision involves the sharing of power in an effort to establish a mutual, reciprocal and non-authoritarian relationship to facilitate optimal therapeutic outcomes. In this context, she focuses on the social history, the socialisation and the relatively powerless structural position that women face, and what she refers to as the general lack of 'real' power. Here, power is used to refer to the unequal distribution and access to resources and privileges that impact differentially on the life experiences of women, often in disadvantageous ways. Taylor (1994) argues that power and gender feature strongly in any therapeutic and supervisory relationship, particularly where clients seeking help themselves feel powerless in many ways, and that supervision has a responsibility to challenge inequalities in power (e.g. gender bias) implicit in our culture. The concept of social power (Cooke and Kipnis, 1986) is also used to describe the differential distribution of, and claim on, power that men and women have and assume in their interactions, including in supervision. Miller (1991) has argued that traditional constructions of power can inhibit women from assuming greater power in interactions for fear of losing or jeopardising the relationship with their interactional partner. She proposes a model of shared power where individuals can be empowered within a connected relationship, also described as relational power (Surrey, 1991). Based on this concept of relational power, Nelson (1997) posits that the supervisor (through the use of their 'expert power') can enable a supervisee to assume greater power over time and to express their personal power within their interactions. Thus, power is conceptualised not simply as a commodity that one has and the other does not, but a dynamic reflecting a social reality that becomes manifest in the interactions within the supervisory relationship.

Others have conceptualised power in relation to ethnicity in similar ways, for example describing power as 'the crucial variable in minority–majority relations and (which) affects the ability of individuals or groups to realise their goals and interests, even in the face of resistance to the power' (Kavanaugh and Kennedy, 1992: 17). In addressing power in what is called 'cross cultural supervisions', Ryde (2000) introduces the following concepts: *role power*, pointing to the power inherent in the role of the supervisor; *cultural power*, pointing to the power of the dominant ethnic grouping; and *individual power*, pointing to the particular power of the individual's personality. Whilst essentialising power, Ryde's contributions enable an analysis of how power manifests and changes depending on the backgrounds of the supervisor, the supervisee and the client: for example, a supervisor may be White, male and from a working-class background; a client may be White, female, working class and able-bodied; and the supervisee may be Black, male, middle class and gay.

Social inequalities are therefore complex, intersecting and multilayered for each person in the supervisory triad (the supervisor, supervisee or the client), reflecting differing social positions and experiences of both privilege and disadvantage. In supervision, power becomes a complex dynamic requiring a sustained, committed and sophisticated social, political and psychological analysis. Here it is argued that it is both the supervisor's and supervisee's ethical and professional responsibility to ensure that the supervisory process attends to social inequalities and their impact on all those involved, and most importantly the client. How this perspective is meaningfully integrated into clinical psychology training and the training and practice of clinical psychology supervisors remains largely a matter of choice in Britain, despite the British Psychological Society's criteria for the accreditation of clinical psychology training programmes (BPS, 2008b), which specify that by the end of training trainees will have 'the skills, knowledge and values to work effectively with clients from a diverse range of backgrounds, understanding and respecting the impact of difference and diversity upon their lives' (accreditation criterion 1.1.2, p. 9). Further, the profession has erred on the side of prescribing an 'understanding' of the impact of differences and social inequalities on clients' lives and an 'appreciation' of power imbalances (e.g. see BPS accreditation criterion 1.37), but demands little in the way of a critical gaze at ourselves, as supervisors and supervisees, or in the way of re-visioning our professional role and all our professional activities (clinical, communication, research, organisational, etc.) in ways that attempt to address difference, inequalities and power.

Some attempts have been made in Britain in clinical psychology (e.g. Dennis, 2001; Patel et al., 2000) and in counselling (Lago and Thompson, 1997) to consider how inequalities and difference, specifically in relation to race, culture and ethnicity, can be integrated into training, supervision and continuing professional development. In the United States there is far more literature in this field and one predominant theme is the focus on describing 'multicultural supervision' and 'cross-cultural supervision'. Both terms have been used to refer to supervision that considers issues of culture and ethnicity, such as differing life experiences, values, beliefs, word views and ethnic identity development in relation to counselling and psychother-apy assessment, intervention, knowledge base and the supervisory and the therapeutic relationships (e.g. Brown and Landrum-Brown, 1995; Con-stantine, 1997; D'Andrea and Daniels, 1997; Gopaul-Nicol and Brice-Baker, 1998; Priest, 1994). In addition, there have been some studies examining cultural and 'race' issues in supervision (for a brief review see Helms and Cook, 1999).

Both in Britain and in the United States, there is a paucity of related literature focusing particularly on clinical psychology supervision and, more poignantly, there is little in the way of guidance on how to incorporate current understandings of power relations, social inequalities and issues of cultural difference and racism into the supervision of clinical psychologists. In addition, as described in Chapter 4, current supervision models are based on specific psychological or psychotherapy theories or developed specifically for supervision, commonly referred to as developmental models. Banks (2001) argues that the use of supervision models based on specific theories or therapeutic models must be questioned, given that the cultural biases within those theories are inevitably reflected in supervision. Developmental models of supervision can also be criticised for presumptions of being universally applicable, regardless of social, cultural and political context.

Before addressing the second and third questions outlined in the introduction, I shall return briefly to the notion of power and empowerment and the implications for supervision.

Foucault's understanding of power (1977, 1988) has been influential and is relevant to interactions within supervision. Foucault's conceptualisation of power pointed to the interactional nature and the constitutive force of power whereby power manifests and shares itself through everyday interactions, language, discourses, social practices, knowledges and the ways in which we come to know of and understand personhood. The notion of resistance is important and he suggests that it can manifest itself within interactions, discourses and in people's attempts to challenge particular definitions of subjectivity. Power is neither seen as lineal, possessed or static, but as relational and as being culturally, socially and historically situated. This analysis of power can enable us to study everyday interactions and institutional practices, as in the supervisory relationship and governing structures, which can sustain regulatory systems of control.

Since supervision is one of the main sites in which particular knowledge is transmitted, where certain skills are fostered as institutionalised social practices and where power permeates every aspect of the supervisory relationship and process, it is appropriate to focus on how issues of difference, inequality and oppression become manifest and how supervision can facilitate and nurture resistance in the struggle against oppression. However, a major criticism of Foucault's analysis and theory of power is that it offered little in the way of encouragement or direction in challenging oppression and illustrating how resistance could be fostered (e.g. Taylor, 1984); also it neglects the material reality of power relations and their impact on people's lives, and their resistance to change. To focus only on power as it operates in everyday interactions, discourses and in regulatory systems can disguise the reality of material, social inequalities, thereby leaving the social order and power relatively unchanged.

Practice implications of an approach to supervision that attempts to address both understandings (discursive and materialist) of power include: (a) a social, cultural, historical and political analysis into every aspect of supervision; (b) developing an awareness of how the client, the supervisee and the supervisor are privileged and oppressed, the impact on their lives and the significance of this in therapy and in supervision; and (c) active exploration of the different levels and ways in which a clinical psychologist could intervene in collaboration with the client, to create maximum change for the client to enhance their emotional, social and political well-being. These practices can be seen as opportunities for resistance in the Foucauldian sense, and hopefully for change in the political and personal sense.

The following sections focus on four main aspects of supervision, each outlining key issues with regard to culture, racism and ethnicity and offering some guidance on how supervision could be enhanced. The four main aspects of supervision to be addressed are: process of supervision; developing knowledge; developing skills; and personal–professional development. To develop confidence and competence in addressing these issues in supervision, both supervisors and supervisees need to acknowledge that learning to think critically is a vital prerequisite to practising in ways that meaningfully acknowledge and address issues of culture, ethnicity and racism.

The process of supervision

As discussed earlier, the roles of the supervisor all accentuate the power imbalance between the supervisor and the supervisee, and also with clients, regardless of differences or similarities between supervisor and client, for example in ethnic or cultural background, or gender, age, class and other aspects.

The scope of this chapter is on the experiences of Black and minority ethnic supervisees being supervised by White majority ethnic supervisors, where clients may be from any majority or minority ethnic backgrounds. Numerous barriers exist in supervision to prevent an exploration of the significance and implications of power and difference in terms of culture, ethnicity and racism, and these are detailed below (for further discussion from Black trainees' perspectives, see Adetimole, Afuape and Vara, 2005).

Colour blindness

Statements such as 'I treat all trainees in the same way, regardless of their ethnicity or colour' exemplify the commonest barrier to discussing power relations and their effects on the supervisee and the client. It is as if all supervisees are seen as colourless, culture-less and denuded of social and political contexts, as if the fact of racism and the reality of its impact on people's lives are not worthy of acknowledgement, let alone discussion in supervision. Ridley (1995) suggests that colour blindness can result from counsellors' (or supervisors' in this context) need to appear impartial, from fears that they may actually be, or be thought of as, racist or from fear of appearing ignorant or incompetent.

Colour consciousness

Ridley (1995) describes colour consciousness as the opposite of colour blindness, the belief that perhaps all of the clients' (and the supervisees') difficulties stem from their being a minority ethnic person, suggesting that 'White guilt' is a common cause. In supervision this can manifest in attributing all difficulties (explicitly or implicitly) to the supervisee being Black, with the implicit assumption that an exploration of relevant issues in the supervisory relationship cannot take place. Thus, the responsibility for change, if any is thought possible or desirable, rests with the supervisee, not the supervisor. Supervisees may themselves avoid raising issues of culture or racism for fear of being themselves positioned as being 'overly' preoccupied with such issues and with their own 'personal' difficulties in relation to their ethnicity or their experiences of racism.

Pathologising the supervisee or the client

Supervisees may describe the process in supervision whereby they come to be held responsible for any client–supervisee or supervisee–supervisor difficulties, or where a supervisee fails to meet the expectations or standards set by the supervisor. Little space is allowed for a discussion of, say, the cultural biases inherent in the expectations or standards set by the supervisor, or of the cultural norms against which the supervisor may be judging the supervisee's competencies, knowledge and learning styles, or of the biases and oppressive functions of certain therapeutic models and interventions espoused by the supervisor. Supervisees, including trainees, thus can easily be labelled as perhaps 'lacking in an adequate level of competence', 'defensive and inflexible', 'resistant to feedback', 'lacking reflective skills' or 'requiring a greater level of instruction, guidance, monitoring or supervision'.

Denying the importance of discussing power, culture and racism

Supervisors may never mention, invite or encourage any discussion of power relations or cultural differences. They may, if challenged or prompted by a supervisee, respond that 'it's not an issue here, most, if not all, of our clients here are White', or 'we never see any Black or minority ethnic people in this particular service/area'. The implication is that power and culture are only salient where there are overt differences in colour; the message to the supervisee is that culture, ethnicity and racism are not worthy of discussion, regardless of the possible differences and inherent power relations between supervisee and supervisor.

Fukuyama's (1994) analysis of critical incidents also suggests that supervisors may tend to minimise supervisees' efforts to attend to their clients' concerns related to racism. Helms and Cook (1999) give examples of 'supervisor minimisation strategies', including insisting that such matters are superficial and not germane to the client's 'real' problem, refusing to discuss such issues or devaluing the supervisee's competence if they address such issues in their work. They suggest that, in response to such strategies, supervisees may feel discouraged and reluctant to explore issues of culture or racism for fear of being negatively evaluated by the supervisor. Further, the fear of being scapegoated, marginalised (e.g. amongst peers) and being failed as a trainee can act as a major deterrent to voicing issues of discrimination, even amongst peers (Patel et al., 2000).

Expressing dissatisfaction with demands to integrate 'new material' into clinical and supervisory practice

Supervisors may often feel dissatisfied, pressured, misunderstood, undervalued and burdened with the increasing demands placed on them to provide a range of experience, to facilitate the development of a range of competencies and to ensure a scholarly and critical approach to the development of knowledge within supervision. Reactions include anger, irritation and outright dismissal of any suggestion or request that supervision should include discussion and exploration of issues of culture, racism and power relations, perhaps because it is experienced as a demand and one that arises out of an explicit criticism of the profession and clinical psychology practice (Patel et al., 2000). Unfortunately, supervisees may be left feeling that they are making unreasonable demands, that they themselves or their training needs are excessive or that these issues are relatively unimportant or unworthy of acknowledgement within the profession and supervision.

Not surprisingly, the supervisory relationship is fraught with complexities, differences in expectations and perhaps mutual mistrust when the supervisee and the supervisor are from different ethnic backgrounds. The majority ethnic supervisor's anxieties about their competence in understanding and addressing issues of power, culture, ethnicity and racism may be compounded by the minority ethnic supervisee's anxieties about how they will be negatively evaluated or misunderstood by the supervisor because of their minority ethnic status. Gopaul-Nicol and Brice-Baker (1998) argue that such levels of anxiety in some minority ethnic supervisees might inhibit them from revealing difficulties in their work or weaknesses.

Crucial to any effective supervision is unquestionably the quality of the supervisory relationship, which is to be prioritised and nurtured if trust and mutuality are to develop in the 'multicultural supervisory relationship' (Martinez and Holloway, 1997) and power is to be meaningfully addressed. According to Holloway (1995) the supervisory relationship is the container of the process in which supervisee and supervisor negotiate a personal way of utilising a structure of power and involvement or attachment that facilitates learning. Gatmon's (2001) study highlights the significance of providing an atmosphere of safety, combined with a depth of dialogue and frequent opportunities to discuss cultural variables in the supervisory relationship, in contributing to building supervisory alliances and increasing supervisee satisfaction.

Improving supervisory practice: The process of supervision

Supervisory practice can be improved to facilitate the process of supervision in several ways:

1   Safety and trust need to be established and nurtured. However, this raises further questions, such as: What does it mean to feel safe, or safe enough, and for whom? How can safety and trust be achieved and maintained? Whose responsibility is it to make the supervisory relationship and process safe?
    Feeling safe can mean essentially the same for both supervisee and supervisor: being able to be open, honest and reflective; being able to take risks in sharing one's concerns and doubts, and being able to take risks in revealing one's own limitations in terms of knowledge and skills in relation to addressing issues of power, culture, ethnicity and racism. It does not mean giving false reassurances that the supervisee (who may be a trainee) is not being evaluated, or that the supervisor will not be challenged if they make biased assumptions, racist comments or advocate a Eurocentric perspective. The supervisor must learn how to model openness and learning about potentially deeply sensitive, often controversial and complex issues of cultural difference and racism spanning the personal, professional and theoretical realms. For the supervisee the challenge is learning to take considered risks in being open, thoughtful, reflexive and challenging within the process of supervision.
    It is the supervisor's responsibility and obligation to create an atmosphere of safety and to develop a trusting relationship with the supervisee. To simply expect that the supervisee should feel safe and trust the supervisor is perhaps naive; trust needs to be earned and safety needs to be demonstrated so that the process of building a relationship conducive to mutual learning can be facilitated.

2   Developing a language to talk about power relations, culture, ethnicity, 'race', racism and oppression in supervision can be extremely difficult and anxiety-provoking but is an essential step towards enhancing supervision. Supervisors can demonstrate a willingness to talk about emotive and sensitive issues without being dismissive, and in doing so they might expose their uncertainties about the language to use or their limitations in knowledge about these concepts and issues.

3   Reflexivity on part of both the supervisor and the supervisee is critical in minimising anxiety and in developing a mutually enabling supervisory relationship. Reflexivity can mean the supervisor examining and reflecting on: (a) their own ethnicity and cultural background; (b) experiences of power and powerlessness in their personal and professional lives and in their own supervision; (c) preferred theoretical models, clinical practice and inherent biases; (d) their assumptions, beliefs, values, biases and racism, which inevitably influence their practice, their supervision and their relationship with the supervisee; (e) their stage in development as a supervisor and the related anxieties, expectations or attitudes to supervisees or to supervision, or to the demand to include newer and challenging approaches into their supervision; and (f) their own anxieties, fears, doubts, limitations, abilities and strengths in thinking about and addressing issues of power, culture and racism. The implications for how and where supervisors might do this will be addressed subsequently.

   Reflexivity extends to the actual supervisory relationship and supervisors can ensure that reflection and discussion about the supervisory relationship itself are permissible, welcomed and a necessary part of the process of learning.

4   It is essential to negotiate within the supervisory relationship several parameters: who can raise these issues, and how and when or what action might result. The contracting process begins at the time of establishing the supervisory relationship, but it is an ongoing process involving regular review (Scaife, 2001). Supervisees should be actively facilitated to contribute to the contracting process and its review, and to include possible contentious issues around difference.

Ideally, a supervision contract that encompasses all the issues raised above should, through honesty and collaboration, enable the establishment of a quality supervisory relationship where mutual learning can flourish.

Developing knowledge

An important function of supervision is to facilitate awareness, understanding and skills in the application of a knowledge base that draws on psychological theories, research and practice-based evidence. The development of competence in this area within supervision is traditionally thought of only in relation to the supervisee's learning. Questions that arise include: Who has the responsibility to impart knowledge to whom? Whose knowledge is being imparted? What is the basis of that knowledge, its construction and limitations, and how has this knowledge come to be produced? Which knowledge is being privileged and which is subjugated?

In clinical psychology training, supervision and practice, the belief that all psychological theories are universally applicable, politically neutral and potentially beneficial rather than being potentially toxic and oppressive remains largely uncontested. Psychology's approach to 'race', racism and cultural difference in its knowledge base has historically been either to ignore them, to focus on 'race' in an exploitative and abusive way (e.g. in examining 'race' and IQ) or to depoliticise it and strip it of its social historical and political context (e.g. in discussing cultural differences as if they are essentialised characteristics or idiosyncrasies located in the 'other'). However, there are powerful contributions to understanding power and racism in psychology's knowledge production (see Henwood and Phoenix, 1999, for a summary). That said, there is no tangible impact as yet on clinical psychology training.

The Eurocentric nature of psychology's knowledge base points to the inherent limitations of this knowledge and to the potential for perpetuating oppression in theory production and in supervisory and clinical practice. The blanket use of and the unquestioning approach to applying such knowledge to Black and minority ethnic clients can be seen as amateurish at best, or as abusive or as 'secondary colonisation' at worst (Patel and Fatimilehin, 1999). In discussing the nature of unintentional racism in the use of psychological theories, Ridley (1995) describes four categories of models of mental health – the deficit, medical, conformity and biopsycho-social models – in an effort to expose their limitations and their potential to perpetrate racism. If supervision is to be able to address the nature and function of power relations in psychology then it is incumbent upon supervisors to integrate an analysis and a critique of psychological knowledge, particularly in relation to their own field.

Improving supervisory practice: Developing knowledge

Supervisors can address issues of power, culture and racism in facilitating the supervisee's general competence in the understanding and application of psychological knowledge in several ways, for example:

1   Supervisors need to examine and critique their own knowledge base and professional trainings with a historical, cultural and political analysis to identify cultural biases, racist assumptions and oppressive

functions of this knowledge. This can be done in private, in their own supervision, with colleagues or in their own training and services.

2   Supervisors need to actively engage in and facilitate ongoing reflection and to discuss and criticise commonly used psychological theories in relation to cultural biases and racism (for examples relevant to particular clinical specialities, see Patel et al., 2000).

3   Supervisors can encourage discussions on identifying the merits and potential benefits of particular theoretical approaches and models, as well as their limitations in application to Black and minority ethnic people.

4   Supervisors can encourage exploration and discussion in supervision of other relevant models and theories not necessarily based on Western psychological approaches, for example contributions from the fields of African psychology, Chinese medicine, Ayurveda, Yoga, Buddhism, sociology, etc.

5   Supervisors can guide supervisees in developing critical thinking skills by modelling a reflective, questioning approach. Posing challenging questions can be helpful, for example inviting reflection on the origins and production of psychological theories, on the role, uses and misuses of research in perpetuating biased and racist theories, on the benefits and limitations of research-based and practice-based evidence in clinical psychology and on the application of biased and racist concepts and theories in clinical practice and in service design and delivery.

Developing skills

Clinical psychology training focuses on developing a range of competencies with a range of clients, across the life span, seen in a range of settings. For supervision to facilitate an understanding and competencies specifically in addressing power relations and oppression in clients' lives, in clinical and research practice, in service development and in the supervisory relationship, both supervisees and supervisors have to be committed to and strive to nurture critical thinking.

In relation to multicultural counselling competence, Helms and Richardson (1997) argue that it is not a unique set of skills per se that is required, but a particular philosophical orientation characterised by a responsivity to the relevant socio-political dynamics of 'race' and to principles of cultural socialisation in all interactions with clients. Of course, such responsivity and a philosophical orientation have to go beyond simply an 'awareness of' and 'sensitivity to' relevant issues. What is needed is the ability to operationalise a social and political analysis of cultural and racial oppression in our psychological thinking skills and in clinical and research practice, and supervision provides an opportunity to consider how critical thinking can be translated into clinical practice.

Improving supervisory practice: Developing skills

The following provides some suggestions regarding what supervisors can do to encourage reflection, discussion, debate and skills development within supervision. The main areas considered are assessment, formulation, intervention and organisational skills.

Assessment

Critical to developing appropriate assessment skills is: (a) the ability to evaluate the validity and the appropriateness of the theoretical basis of assessment methods used; (b) the ability to critically analyse how difference has been constructed during the referral process and within the chosen theoretical approach; and (c) the ability to evaluate the role and function of power within the entire process of referring, assessment and the process of establishing theory–practice links during the assessment. Table 7.1 (next page) summarises questions that may be useful in supervision.

Formulation

Almost all approaches to psychological formulation are based on particular theoretical approaches, models that themselves are invariably Eurocentric and often decontextualised, de-politicised and sanitised of understandings of power. As such, psychological formulations rarely address power relations and rarely do they suggest anything in the way of social action. Useful contributions in clinical psychology can be found by Hagan and Smail (1997), who advocate power-mapping as a methodology, and by Holland (1990, 1992), who illustrates the use of a material understanding of power and its impact in her model of social action psychotherapy.

The processes of assessment and formulation inevitably develop simultaneously, and the wheel of assessment and formulation (Figure 7.1 on p. 109) highlights the ongoing and cyclical nature of this process and the different arenas where understandings of culture and racism can be integrated into the formulation. The suggested questions in Table 7.2 (p. 110) correspond to the different segments in the wheel and may facilitate supervision.

Intervention

The ability to explain and to negotiate and renegotiate with the client an appropriate approach to intervention relevant to the client, based on an evolving formulation, requires many skills. In supervision these skills can be articulated, rehearsed and debated. It is particularly important to this process that both supervisor and supervisee can demonstrate reflexivity and critical thinking, and can re-evaluate the potential for abuse and oppression in the use of existing theoretical models and interventions. Perhaps most important is the willingness and commitment to re-conceptualising what can

Table 7.1 The referral process and assessment

1 What aspects of your 'self' (e.g. culture, ethnicity, heritage, gender, age, class, etc.) could be influencing your understanding of the client referred, of the referral request and of the assessment process?

2 Who is the referrer? What might be their personal and professional understanding of the client referred to you? Could their ethnicity (or gender, etc.) or their professional context have influenced how they have described the client, or how they construct the client's present difficulties or possible interventions they suggest? Which theoretical constructs are used in the referral letter (e.g. 'separation problems' or 'somatisation')? To what extent are those constructs Eurocentric? What are the implications?

3 In the referral process, who else or which other services influenced the referral being made to you in particular (or to clinical psychology)? Which assumptions, values, stereotypes and personal/professional beliefs might have influenced the referral route, and how transparent were they to the client? What might be the client's fears, suspicions, expectations or understanding of what a clinical psychologist does, how and why?

4 What might be the implications of the way in which a referral letter constructs, say, culture (e.g. is culture the only central construct, or is it invisible and unimportant)? What are the implications for the client and for the type of service offered to the client (or withheld from them)?

5 Who might you need to consult to enable you to conduct an appropriate assessment (e.g. which family members, which colleagues or community organisations or religious practitioners, etc.)?

6 Which language is the most appropriate for conducting the assessment? What assumptions are being made by you, your supervisor, manager or service in deciding whether a professional interpreter is needed or not? Do you need to find a bilingual therapist or co-worker, or a professional interpreter? What do you need to know in order to decide or to find an appropriate interpreter (e.g. language or dialect spoken or preferred by the client, gender of interpreter, etc.)? Who might you consult to help you decide? What are the consequences (legal, professional and clinical) of offering a service, having decided against using a professional interpreter, where a client/family does not speak English?

7 What are you and the client bringing to the assessment in your own cultural understandings, values, stereotypes, histories and experiences of privilege and oppression and your expectations of an assessment or subsequent services? How might this influence the client's experience of the assessment process and the process of trying to establish a therapeutic alliance? How can this be addressed so that the assessment can be experienced as collaborative and empowering?

8 Have you made transparent and explicit to the client how and why they have been referred to clinical psychology, and why to you? Have you explained the 'professional' and the 'organisational/service' rationale for the referral? Have you sought their understanding of the referral process and its implications? Have you discussed the possible limitations and biases in the process of psychological assessment and therapy-related services offered to them? For example, have you explained and discussed with the client how the psychological therapies used have commonly been developed in the West and rest largely on the assumption that 'talking' helps? How have confidentiality and informed consent been discussed (e.g. noting the Western biases in such concepts, as well as in most psychological therapies) and are clients' understandings of these fully explored?

9 If you have chosen to use formal assessment tools (standardised tests or measures), can you justify their use and their validity for the client in question? What might be

Table 7.1 (continued)

the inherent biases (e.g. cultural), limitations and the potential for abuse in these assessment tools? What are the ethical implications of using assessment methods and tools that are not reliable or valid for the client in question?

10 How is power salient in the assessment process? Where is power significant: for example, as a White, male, trainee clinical psychologist how might your ethnicity, gender and position as a trainee professional be significant in relation to a Black, male, older client referred to you for a cognitive assessment whilst under the Mental Health Act? What are the implications for the process of assessment or the possible outcomes of the assessment?

11 What are the contexts relevant to talking with and understanding the client and their presenting difficulties? For example, what is the client's/family's economic context, their familial context or the impact of poverty and racism on their lives? How can an awareness of these be integrated into an assessment that understands the client's difficulties? In seeking to understand these issues, how can an assessment be conducted in a way that does not unquestioningly mirror and reinforce power relations experienced by the client in their own lives?

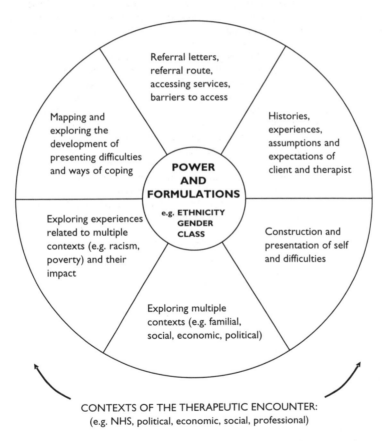

CONTEXTS OF THE THERAPEUTIC ENCOUNTER:
(e.g. NHS, political, economic, social, professional)

Figure 7.1 Assessments and formulations: Integrating issues of difference and power.

Table 7.2 The process of assessment and formulation

1 How are referral letters written (e.g. language used, constructs employed) and by whom? What is the referral route and what assumptions are being made by the referrer? Which services are made available to the client by the referral and which have been excluded or withheld? What culturally biased assumptions, stereotypes or values may have influenced this process? What are the implications for the client (e.g. in terms of informed consent, informed choice versus coercion in the referral process)? Would the client be able to request a particular therapeutic approach or a therapist from a Black or minority ethnic background? Would the client have been given an opportunity to discuss their own understanding or preferences in terms of healthcare approaches (e.g. traditional to the client rather than traditional Western approaches offered within the NHS) or in needing a professional interpreter (as opposed to a family member acting as a lay interpreter)?

2 What are the histories (personal and political) that clients and practitioners bring to the assessment? How can we explore the client's expectations and assumptions of who the practitioner is, what they will do and what their views may be regarding the client's presenting difficulties (e.g. Black and minority ethnic clients may have many assumptions about a White practitioner and they may utilise effective survival strategies of adopting a distant, questioning and mistrusting stance towards them)? Similarly, what are the assumptions, stereotypes, values, biases and expectations of the practitioner in relation to the client and how might they impact on the process of the assessment and formulation? What are the implications for the validity and utility of the emerging formulation? How might such formulations influence the interventions (and their related models) chosen, offered or imposed on the client? What are likely to be the enabling or disabling and potentially oppressive consequences for the client?

3 How does the client talk about and construct 'self', identity or personhood (e.g. how does the person construct identity, explicitly as racialised, gendered or in terms of an individual autonomous self or a collective identity)? To what extent do the assessment and formulation explore the significance of the points of convergence or divergence in the client's and the practitioner's understanding of the 'self'? What is your understanding of 'self'? To what extent is this influenced by your own personal cultural history, or perhaps by your professional and academic training in psychology (e.g. the dominance of the Cartesian dualist notion of self in psychological theorising)? What are the implications for the choice of interventions or psychological models for interventions? How can this be discussed and negotiated with the client?

4 How does the client talk about and explain their difficulties and ways of managing? Which meaning-making systems (e.g. religious, political, cultural) do they draw on? To what extent are these ways of understanding their distress respected, explored, privileged, superficially acknowledged or integrated into the psychological meaning-making systems (e.g. psychological models) that you might be using in the assessment and formulation?

5 How does the client present themselves and their difficulties to you? How do these ways of presenting make sense to the client in terms of their own cultural etiquette (e.g. how to respond to elders, to men or to professionals) or their own histories of oppression (e.g. how to talk or protect yourself with those in authority, or with White people in 'White institutions')? Clients present themselves and their difficulties often in ways that make sense to them, feel safe for them and may determine what they are offered. How can a formulation take these factors into account?

6 What are the multiple contexts (social, cultural, economic, political, familial, service) influencing the client and their difficulties? How might these influences be important in understanding which resources and opportunities clients have for change, and what are the impasses to change? For example, what is the significance and the impact of

Table 7.2 *(continued)*

the marital or familial context for the client and related cultural factors? What are the influences of power in the client's economic and political context (e.g. not being able to work as an asylum seeker or not being able to find employment) and how might this be linked to the history of racism for Black and minority ethnic people in Britain, and specifically for the client? How realistic is it that a client can change accommodation where they have experienced racism from neighbours and where this has had an adverse impact on their well-being? To what extent might poverty and institutional racism be important considerations in an assessment and formulation? Is feeling powerless as a practitioner a justification for not addressing disadvantage and oppression in a formulation? What might be the ethical and practical implications for intervention and for the evaluation of such interventions (or for the absence of any interventions) addressing such material inequalities and injustices?

7 What are the client's experiences in relation to the multiple contexts identified in the assessment? For example, which opportunities in life have they been afforded, or denied, because of who they are (e.g. as a White, able-bodied, middle-class male or as a Black gay male)? Which negative experiences have they had (e.g. experiences as a Black gay man of racism at work, racist verbal or physical attacks on the streets, homophobia within their own family and religious community as well as within the majority, White gay community)? What might be the impact and influences of these experiences on the client, their life, their relationships, their view of the world or their interactions with you? What are the implications for the models that you use, the interventions that are planned, the appropriateness of the practitioner themselves or for the roles of a clinical psychologist?

8 With respect to mapping and exploring the development of presenting difficulties and ways of coping, how does the experience of racism in the client's life, in education, employment, in the lack of opportunities, etc. manifest in and account for the presenting difficulties, and for the way in which the client (or their family) attempted to manage/cope to date and draw on their own resources? How can a formulation effectively address the aforementioned questions and suggest an ethical and just approach to interventions?

be considered 'therapeutic', using a range of approaches and reconfiguring professional roles and responsibilities in order to practise a just psychology.

It is contended here that no single Western psychological approach currently exists that can adequately address the reality of both material and relational power and powerlessness and the impact on people's lives and distress. Contributions from narrative approaches to therapy (White and Epston, 1991), social action approaches to therapy (e.g. Holland, 1990, 1992) and community psychology (for excellent examples, see DCP, 2005, 2006) provide both hope and indication that perhaps psychological approaches can contribute to social change and address power. So-called 'alternatives' to Western psychological approaches (e.g. approaches drawing on cultural or religious rituals or practices, or using political/quasi-legal methods such as taking detailed testimonies of abuses and atrocities suffered, sometimes to be used in legal proceedings and intended to be therapeutic) are generally not acknowledged as 'psychological', partly accounting for their limited influence. The question remains: Are psychology and psychological interventions, as currently configured in the West, the only or indeed the most effective way to address social inequalities and their impact on people's well-being? Re-conceptualising 'psychological' practice demands that our theories address social context and power, necessitating theoretical integration drawing on other disciplines such as sociology, political science and law. It also requires psychological practice that includes activities beyond 'therapy', but that nonetheless have a positive impact on people's social and political environment and subsequent well-being. Table 7.3 highlights questions that might stimulate relevant discussion and facilitate the development of intervention skills within supervision.

Understanding organisational contexts

Competencies related to understanding the organisational contexts and to developing ethical, professional and 'just' psychological practice within those contexts is an important area for consideration in supervision. Again it is crucial that there is unequivocal commitment to developing services that best serve clients from all sections of the population, equally and in ways that are relevant and meaningful to service users and the diverse communities that services are intended to serve.

Supervision can enable reflection on how power operates within the organisational systems (e.g. at team, service and management levels) as well as in the legislative developments relevant to health and social care in particular specialist areas. Reflection on power and its workings within the profession, our code of conduct and ethics, and professional practice guidelines can also be an important aspect of supervision that allows us to examine the role of clinical psychologists in challenging discriminatory and oppressive structures that exclude and abuse some groups. Working with Black service users to better understand their experiences of psychological and mental health services and addressing their concerns is also an essential area for exploration in supervision (for excellent discussion from Black service users' perspectives, see Trivedi, 2002, 2009, and Jones, 2009). The role of psychologists as potential change agents in developing more equitable and appropriate services for Black and minority ethnic people is advocated by Nadirshaw (2000) and by the Division of Clinical Psychology in their Briefing paper on services to Black and minority ethnic people (DCP, 1998, currently being updated).

Questions that could contribute to relevant discussions and to the development of organisational skills within supervision can be found in Table 7.4 (on p. 115).

Personal and professional development

In learning how to understand and manage the dynamics related to culture and 'race', Helms and Cook (1999) argue that supervision is indeed the most

Table 7.3 Interventions

1 Given your formulation, which psychological models or specific interventions might most effectively address the varying layers of the client's/family's experiences and distress that may be related to racism, marginalisation and oppression? How might your planned intervention address the reality of racism and poverty? For example, if a client who did not speak English was assessed by a colleague without an interpreter and subsequently denied a service that you believed would be crucial or preferred by the client, how would you proceed? Would you simply organise a referral or access to the denied service in question? Would you also discuss with, and challenge where necessary, the colleague who conducted the initial assessment, or would you alert the client to their rights and enable them to lodge a complaint or make a formal complaint yourself? How far would you be prepared to proceed (or not), for whom, with whom and why?

2 What are the possible assumptions, values and cultural biases inherent in the psychological models and resulting interventions you have planned? What might be the implications of using such interventions with the client (e.g. in locating 'the problem' within the client, or acknowledging the importance of social context and external realities of discrimination, whilst still locating responsibility for change solely with the client/family)?

3 How will you explain to the client the rationale for the type of model and interventions you plan to implement? How will you facilitate the ability and create genuine opportunities for the client to question the utility, validity or appropriateness of your planned interventions?

4 What might be possible parallel processes in the therapeutic process and relationship that mirror, replicate and perpetuate experiences of discrimination experienced by the client? How can these processes be identified, acknowledged and explored with the client?

5 How might you reflect on and challenge your own prejudices and racism, however unintentional, in the therapeutic process? How would you know when your interventions were oppressive or racist in their outcome? How would you enable and facilitate an exploration of these issues during therapy? Where and with whom might you want to reflect on these issues in safety?

6 To what extent do your interventions focus on problems, weaknesses and vulnerability of the client in a way that might be experienced as pathologising or blaming the client, for example, for their experiences of racist abuse in their workplace? Could strategies for helping the client to be 'more assertive' or to re-evaluate their perception that 'everyone is out to get me at work . . . they're constantly watching and waiting to pick on me' or to explore the reasons why they perhaps repeatedly find themselves in situations or relationships (both personally and at work) where they are victimised be experienced as, and function as being, oppressive and racist?

7 How could you assess the impact of racism on a client's life and formulate effective intervention strategies? How could your interventions challenge racism in the client's life, as well as in the therapeutic relationship, in the therapeutic work and in the related professional network/team? Which personal and professional resources would enable you to effectively challenge such racism? What would 'challenging racism' look like in practice?

8 To what extent are your interventions or your therapeutic approach designed, adapted or chosen specifically for the client in question? Alternatively, to what extent is the client expected to fit into and respond to your own preferred approach, or

continues overleaf

Table 7.3 (continued)

into the dominant model within your service? What are the implications of this for the client?

9 To what extent do your interventions assume that all of the client's presenting difficulties can be attributed to their culture (and how is culture understood?) or to experiences of racism, or, conversely, that culture and racism are irrelevant to understanding the client's distress, difficulties and ways of managing? What are the implications of this for the client?

10 When might it be necessary to work with a bilingual co-worker or a professional interpreter in therapeutic practice? What are your beliefs and assumptions about the value of working with such colleagues in therapeutic practice? To what extent do your own anxieties or possible lack of experience and skills in working with interpreters influence your choice to either deny some clients psychological therapy or deny them a right to a professional interpreter? What might this illuminate about power relations and unintentional racism? What might be the implications for clients or 'potential' clients (those who cannot access our services)?

11 What are the range of ways in which your therapeutic interventions could be evaluated, particularly with regard to their validity and their effectiveness in addressing issues of culture and/or racism significant to the client? What role might the client themselves be entitled to and be allowed to use in enabling an honest and just evaluation to take place?

logical and primary vehicle for influencing personal and professional growth and development for both supervisee and supervisor. Scaife and Walsh (2001) describe personal and professional development as an ongoing learning process about aspects of the self in relation to others. They identify three categories of aspects of self relevant to supervision: acknowledging the personal impact of client work; the influence of events outside work on relationships at work; and the influence of personal life history, values, beliefs and personal characteristics on relationships at work. The primary focus is on ensuring professional practice that will benefit the client. If supervision is to facilitate personal and professional development effectively then it is an obligation for both supervisees and supervisors, separately and together, to explore aspects of self relevant to the supervisory relationship and to the process of supervision itself.

Who we are, how we experience and see the world, our notions of personhood, how we relate to one another, how we practise in a professional context and the baggage and resources we bring to supervision and to our overall work are all relevant to personal and professional development. Learning to be a clinical psychologist is thus more than just learning about clinical psychology, it is about learning how to reflect on the interface between our personal and professional identities, that is, our multiple identities in terms of gender, ethnicity, age, sexuality, class, etc., and learning how to use this understanding to improve practice. In supervision that can mean, for example: a supervisee being encouraged and facilitated in learning what it means to them to be a Black, female, clinical psychologist; learning how it

Table 7.4 Understanding organisational contexts

1 What were the historical, social, legal and cultural contexts within which the service you work in was first conceived and developed? How did these contexts and related motives operate in a way that some sections of the population were excluded, marginalised or ill-served? What professional, theoretical or service justifications are made to defend such inequities in service delivery?

2 What is the composition of the local population that your organisation serves? What are the numbers of Black and minority ethnic people in your area, and what are their backgrounds, histories and differing needs? Are they aware of the availability (or not) of local psychological services, both statutory and voluntary? What are the range of perceptions, assumptions, fears and expectations of these services or of those that work within them? What evidence exists to reveal their use of, avoidance of or exclusion by these services? In the absence of such evidence, what would we need to do to find out and develop more appropriate services?

3 What is the composition of the client population referred to and seen by clinical psychologists, and does this compare with the composition of the local population? How is this monitored within your service, your team or by yourself in your own caseload? How does such monitoring impact on the design and ongoing development of services and clinical practice? If service design and delivery is changed in response to monitoring exercises, then how is this change evaluated and by whom?

4 What might be some of the reasons for the relatively very low numbers (or absence) of Black and minority ethnic people within your service? What issues affect the availability of and accessibility to psychological services? Or, conversely, what might be some of the reasons for an over-representation or disproportionately high number of Black and minority ethnic people in certain services, such as in acute mental health wards or in forensic settings? What are the implications of this for clients, for the local Black and minority ethnic communities or for the service? What are the roles and the ethical responsibilities of clinical psychologists in addressing these factors? What would it mean for psychologists to remain curious bystanders or to remain disinterested or comfortably blind to the contributory processes and functions of power, and to exclusion and oppression?

5 How might clients who do not speak English be able to access and utilise psychological services? Which services are made available to them or denied them, and on what grounds? For example, particular psychological services may be denied to people who do not speak English because of practitioners'/managers' beliefs that psychological therapy is compromised, impossible or ineffective with the use of interpreters. Practitioners may deny their own lack of competence in working with interpreters or attempt to obscure their lack of commitment to providing appropriate services equitably to all those in their local population. What are the implications for would-be clients of such practices and defences offered? What might be some of the ethical, professional and legal obligations of clinical psychologists to address these issues effectively? Which policies might need to be implemented and effectively monitored within the organisation? Which resources would be needed and how could psychological services be developed to be able to serve all those in the local population?

6 Which policies exist within the organisation and within psychological services to ensure equal opportunity to access healthcare services? How are such policies operationalised within your own service or team? How are these service measures monitored and evaluated? What is the role of clinical psychologists in this process? What steps are taken when such policies are breached? What might be your own professional and legal obligations in situations where such policies are breached?

impacts on both her professional relationships and on her clinical work; how to make oneself safe as a Black professional at work where subtle and perhaps unintentional institutional discrimination is pervasive; or how to recognise, challenge and manage racism when encountered within a clinical session, within clinical supervision or within management supervision. For a supervisor, this also requires an openness and courage to explore what being White (or from any ethnic background) may mean to them and to the supervisee and the implications for the supervisory relationship.

D'Andrea and Daniels (1997) emphasise that ethnic and racial identity development, that is, 'the way individuals view themselves as cultural/ethnic/ racial beings', is important to discuss in supervision. They describe the range of ethnic identity development models, such as Cross's (1971, 1995) model of Black racial identity development, the minority identity development model (MID; Atkinson, Marten and Sue, 1993), and White identity development models (Helms, 1995; Ponterotto and Pedersen, 1993), asserting that assessing at which stage(s) of ethnic–racial identity development supervisors and supervisees are likely to be functioning is of critical importance in understanding the process of what they call multicultural supervision. For supervision, facilitating personal and professional development requires the ability and willingness for both supervisee and supervisor to reflect on their and perhaps each other's ethnic identity development stages in relation to practice.

Improving supervisory practice: Personal and professional development

Supervision that values and facilitates personal and professional development is one where safety is fostered, reflection is encouraged and modelled, permission is given to explore the personal–professional interface and where related uncertainty, confusion, anxiety, fears and ambivalence are normalised, accepted and not judged. Some examples of personal and professional development issues of culture, racism and power are:

1   Supervisors and supervisees can examine their own values and beliefs as they manifest in the supervisory relationship and in the supervisory process itself, making this explicit in the supervision contract. Scaife and Walsh (2001) provide excellent examples of how supervision can be used in this way, for example by audiotaping a supervision session with a view to reviewing it specifically to identify the values and beliefs of both supervisor and supervisee.

2   Supervisors and supervisees can reflect privately or with colleagues and perhaps discuss models of ethnic and racial identity development and how they may apply to their own supervisory relationship and to the supervision and organisational context of clinical work.

3   Supervisors can seek further training to develop their knowledge, understanding and skills related to working with Black and minority ethnic clients, and to providing supervision to supervisees from diverse ethnic (majority or minority) backgrounds.

4   Supervisors and supervisees could consult Black Service User groups and networks, minority ethnic community groups and Black and minority ethnic colleagues to enhance their own knowledge and understanding of issues related to culture, individual and institutional racism, etc.

5   Supervisors and supervisees could identify and reflect on their own experiences of inequality, racism, disadvantage, marginalisation and privilege in their personal and professional lives. As an ongoing supervision theme they could consider how this may influence their identities, values and expectations, their relationships at work, their professional activities and especially their work with clients.

6   Supervisors and supervisees may need to identify and use existing or potential sources of support for themselves, particularly sources that would facilitate their confidence and competence in talking about and addressing issues of culture, racism and power in all areas of their professional practice. Sources of support could include professional relationships, personal relationships, professional networks and user networks.

Summary

This chapter has attempted to explore some key issues and some of the ways of improving supervisory practice in clinical psychology to enable us to develop greater understanding, confidence and competence in addressing power, cultural differences and racism. Whilst some implications for supervisors and supervisees have been outlined, the overall implications for the profession also require attention, although these will be mentioned only briefly here. Key implications include the responsibilities for our professional body in examining its own structure, policies and procedures and its own organisational processes that reinforce a Eurocentric bias in every aspect of clinical psychology. Clinical psychology training programmes also need to review and revise the content and methods of training, to examine their own biases and institutional racism and to pay particular attention to the potential abuses within supervision (clinical, academic and research supervision) in relation to cultural and racial oppression. Finally, and inevitably, the content and nature of training for supervisors and the monitoring of supervisors and supervision with respect to issues of culture and racism remain important challenges for the profession.

Chapter 8

Incorporating gender issues in clinical supervision

Gill Aitken and Maxine Dennis

Most women still have very different life experiences from most men . . . because women's lives are different from men's they need different things from public services. Meeting their needs often means changing the content of services and how they are delivered . . .

(Equal Opportunities Commission, 2004: 1)

A further major dimension of (clinical) supervision concerns diversity. Diversity can be recognized against the ADDRESSING[1] influences, but the main implication is to treat diversity issues in supervision (e.g. cultural differences) as a result of the interaction between you both. It is a dimension of your relationship that requires your usual professionalism, particularly a willingness to discuss such interactions openly and constructively (e.g. in order to enhance your sensitivity and hence effectiveness).

(Milne, 2008: 29)

Introduction

Since 2003 there has been a wealth of gender-related legislation, policy and guidance to address the adverse impact of (Trans[2]) gendered social, health and economic inequalities (see Table 8.1). Organisations and individuals are targeted to enact positive and inclusive social and human values and outcomes. However, legislation and policies do not effect change: individuals do. For positive and informed gender relating, we need to be receptive to two main ideas: first, that growing into becoming a man or woman affects how we feel and think about, and act and relate towards, ourselves and others; and second, whilst there may be commonalities of experiences and consequences within and across gendered lives, there are also differences. In brief, at any moment in time, we can be influenced by legacies from past gendered and early experiences or from anticipations and hopes for the future (notions of transference, counter-transference and projection can be helpful here).

Table 8.1 Summary of gender equality developments

Time scale (years)	Gender equality development
100+	Women's equality and social justice campaigning and activism (peripheral)
100+	British Psychological Society founded (1901)
60+	National Health Service founded
35+	Equalities legislation first introduced (e.g. Sex Discrimination Act 1975)
17+	BPS: Society Sections and Faculties (e.g. Psychology of Women Section, 1988; and later: Psychology of Sexualities Section; Faculty of Race and Culture)
12+	Person-centred and integrated public services reform (e.g. National Service Frameworks, 1999)
9+	Public sector duties (race, 2000; disability, 2006; gender, 2007)
6+	First national Gender Mental Health guidance (e.g. from the DH: *Mainstreaming Gender & Women's Mental Health*, 2003; *Scoping the Needs of Men*, 2009)
5+	Transgender legislation (e.g. Gender Recognition Act 2004)
2+	Transpeople guidance (e.g. *Trans – A Practical Guide for the NHS*, for Trans employment and healthcare in the NHS, 2009)
<2	Equality and Human Rights Commission founded (2007)
<1	Single Equalities Bill published (2009)

In this chapter, we consider how clinical supervision can create a space and means of opening up different perspectives and dialogues for issues of diversity and power to be considered (McQueen, 2000). This is for the benefit of ourselves as well as the clients, colleagues and supervisees we (may) work with.

Throughout this book there is implicit, if not always explicit, acknowledgement of differences in structural relations of privilege and power along the supervisor–supervisee dimension. In clinical psychology the supervision process aims to enable supervisees to learn to bring together theory, techniques and interpersonal interventions:

> Supervisors are vested with the power and responsibility, by their institutions and training programmes to evaluate, influence and judge trainees. They are also supposed to provide to the less skilled and inexperienced and less knowledgeable student therapist the skill, knowledge, and personal awareness, to help the client in a professional and ethical manner.
>
> (Carter, 1995: 237–238)

When writing in 2003, we noted that reactions to running workshops on gender issues included: 'not relevant . . . we now live in a more equal society . . . we treat everyone as an individual . . . we work collaboratively' (Aitken and Dennis, 2004: 136). Our experience now is of a shift to 'how do we *do* gender in supervision . . . what set of *skills/techniques* do we need to learn?'

Such a shift reflects a dominance of knowledge and skills competence models in the professions and public sector services. Within supervision we are mindful of the pressures on supervisees (and supervisors) to take a gender neutral perspective to meet the demands of the profession, particularly when 'core' competences and evaluation of trainee placements and services do not explicitly identify inequality or gender as an evaluation measure. When gender competences are included, knowledge and skills are important but are not sufficient and so risk being applied in mechanistic ways. For example, in supervision, knowledge of a woman or man not fluent in English could mean that we focus on ensuring access to an interpreter, leaving our own values and views or our relationship with the client unreflected upon.

A knowledge and skills approach can be experienced as a ready solution to feeling paralysed or overwhelmed as we begin to personally and professionally become aware of the privileges and access to power resources we have. This can also feel like a solution to address the 'gap' arising from the legacy of gender and culturally neutral approaches of the dominant scientist-practitioner model of clinical psychology training (Nadirshaw, 2000; Sayal-Bennett, 1991). In such models, 'doing' and activity are privileged relative to facilitating a creative thinking and practising environment. We would argue that such an approach characterises necessary but early developmental phases of practice (as therapist and supervisor).

Such an approach can also meet our need for certainty in contexts of anxiety when working with tension and conflicts arising from perceived differences and the risk of 'getting it wrong'. Indeed, equalities legislation and policy tends to focus our thinking on experienced negative effects (discrimination), with little account taken of participants' intentions or their relational histories. All too common are accounts of the use of grievance procedures and legislation as 'sticks', which close down thinking and talking with one another about sometimes difficult and emotive issues around gender and 'race'.[3] If this is our experience as practitioners and co-workers, what might be happening between clients and practitioners? Recently, diversity was included in *Introduction to Clinical Supervision: A Tutor's Guide* (Milne, 2008). However, findings from the piloting of this guide generated no information on whether and how issues of diversity were addressed (Milne, personal communication, 2009). In summary, the mainstreaming of gender and equalities in training (and likely thinking and practice) remains far from robustly embedded. Indeed, at a 2008 regional supervisors' training event facilitated by one of us (Gill Aitken), over 90% reported no previous experience of 'race' and gender training in clinical supervision. Positively this was followed up by a request for a 2-day residential in 2010 to explore such issues.

Developing knowledge and skills about different social groups is part of the process. However, we are personally and professionally members of

Confidence based on clarity of own values and how these enter a context

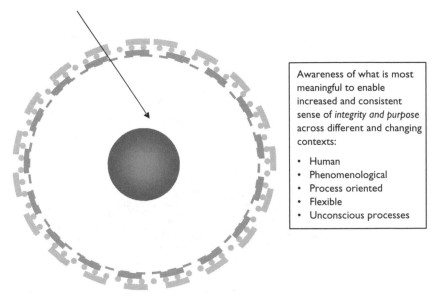

Awareness of what is most
meaningful to enable
increased and consistent
sense of *integrity and purpose*
across different and changing
contexts:

• Human
• Phenomenological
• Process oriented
• Flexible
• Unconscious processes

Figure 8.1 The aware–authentic supervisor (adapted from Aitken and Franks, 2009).

those very groups: The implication is that we also need to take a look at ourselves and develop awareness and curiosity about how our own supervisory and clinical practice is influenced by the (ad)vantage point of personal and various referent group values (Figure 8.1). How aware are we of how we might embody these influences in our practice and how these may be played out in the operation of power? For some, the recognition or realisation of how power relations are played out and their differential effects may be anticipated or experienced as too painful or too threatening to voice, so that 'that which is unspeakable cannot be challenged'. This can mean that habitual patterns and dominant–subordinate relations are reproduced (Font, Vecchio and Almeida, 1998; Miller, 1986). Developing and responding from a more aware or 'authentic' self can feel too risky, as the process requires that we move away from a more expert-certain position (beyond self) to one of uncertainty and one that is more relationally attuned.

In this chapter, we positively contribute to debates about how clinical psychology can incorporate gendered issues and how these can be thought about in supervision. We do not propose the use of a prescriptive model or 'recipe cook book' of techniques or strategies. We do, however, highlight the importance of supervisors and supervisees being both grounded and experienced (practised) rather than attached and fixed to known tools and techniques or, at the other extreme, reaching out for the latest model or

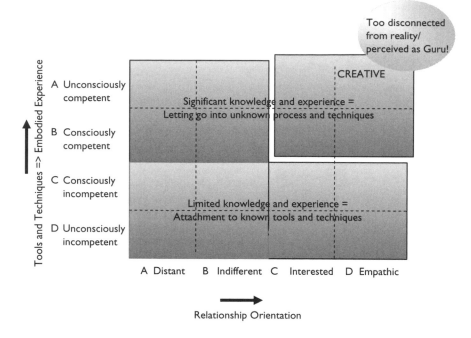

Figure 8.2 Model of supervisory development (Aitken and Franks, 2009).

technique without consolidation and integration. As Figure 8.2 indicates, the risk of simply acquiring more and more models or techniques would be to move beyond a creative space to a position of becoming disconnected with the realities of our social environments or being related to by supervisees as a 'guru' (intersecting with professional status) with possible exploitation of power relations. Figure 8.2 presents a developmental model that can be used as an aid to position ourselves individually or relationally at any time.

The rest of this chapter is divided into eight main sections. In the first section we briefly provide a context of why we are interested in the topic of gender and power. In the second section we review some terms and definitions (e.g. gender, power and empowerment) that are often used in working with diversity issues. This is to make clearer what we understand by these and to think about how we might need to support ourselves in preparing to reflect on and explore these issues. In the third and fourth sections we outline a 'process' model of supervision as a framework to illustrate the complex web of relationships and contexts that enter the supervisor–supervisee relationship and also provide some of the research evidence on the impact of wider social-political contexts (fourth section), including clinical psychology developments (fifth section). We then focus on possible gender influences and effects on the process of supervision, including the supervisee–client relationship and supervisee–supervisor relationship (sixth section). In the seventh section we take this back out to implications for working with a client (as gendered). In the final section we discuss a case to work through and questions we might ask ourselves.

About ourselves

We first met in 1994 as executive members of the BPS 'Race' and Culture group and subsequently have taught and presented at conferences together. As Black-identified and White-identified women we clearly bring our histories, and through our relationship we aim to use our experiences in a constructive way to offer some thought to this area.

Over the years, we have both been concerned and interested in how supervisory practice addresses culture, racism and oppression as well as the provision of culturally- and gender-informed appropriate services. For us, personally and professionally, directly tackling issues of gender bias, racism and factors that may hinder various communities' access and experience of supervision and therapy requires ongoing interrogation.

There is much literature that suggests that many Black women and men experience the impact of racism as a more significant oppressive force than sexism (McKay, 1992). Relatedly, early strands of White feminist liberation movements were charged with being narrow and irrelevant to Black women's lives. However, to separate being Black from being a woman or man does an injustice to a whole area of Black people's existence and experience. We have been moved by the dialogue and developments within feminist models over the decades to attend to 'race', class, sexual orientation, age, etc. – the multifaceted aspects and dynamic dimensions of being human. The work of many theorists, for example Chesler (1974), Collins (1990), hooks (1990, 1993), Lorde (1984), Miller (1986) and Morrison (1992) among others, has had a great impact on our thinking, understanding and practice.

Temperely (1984) points to the ambivalence all of us feel towards the complementarity of the sexes. She states that it is easy to blame one sex or adopt an adversarial/rivalrous position that may eclipse the importance of sexual interdependence, union and creativity. This chapter aims to demonstrate this in a clear way.

We aim to approach our clinical and supervisory work with openness and readiness to work with what a patient or supervisee brings, to provide a container to promote some growth and understanding (Bion, 1959, 1962, 1970). An awareness of the socio-economic and political inequalities, together with a person's connection with their community, is integral to our work. However, we continue to reflect on our practice and in so doing allow space for continuing evolvement.

We hope that this joint chapter helps take us in some small way towards a greater understanding and appreciation of these interrelated issues within the practice of supervision.

Definition and concepts

Here we briefly present definitions for sex, gender, sexual orientation, power and empowerment. The definition we draw on will both reflect and construct our practice in supervisory and therapeutic relational encounters.

Sex and gender

For some, 'sex' is differentiated from gender: sex is located in biological differences whereas gender is a social construct. Others argue that *both* sex and gender are social constructs rooted in social judgements and expectations.

Sex (Organisation Intersex International, undated)

- Defined and assigned in legal, anatomical, biological, genetic and chromosomal terms: can be male by one definition and female by another.
- Single sex and intersex people may be of any gender identity and sexual orientation.

Gender

- The social characteristics of sex.
- A process through which social life is organised at the level of the individual and the family, and the central feature is power.
- Gender identity is the inner sense of being female, male, both or neither. It may may not be the same as the sex and/or gender assigned to an individual by others.

Sexual orientation

- Is the complex interplay of a person's 'affectional orientation' (who they like), 'erotic orientation' (to whom they are sexually attracted) and 'romantic orientation' (with whom they fall in love).
- May remain consistent over a person's life time or evolve and change over a life course.
- Is different from sexual behaviour and also from gender identity.

Some argue that socialisation processes differentially affect boys and girls. Boys 'psychologically expand' to have increased cultural expectation about the development of an autonomous self and identity, whilst girls 'psycho-logically contract' to develop a sense of self in relation to the needs and desires of others (Larkin and Popaleni, 1994). Of course, there are vari-ations in degrees of expression, influenced by personal development and social positions (e.g. class, 'race', ability). Additionally, the concept of Trans has in some contexts been extended to include women and men who do not conform to or transgress stereotypical normative-gendered expec-tations (e.g. dress codes, behaviours).

Evidence for the above comes from study findings that, as a group, men take more instrumental roles with greater agency (particularly in external or public spheres) and women take more expressive or more communion roles (particularly in internal or domestic spheres). Whilst we question this separation of public/private spheres, it can be a starting point to explore the impact of differentiated gendered aspects of everyday life as acknowledged by World, European and UK Equality and Human Rights organisations:

> a first step in creating change lies in an evolving consciousness of the straightjacket that gender norms and heterosexism impose . . . In this sense therapy becomes one vehicle for the construction of male identity. It challenges roles; it positions itself as commentator on structural aspects of class and culture that intersects with gender to create oppression. Our therapy must . . . promote values in keeping with changing, positive definitions for both men and women. These values would include a mandate for collaboration, partnership, and equality.
>
> (Bepko et al., 1998: 79)

A central question for us might be: What are the implications for us as (trainee) clinical psychologists if we internalise or reject various gender role stereotypes or attitudes, either in relation to self or other women or men? Developing awareness of and acknowledging our own gendered assump-tions and premises enables us to attend to these issues in our constructions of self, supervisees and clients. Further, we can then develop an awareness of possible constructions by others and the impact of such constructions arising in therapy and supervision encounters.

Power

Power as a concept has been variously defined and has generated numerous typologies. We draw on the following:

- An awareness, an understanding, a realisation that you already have power, albeit power that the culture does not recognise (Kitzinger, 1991).
- (Power as) positive, as the capacity to produce change (Mitchell, 1974; Taylor, 1994).

Power is often conceptualised as located in the individual and as a 'thing' that is possessed: to be held on to or 'given away'. Such a perspective ignores the relational aspects of power. Power enters our everyday discourses, often signifying the value of male behaviour and the devaluing of female behaviour. For people identifying with disadvantaged or oppressed groups, acknowledgement and acceptance of access to forms of power can be uncomfortable, as explicit use of power is typically associated with misuse and abuse. Relational power is not only about exercising power over others more effectively, but also about facilitating power in others (Cassell and Walsh, 1993). The notion of relational power as both potentially oppressive and enabling is the province of this chapter.

In considering the exercise of power in a supervisory context, the supervisor typically defines the relationship and is assumed to have a greater knowledge base, objectivity and status than the trainee as supervisee (Carter, 1995). As such a supervisor can maximise or minimise a supervisee's sense of powerlessness, which is present in the relationship. These feelings may be more evident for new trainees. Therapy and supervisory encounters encompass complex dynamic aspects, where one's identification with aspects of colour, history and role can be more or less prominent at any one time and in different configurations. As supervisors and therapists we need to hold these in mind to be receptive enough to what is brought into these encounters and to respond to the human being in front of us.

For supervisors, as (institutionally accredited) experts, power advantage includes enhanced credibility. Even in clear-cut conflicts such as lack of supervision time or different styles in thinking about and applying a particular therapeutic model, it is likely to be a trainee's word against the supervisor's with well respected supervisors. If gender issues are not acknowledged as valid or legitimate areas of exploration by a supervisor, then how power relations are played out will have differential effects, possibly with a greater bearing within the supervisory relationship when the supervisee is training, and once qualified if the supervisor has a future managerial role.[4]

Pinderhughes argues that a 'supervisor may use the helping role to reinforce . . . (his or her) own sense of competence by keeping subordinates in a one-down position' (1989: 111). If supervisees internalise such models, then they become vulnerable to replicating aspects of such harmful, or at the very least unhelpful, interactions in a parallel process with clients. This in effect extends the influence of an unhelpful supervisor onto clients (see also Figure 8.2, left-hand quadrants)

Empowerment

Three different definitions of empowerment are:

- A person experiences herself as having a legitimate right to claim her voice and having expertise and a referent framework from which to act (Hewson, 1999).
- Empowerment can be felt momentarily or can be transformative when it is linked to a permanent shift in the distribution of social power (Yuval Davis, 1994).
- Empowerment involves rejecting the dimensions of knowledge, whether personal, cultural or institutional, that perpetuate objectification and dehumanization (Hill Collins, 1990).

Work around empowerment and empowering strategies typically reflects individualised approaches that 'rely on developing in women this sense of personal agency . . . create in women a certain state of mind (feeling powerful, competent, worthy of esteem, able to make free choices and influence their world)' (Kitzinger, 1991: 122). However, the lived reality of being able to make free choices and significantly influence the world may be more restrictive than we would like to think. Skills training, such as positive thinking and learning how to voice or be assertive, may not be enough.

Hewson's (1999) statement helps us to prepare ourselves for thinking about these issues:

> In western culture many men are trained to have a confident, self advertising presentation, which can earn expert power even when they do not have relevant expertise. On the other hand, women are often trained to have a collaborative, self-effacing presentation which does not tend to earn expert power even when they have the expertise.
>
> (Hewson, 1999: 407)

Supervision is an opportunity to attend to pre-existing beliefs, perceptions and feelings that affect how we relate with and behave towards ourselves and others, as well as attending to more subtle aspects of gender in the (counter-)transference.

In exploring and speaking about such issues, supervisors and clinicians need to be familiar with some of the debates, research and publications relevant to gender and related social inequalities (see also Table 8.1). There is a wealth of evidence that gender (of therapist and client) can impact on clinical judgements of mental health needs and risks that are played out in the intersection of gender with 'race', class and age.

In our view, it is the (ultimate) responsibility of supervisors to create the conditions for supervisees to actively explore values and beliefs. One way is for supervisors to name that being challenged and exploring different viewpoints aids the supervisor's learning and development as much as the supervisee's.

The initial placement contract can be the starting point for supervisor and trainee to name, acknowledge and discuss understandings of power imbalances and commit to be alert to how and when these are played out. Clear boundaries and an awareness of respective roles, responsibilities and accountabilities can provide a basis from which a range of issues can be explored in non-condemnatory and non-defended ways. This will of course depend on the supervisor's own confidence and receptiveness to being challenged by a supervisee raising potentially contentious areas or indeed in challenging a supervisee.

As supervisors, where do we locate ourselves in the supervisor develop-ment model in general or in relation to a particular supervisee (see Figure 8.2)? As supervisors we are not immune to developing rigid or inflexible patterns of relating or indeed, at the other extreme, where we have devel-oped practices that have remained unchecked or unchallenged because of our institutional power positions or because we rationalise or defend them as grounded in our form of reality or rooted in our expert positions (see top right-hand quadrant of Figure 8.2). Perhaps some cases reaching BPS disciplinary hearings (often reflecting gross misuse of power abuse against clients and supervisees) might be indicative of this.

Similarly, supervisees can project false competence or arrogant confi-dence (based on sense of entitlement or unconscious incompetence), which can also adversely affect a supervisor's capacity to explore areas because of the latter's anxiety or fear of creating tension, being subject to claims of discrimination or of appearing less competent than the supervisee. This might be particularly the case when supervisees have also not been chal-lenged over time by different tutors, supervisors or managers out of fear of allegations of discrimination. These dynamics can interface with those arising out of both 'visible' differences of 'race', gender, etc. as well as more 'invisible' differences of sexual orientation, class, etc. Further, Patel (1998) noted that when occupying contradictory positions of 'perceived' subordi-nate (Black-identified group membership) and dominant (e.g. clinical psy-chologist), practitioners may draw on strategies and tactics to reflect increased professional power to enhance credibility with a client expecting a dominant 'valued' position (e.g. White-identified therapist). This may be heightened when weaving in a gendered perspective (see also Aitken, 1998; Leary, 1998). This will have implications for supervision and issues that need to be addressed throughout placement and supervision experiences (see also McQueen, 2000). Any opportunity for self-reflection requires dialogue and recognition that our learning is an ongoing process.

A supervisee's feelings towards and about the supervisor, how they are treated and whether and how conflict is addressed in supervision can provide a parallel frame in deepening our understanding of direct clinical work with clients. The enabling and containing aspect of the supervisory relationship is crucial. It may be that, as supervisors, we need to look at flexible formats and conditions for supervision in order to provide 'safe' spaces for supervision across (and within) gender contexts (Milne and Oliver, 2000).

Process model of supervision

Hawkins and Shohet's (2006) process model of supervision highlights the richness and complexity of any supervision or therapy encounter reflecting client, supervisee and supervisor as individuals, as well as in various relations to one another (e.g. therapy matrix and supervision matrices). Their model makes explicit how individual encounters are embedded within and affected by (particular) socio-economic, political, cultural and organisational contexts. *How* we understand the effects of these wider contexts on supervision and therapy will, in part, be dependent on our 'conscious' awareness of such issues.

For example, in considering the wider social context, if we adopt a consensus view of society (i.e. there is no conflict in wider society) then undertaking a gender-neutral approach to relational encounters will not be experienced as problematic or limited. Here, psychological distress would be understood as reflective of individualised 'breakdown' to be 'fixed' through individualised solutions, including psycho-educative ones. This may involve the sharing of individualised techniques, including learning more adaptive cognitions and behaviours, but these risk leaving the person as still unknowing about herself and her personal histories, connections and commonalities with others, and leave structural conditions unchanged. Such a societal view is one that still permeates clinical psychology training.

This is contrasted when holding a conflicting view of society as structured by social inequalities, through which different individuals share commonalities (of exclusions and strengths) along dimensions of gender, 'race', class and the intersections of these. This approach requires the clinician's and supervisor's awareness and knowledge of social inequalities and how these organise our existence *internally* and *externally*. Here a person is understood as a social being, and institutionalised structures and systems of gender, ascribed 'race' and class are differently oppressive, constraining and enabling, both in therapy as well as in any supervisory encounters.

All of us have likely internalised powerful gendered and cultural messages about what is (un)acceptable and (de)valued, just as our women/ men clients have. We would question the extent to which the conditions are created in supervisory encounters to bring to awareness (consciousness) such internalisations and how these affect our professional as well as personal relating (see Green, 1998). Within supervision, it may feel that to raise such issues from a structurally less powerful position (supervisee) risks positioning ourselves in relation to the supervisor as 'less than professional'.

As 'professional' men and women practitioners, how do we feel and relate to a crying or angry male or female client or witness our male or female supervisor or supervisee crying in session (therapy or supervision)? How do we discern if we are engaging in skilful clinical practice, violating boundaries or appropriately responding on a human and therapeutic level? How does this differ if the client or supervisor/supervisee identifies as the same or other gender to us and/or sexual orientation? Exploring such issues within supervision enables the beginning of the supervisee's own capacity for self-reflection, which Casement (1988) calls the internal supervisor or Third Eye. The role of the external supervisor is to support the development of this internal capacity pre- and post-qualification. At post-qualification we would expect practitioners to move towards more autonomous functioning and an increased capacity to draw on the internal Third Eye, and not react from personal and gendered ego-driven positions.

Impact of wider social political context

In this section, we summarise background research findings that have implications for supervision in connecting the external world (of out there) with the internal world (of psychology, of a supervisory relationship and of the individuals who come together). It is important to reflect on how the specific knowledge base we draw on influences what is understood as significant and what is then validated.

Research provides consistent evidence of differential effects that seem to cut across cultural and class identifications and over time. Bostock (1997) summarises these under three broad headings.

Status and role expectations

Relative to men, women are accorded lower social status and more restrictive role expectations than men. Evidence for this is drawn from gendered representation in structural positions of power in wider society, from the political sphere to the private and public sectors. Women continue to be over-represented in heading lone-parent families, as primary carers of children, adults and older adults and working at grass roots in the identified 'caring professions'.

In supervision, if discussing the needs of a male primary carer of children we may idealise his role and/or work hard to offer greater practical and emotional support to him than we would a woman carer. By contrast, women who reject a parenting role or harm their children are more readily demonised, typically viewed as having transgressed both their mothering and caring roles.

Abuse and neglect experiences

Relative to men, women have greater exposure to adverse emotional, physical and sexual abuse and neglect experiences from childhood continuing into adulthood, with increased risk of social isolation – particularly from people known to them. A significant number of men have also been subject to such experiences, and normative expectations around masculinity can be a factor in inhibiting disclosure.

As practitioners, psychologists' focus is typically directed outwards towards clients; given that we are gendered, these issues are relevant to us as individuals. How do we as men or women identify or un-identify with clients who may be the abusers/perpetrators and the abused/survivors? Do we take any of these issues to supervision? What are the therapeutic boundaries we consider and do we operate different boundaries when relating to women and men across cultures? What happens if we experience sexual attraction or disgust/anger towards a client? What happens if we ourselves become perpetrators or if we suspect a colleague or supervisor? Do we rationalise, do we justify or do we even talk about such issues with others? At a more subtle level, when we hear about the grooming and silencing strategies of abusers, do we link this with our attempts to socialise our clients or indeed supervisees into our particular models?

Access to societal resources

Women have more limited access to economic, material and social resources. Women continue to be paid less than men and form the majority living below the poverty line and dependent on benefits. Lower income adversely affects quality of housing, access to facilities and amenities and increased contact with statutory agencies.

Failure of clients to attend for therapy is one example. As supervisees and supervisors, we are often governed by narrow rules with pressures of waiting list times, where failure to attend is often assumed to reflect a client's lack of motivation. What understanding do we have, and how do we support women with childcare issues who have a restricted social support network and where our service may be one statutory appointment among many (social services, housing, general practitioners, etc.)? Do we consider such practical issues to be the province of clinical psychology? In supervision we have explored with supervisees how we can try to engage with a woman to explore possible conflicting needs. Given our earlier arguments about women's possible socialisation to meet the needs of others, it is important to explore how being available to her children may be experienced as in opposition to a woman having the space to explore her (internal) needs. This can be done without the therapist taking up the position of a persecutory figure. Often client attrition can (privately) become a way to manage a waiting list without publicly rejecting a client.

Drawing these threads together, the content and process of case formulation in supervision would need to be aware of different frameworks in thinking about men and women's presenting distress. From a social inequalities perspective, women and men are differently socialised into subordinate and dominant positions, respectively. In a psychology of subordination model, women are at risk of developing 'emotional/psychiatric disorder' or finding ways to exert control in indirect ways (e.g. use of alcohol, difficulties with eating and self-injury) to alleviate internal distress. The heightened use of such coping strategies has also been found in studies of gay, lesbian, bisexual and transgender populations.

We might argue that this is an extreme position to take, yet we see female, gay, lesbian, bisexual and transgender populations over-represented in categories of affective related disorders (e.g. depression, anxiety, borderline personality disorder and affective psychoses) whereas heterosexual men appear more often in the figures for substance misuse and anti-social personality disorders. Again a focus on clients can mask our own gendered needs as part of the workforce. The published *Independent Inquiry into the Care and Treatment of Daksha Emson and her Daughter Freya* (North East London Strategic Health Authority, 2003) highlighted how gendered, racialised and professional issues for (mental) health practitioners affected the availability and access to timely and appropriate occupational and support services.

Our particular understanding of presenting distress will impact on the way we talk about and open up therapeutic possibilities. Societal acknowledgement of inequalities is indicated in changes in legislation over the years. Although women comprise over 50% of the total population numerically, as a category women have been considered a psychologically and economically oppressed or dominated group, as evidenced by being routinely and legally discriminated against in society. Attempts to legislate out such discriminations in the UK are evident (see Table 8.1), including the gender public sector duty in 2007.

Placing clinical psychology in context

How aware and interested are we, as supervisors or supervisees, of the critiques of our profession and the wider push within the public sector to shift the balance of power so that services become influenced by and accountable to wider communities (see also *New Ways of Working*, BPS, 2007b)? In approaching supervision, we attempt to engage supervisees with such literature and debates. In so doing we aim to manage the tension between trainees getting through a clinical programme's requirements and how to develop a (de)stabilising critical thinking faculty rather than a passive acceptance of the mainstream status quo. This means, as supervisor, being open to moving from an ascribed expert position to be alongside the supervisee in a relationship characterised by positions of potential conflict; this can feel difficult when the supervisee himself may desire certainty.[5] This could also mean that a supervisor moves from feeling consciously competent to consciously incompetent or unconsciously competent (see Figure 8.2).

In the United States and the UK, clinical psychology has been critiqued as a cultural mechanism that sustains the interests of those in power and rarely challenges prevailing beliefs and stereotypes. This seems a paradox as clinical psychology positions itself to achieve the alleviation of psychological distress and dysfunction and the promotion of psychological health and well-being. Over the years, psychological theories, models and the research on which they are predicated have been critiqued for being partial, specifically reflecting 'idealised' (white, middle class, male and heterosexist) assumptions and norms about what is normative and acceptable, and for focusing on the individual as the site of both the problem and the solution (Fernando, 1995; Patel et al., 2000). Such theories and practices have been identified as excluding particular groups from accessing psychological services or for problematising the individual as being 'deficient' when in services. Although thinking and practice around issues of diversity are developing, they are not yet robustly embedded.

Given our earlier arguments about the gendered socialisation of women and men in our society, there are a number of apparent paradoxes at work. Since 2001, clinical psychology has become a predominantly female occupation and women comprise over 60% of registered DCP members. The increased 'feminisation' of clinical psychology has been more recently responded to with requests for more men to apply. The interrelationship between gender and 'race' still continues not to be analysed. In 2008/9 people of minority ethnic heritages (including mixed parentage) comprised 10% of all successful applicants and women overall comprised 85%.

If women comprise the majority of workers and clients, we might expect arguments about the adverse effects of gender bias operating within psychology to be countered and those structural inequalities mitigated. One explanation for the reproduction of inequalities is that women as a group, and men as a group, are not homogeneous, and inequalities intersect with class, 'race', sexuality and professional dimensions. Further, few women perceive or experience themselves as members of an oppressed group (Ussher and Nicolson, 1992). In part, this could reflect internalisation as a subordinated group – i.e. socialised to the normalcy of society or the dominant models of clinical psychology, engaged in denial of oppression or identifying with the dominant group (psychology and male) norms. Thus women and men reproduce rather than bring about change to the status quo. There is a parallel process and these issues are then seen as unimportant, split off and located in a few to examine or push for change. Nadirshaw (2000) has argued consistently for changes to the structure of the profession and in our opinion this still stands. In supervision, a change in emphasis about what are considered valid topics for exploration may be a necessary step.

Gender in the supervisory relationship

> A social movement that is transformative must break the isomorphism of power that it critiques.
>
> (Almeida, 1998: 2)

Hawkins and Shohet (2006) suggest that there are two main supervisory styles: attending to the therapy matrix via reports, written notes and tapes and attending via the 'here and now' of the supervisory process. In thinking through gender issues for supervision, to engage with the second supervisory style (the here and now relationship), gender issues would be explored and discussed early in the supervisory relationship to clarify what might belong to the client, supervisee and supervisor. Questions to support such exploration could include:

• How do we develop clarity about what informs (our decisions on) how we attend to diversity issues in our clinical supervisory–leadership roles?
• How do we understand how our own diversity-related attitudes and actions are evaluated by others and influence what is relationally possible?
• How aware and knowledgeable are we of personal, group, organisational and wider social forces that act against skilful/useful diversity relating and the personal practices and strategies needed to address them?
• How can we develop confidence to talk about and address potentially challenging diversity issues?

Hawkins and Shohet (2006) identify six modes of supervising in the 'here and now':

1   Reflection on the content of the session so that the supervisee is helped to become more aware of their work with clients.
2   Focusing on the what, why and how of strategies and interventions, and the next step with the client.
3   Focusing on the therapy process as a co-creation, including the conscious and unconscious interaction between the therapist and client (i.e. client's transference).

4   Supervisee's counter-transference. What does the client stir up? Influences such as conscious prejudice, racism, sexism and other assumptions
that colour the way we mis-see, mishear or misrelate to the client.
5   Supervisory relationship (the importance of this is addressed in earlier
chapters of this volume).
6   Supervisor's counter-transference. Here, sudden changes and disrup-
tions to the therapeutic alliance are used to examine the fantasy
relationship between supervisor and client.

According to this model, effective and useful supervision must integrate all
aspects and have some awareness of the developmental stage of the
supervisee. At the beginning, the focus may be on the first two aspects, to
facilitate holding an overview as supervisees begin to look at what is
actually happening rather than acting prematurely and speculating. The
latter aspects become central as the supervisee becomes more sophisticated.
Additionally, a number of tasks need to be addressed, such as the nature
and style of the work of the supervisee, personality of supervisee, openness
and trust established in the relationship, and personal exploration.[6] From
what we have argued throughout this chapter, gender issues can be integrated into all aspects of this work.

Considering the client

Therapy is never a neutral space. A task is to make more visible or explicit
how we negotiate power relations and develop trust through shared understandings, transparency, collaboration and honesty. Tensions or 'ruptures'
to a seemingly 'collaborative' alliance can be important resources and
provide the conditions to re-negotiate power relations. If, at the minimum,
visible or structural differences (e.g. 'race' and gender, professional–client,
supervisor–supervisee) are acknowledged explicitly early in the relationship,
this can enable a supervisee or client to return to these later when they feel
more secure within the relationship. It is incumbent on the therapist/
supervisor to hold in mind how difficult it may be for the client/supervisee
to name visible or structural difference and power. It is ultimately the
supervisor's responsibility and accountability to create a space and conditions to enable possibilities for issues to be revisited at any point in supervision. It is important for the supervisor to be alert to their own defended
or closed positions (see Figure 8.2).

The contexts of therapy (and supervision), such as how the client accesses
care, appropriate therapy and whether the psychologist is seen as the
'acceptable' face of authority or oppression, are going to be salient to
engagement and continued contact issues. Clearly, social norms and cultural discourses impact on assessments (Harris et al., 2001) and the social
constructions of gender and power. Although significantly influenced by

cultural ideologies, they are receptive to training (Leslie and Clossick, 1996).

In therapy a good experience is important. Commitment and articulation of support to women/men with mental health needs is important but not enough. We need to recognise and have the confidence and capacity to appropriately respond to the impact of early childhood and socialisation of women's and men's emotional development, as well as ongoing experiences of disadvantage, oppression and injustice. Individuals, struggling for survival, can feel vulnerable to threats from within the external as well as internal worlds and may not have the emotional reserves/energy to bring about change. What might be required are resources from the outside in the form of care and other nurturing experiences, so that energy can become self-generating.

Parallel processes can operate in the supervisory encounter. In supervision, containment of this complex (therapy and supervision) matrix can be compromised without clear boundaries to allow for the emergence of trust and a relational history that can withstand, contain or work through tensions. A clear contract about the parameters of supervision may enable a discussion about the supervisory relationship and needs to be on the agenda throughout the supervision.

The supervisor needs to be committed and cognisant of the effect that interruptions or planned and unplanned cancellation of supervision sessions can have on establishing and maintaining a robust working alliance. To provide a space that integrates new ways of thinking and practice, a supervisor may draw on their own power resources to the benefit of the trainee by sharing but not imposing their knowledge (Wheeler et al., 1986). Identifying supervisees' competences, thus affirming the role of critical and reflective thinking and practice, can also provide a foundation for a respectful relationship and for constructive criticism to be heard.

Case study

This case study demonstrates how thinking about gender issues can enter therapy and supervisory contexts. In this example, we position an older male supervisor with a young female trainee; the male client is a similar age to the trainee.

A client is referred for panic attacks[7] and upon allocation was seen as a 'straightforward cognitive behavioural therapy (CBT) referral'. During the initial assessment, the trainee (privately) felt she could have been friends with the client if they had met outside of therapy. The client was able to use the therapy to good effect, as seen by his self-reported reduction in the Beck Anxiety Inventory (BAI; Beck and Steer, 1990) scores and the trainee's observations.

The trainee looked forward to the sessions as she felt there was good rapport and the client appeared to make use of the therapy. Mid-point during therapy the client starts to wear excessive amounts of aftershave, complimenting the trainee and requesting self-disclosure about her social life. The trainee attempts to play down and ignores comments about her clothing and attractiveness. Increasingly she becomes aware and self-conscious about how she is dressed and the different degrees of exposure of her body.

She attempts to bring this to supervision by wondering whether the collaborative therapy relationship is breaking down. She explicitly names 'friendliness' as interfering with the homework and tasks within her clinical sessions. The supervisor focuses on providing strategies and techniques to orient the client back to the tasks of therapy. There is no explicit discussion around gendered issues, power or acknowledging the threat (awkwardness) the trainee is experiencing. The trainee does not feel able to bring these concerns again to supervision and the supervisor does not raise the issue.

Nearing the end of therapy, the client says 'he has got something for her and he will give it to her in the last session'. She becomes increasingly worried regarding what the 'something' is. In fact he does not turn up to the last session. She is left with feelings of unease, but also relief. At the penultimate session, the client's symptoms have objectively improved. The supervisor seemingly validates the trainee's competency by naming that the client attended most of his sessions and his BAI scores were reduced.

A man presenting with anxiety can set up the dynamic in a mixed-gender therapy for the woman trainee wishing to rescue a vulnerable male (see also Walker and Goldner, 1995). In our experience, this is often (but not always) different for a woman working with a woman referred for anger issues, in part because the latter reflects a non-normative expectation about acceptable women's behaviours, and also can challenge a woman practitioner's awareness and acceptance of anger within herself, which might be different to a male practitioner's awareness and acceptance.

The supervisee's attempt to bring the (erotic) transference to supervision was named through wondering whether the collaborative therapy relationship was breaking down. She explicitly referred to 'friendliness', however the supervisor's emphasis on re-orienting the client back to task was to the exclusion of any explicit discussion around gendered issues, power or the transference relationship. Without the space in supervision to explore these issues, the trainee plays down her awkward feelings. However, she becomes increasingly aware of what a gendered response is: being an object of desire and how different clothing is relational to body exposure. She thus starts to wear trousers: a concrete solution to a tricky therapeutic encounter. She also experiences guilt when recalling that she felt she could have been friends with the client under different circumstances.

Our approach would be to explore from the outset possible identifications and playing out of power relations with a client around age-related issues and sexualised attraction, as well as a supervisee's wish to be an effective practitioner. As supervisors, we pay special attention to the language that supervisees bring to supervision. Words such as 'friendliness' would be explored for a possible sexualised presentation and as a valid supervision topic. This might be done through referring to male–female relations in general, literature that refers to erotic transference (Bollas, 1994) and counter-transference in same and cross-gender therapy. From the scenario, the trainee experienced a blurring of boundaries, causing her to worry that her appearance was provocative (women as causal of male desire). In not creating opportunities for exploration, the supervisor effectively silenced the trainee. In our experience, some women supervisees have experienced such requests for personal disclosure by males as intrusive (violation of boundaries) and disabling, whatever their stage of training. However, when requested by woman clients, supervisees are more likely to experience these as attempts at connection.

Making more explicit possible identificatory and power relations issues can support understandings of gendered perspectives, such as why a client may make comments in the context of gendered positions in wider society. Therapy (and supervisory) encounters are a microcosm of wider social systems. We aim to enable the trainee to be aware of how to speak with the client to pick up on his anxieties in order to contain his vulnerability, rather than it being reversed: that is, the client's vulnerability has become the supervisee's. The trainee's need to be looked after undermines her professional position and sense of competency, as she feels her need is not legitimated or validated in supervision.

We might ask: 'If the supervisor and supervisee were both women, would the trainee feel more able to bring this to supervision? If all three participants were women, would the comments on the part of the client engender different feelings or interpretations? How would this differ, if at all, if the trainee (or supervisor) was a self-identified transperson, lesbian or bisexual?'

It is important not to portray a scenario of an 'all knowing' supervisor without recognition of the supervisee within this relationship. What the supervisee brings to this relationship and how this affects her understanding and expression of the therapeutic encounter, as well as her readiness and willingness to use supervision, has to be considered an important part of the equation. In summary, both supervisor and supervisee are active participants in the supervisory relationship.

Supervisees (later to become supervisors) will enter supervisory encounters with their own motivations for becoming a therapist or clinical psychologist. Just like the supervisor, the trainee may or may not have the privilege of a theoretical or experiential framework that values considering the impact of wider cultural contexts on therapeutic and supervisory encounters. Part of our task is to think through how to support and facilitate a learning environment in which the cultural contexts (of which we are all part) can be reflected upon. We suggest some examples of learning outcomes that may be usefully agreed at the beginning of supervision as follows: (a) to highlight why psychologists need to be concerned with gender, 'race' and culture and diversity; (b) to be aware of how cultural heritage impacts on personal, professional and institutional relationships; (c) to enable supervisors and supervisees to integrate dimensions of equality into applied practice; (d) to increase our ability to attend to the subtlety and complexity of clinical encounters; and (e) to identify future learning needs.

We have used a CBT case, but note that particular therapy approaches that attend more to the process (e.g. exploratory therapy) more readily lend themselves to attend to issues raised as part of therapy. In saying that, regardless of therapeutic approach, conceptual vacuums and defensiveness can still arise within supervisors and supervisees. Supervision can help the supervisee to become aware of and develop the capacity and confidence to work with tensions, difficulties and ambiguities that emerge in therapy encounters. The supervisory context can offer a space for creative development for both participants that is informed by and adds to skills and techniques (see Figure 8.2: quadrants CD).

At the same time supervision needs to pay attention to the beginning, middle and ending phases of therapeutic relationships, otherwise a focus on obvious differences may function as a distraction from the more general anxieties about therapeutic engagement, dependency dynamics and concerns about separation and endings, respectively.

Summary

In this chapter, we have argued for a move away from additive gender, 'race' or culture packages into supervisory and clinical practices towards a more integrative and transformative process. We tend to separate out the different dimensions of inequalities (e.g. gender and race) but in practice these are all instrumental to our deeper understanding of any individual. We are aware of how the supervisor–supervisee or therapist–client can become caught up focusing through a single lens of understanding and practice (such as gender) or ignoring difference. Without some awareness of the interrelationship of social identifications, this can act as blockages to deeper understanding. To do this we must be able critically to appraise our established assumptions and practices. This may require the capacity to engage more with uncertainty within supervisory relationships. There is a need to move beyond packages of competency tools and techniques and utilise a more fluid approach that attends to process, including transference dynamics, values and meaning.

Supervisory encounters are a microcosm of wider societal processes, and so values, meanings and experiences associated with differences and similarities can still (implicitly or explicitly) figure in therapy and supervisory encounters. The socio-politico-historical context of clinical psychology and the cultural heritage of those training (in terms of 'race', gender and/or class as exemplifiers of differences) need to be made explicit. Therapists and supervisees need conditions in which to feel safe (this does not mean unchallenged) to explore uncertainties and the powerful feelings that emerge when dealing with issues relating to structural differences and power. Otherwise, how can we provide the conditions for clients to raise such issues without them feeling vulnerable to further pathologisation and/ or exclusion by professionals? It may be that clinical psychology and practitioners can consider crossing disciplinary and professional boundaries to inform ourselves of alternative forms of analyses and practices (see also Holland, 1995). In brief, our capacity to tolerate self-reflection about our own personal and professional cultural heritage is central to us becoming curious, questioning and bringing about positive change.

Acknowledgements

We would like to thank the clients, supervisees and colleagues we have worked with over the years, who inform our thinking and practice. The views expressed here are personal and do not necessarily reflect those of our employing institutions.

Notes

1 ADDRESSING is taken from Hays (2001), who developed this acronym as follows: A: age and generational influences, D: developmental, D: disabilities, R: religion and spirituality, E: ethnicity, S: socio-economic status, S: sexual orientation, I: indigenous heritage, N: national origin, G: gender.
2 Unless otherwise specified the term Trans used throughout this chapter encompasses more common reference to: transsexual (e.g. pre–post and non-operative transsexuals); transgendered (e.g. people identifying as transvestites, drag queens and drag kings, etc.); gender variant (people engaging in behaviours, dress codes, etc. stereotypically associated with a particular gender). As a term it contrasts with the notion of a person being, appearing, acting and relating in conventional-stereotypical masculine or feminine gendered forms and ways.
3 The present authors use the term 'race' as a political marker of the racism experienced by Black and minority ethnic groups and is used so as not to obscure the existence of racism. The authors do not subscribe to notions of 'race' as reflecting biological or cultural essentialism.

4 For further reading around issues of power across different dimensions and contexts relevant to clinical psychology (professional, class, in therapy), see also Beckwith (1999) and McQueen (2000).

5 As supervisors we accept our authority, responsibility and accountability in relation to supervisees, but we aim to challenge the view that we are sole bearers of expertise in particular areas. To accept the expert position prevents others from recognising the necessary struggle that is part of the process of development.

6 Carroll (1996) uses a social role model to differentiate among the tasks of supervision. These include the learning relationship, pedagogological features, evaluation, monitoring of professional ethical issues, advisory role, consultancy role and monitoring administrative aspects.

7 A male patient diagnosed with panic attacks is a reversal of the usual picture where 70–95% of anxiety-related disorders are diagnosed in women.

Chapter 9

High fidelity in clinical supervision research

Derek Milne, Caroline Leck, Ian James, Maria Wilson, Rachel Procter, Laura Ramm, Judith Wilkinson and James Weetman

Introduction

We start our account of research by outlining the distinctive 'scientist-practitioner' tradition in clinical psychology, bringing it up-to-date by suggesting that the UK government's ongoing commitment to research and development affords an exceptionally conducive environment for supervision research. Drawing on systematic reviews, we then summarise the status of this research field in general, benchmarking it at roughly the same stage of development as was psychotherapy research in the 1960s, partly due to problems with measurement. For example, Bambling et al. (2006) conducted one of the few randomised controlled trials (RCTs) of supervision (hence providing good rigour), but they relied on a purpose-made instrument to measure adherence in supervision (i.e. adherence to either a cognitive behavioural therapy or psychodynamic supervision approach). Although this had good reliability, there were no validity data. This study illustrates the state of research in the supervision field and underlines the measurement problem.

Following this introduction, the majority of the chapter is then devoted to a detailed example of how we might take supervision research forward through the use of the 'fidelity framework', a systematic approach to the problem of imprecise measurement. Because it is highly topical and unusually well specified, we will apply this framework to clinical supervision within the Improving Access to Psychological Therapies (IAPT) initiative (Layard, 2005a) to illustrate how it can contribute to the improvement of research instruments.

In summary, the chapter will attempt to 'revitalise' research in clinical supervision (Ellis, 1991) by formulating the measurement part of the supervision research problem and by outlining some promising new instruments and approaches.

Research and clinical psychology

Defined in suitably inclusive terms, research is surely essential for clinical supervision. As a process for better grasping our world, it affords a secure foundation on which to develop concepts, definitions, descriptions, explanations, predictions and experimental control (Kerlinger, 1986). Although some question the reliance on such conventional research methods as the traditional experiment (e.g. Barkham and Mellor-Clark, 2003; Davy, 2002), the variants of research activity can still be viewed as united in their efforts to achieve these familiar goals of research. For instance, advocates of routine outcome monitoring may eschew the usual emphasis on the 'very time-consuming and expensive' tasks that experimentation entails (e.g. instrument refinement; Iberg, 1991: 575) but still enthuse about improving therapists' clinical performance. Similarly, advocates of 'small N' research highlight the profound difficulties entailed in generalising from carefully selected experimental groups in 'grand collaborative studies' using the RCT design (e.g. Barlow, Nock and Hersen, 2009: 49), but they share their research colleagues' curiosity about what determines treatment effectiveness.

Within mainstream clinical psychology, research has traditionally enjoyed a prized place, enshrined in the scientist-practitioner model (Barlow, Hayes and Nelson, 1984). This model afforded an integrative alliance, allowing those clinicians with profound objections to research (as based on the assumptions and criteria associated with the RCT) to join forces with their more empirically minded colleagues, all of them committed to an applied science of behaviour change in the clinical context. Although prominent figures (e.g. Carl Rogers) and the results of surveys (Cohen, 1979) suggested that this alliance was something of a myth, detailed enquiry into what clinical psychologists reported doing in the name of research gave some basis for believing that the scientist-practitioner was at least a modest reality (Milne, Britton and Wilkinson, 1990; Milne et al., 2000).

The scientist-practitioner appears to have been bolstered in the UK by the government's policy of evidence-based practice (EBP; DH, 1994). EBP is based on a suitably broad definition of research and development, encompassing as it does explanatory studies (i.e. basic, laboratory-style research on efficacy), pragmatic research (i.e. service-based evaluations of effectiveness) and associated research activities (such as audit, guideline implementation, staff development). These are all intended to work symbiotically, fostering improved patient care (Peckham, 1991; Roth, Fonagy and Parry, 1996). Furthermore, they are all viewed as essential parts of the research 'engine', that is, as necessarily interlinked research activities. They have subsequently been elaborated to emphasise the most viable range of options available to clinicians, such as service system research (Barkham and Mellor-Clark, 2003) and service improvement research (Milne et al., 2008b).

In summary, after a troubled start for the solo scientist-practitioner, the EBP initiative within the UK has latterly provided what can be construed as a secure and collaborative environment, one that fosters suitably reformulated variants of research activity (e.g. developing and implementing supervision guidelines; for more on this formulation, see Milne and Paxton, 1998). The implication of this sanguine perspective is that supervision can be researched by clinical psychologists in their routine practice as never before, aided by an attractive range of methods that are government endorsed and scientist-practitioner congruent. From this fortunate platform, we next consider the unfortunate state of research in clinical supervision.

Research on clinical supervision

If one applies to clinical supervision research the benchmark that has been applied to psychotherapy research (Orlinsky and Russell, 1994), then one might say that we are currently about 'half-way there', working on the 'search for scientific rigour' (i.e. phase 2 of 4). Expressed historically, supervision research is now grappling with issues that concerned psychotherapy research in the 1950s and 1960s. This phase 2 activity concerns tasks such as the development of objective approaches to measurement and attempts to demonstrate effectiveness. This is not to say that we are entirely finished with phase 1 (i.e. pioneering work to clarify a role for research, or a shared paradigm), nor completely un-involved in phase 3 (i.e. increasingly sophisticated conceptual and methodological developments), but this benchmark may help to provide a rough indication of the current status of supervision research.

Support for this benchmark can be found in most reviews of the clinical supervision field, particularly the systematic reviews. For instance, the two related reviews by Ellis et al. (1996) and Ellis and Ladany (1997) concluded with broadly negative appraisals of supervision research reported between 1981 and 1997: the methodological quality of these studies was deemed 'substandard', meaning that few firm conclusions could be drawn (Ellis and Ladany, 1997: 492). Specifically, they noted the 'dearth of viable measures specific to clinical supervision' (p. 493). However, in the latter paper they did conclude that our scientific understanding had improved.

This more optimistic view is supported by a series of more recent systematic reviews, ones that have attempted to overcome the problems inherent in the all-inclusive approach that Ellis and his colleagues have utilised (i.e. they reviewed over 100 studies in each of their reviews, resulting in significant sample heterogeneity and variable study rigour). To redress these problems, these latter reviews (e.g. Milne, 2007; Milne and James, 2000; Milne et al., 2008a) adopted the 'best evidence synthesis'

(BES) approach to the systematic review (Petticrew and Roberts, 2006). Unlike the standard review approach adopted by Ellis and colleagues, the BES approach extracts the smaller seams of rigorous supervision research in order to draw pragmatic conclusions inductively. At least as a short-term pragmatic exercise, this can enable us to address issues such as how we should define and model clinical supervision, and to clarify which supervision methods appear to work. As a result, best practice guidelines can be developed and disseminated, to foster EBP (Milne, 2009). In the medium term this reliance on induction should lead to empirical attempts at falsifying the kind of understanding that has emerged from the BES work.

This BES work meant selecting only those supervision studies with interpretable designs (and meeting other criteria), so that we were able to draw more favourable, well-founded summaries of supervision research than Ellis and his colleagues. For example, in the review concerned with developing an empirical definition of clinical supervision (Milne, 2007), a simple 7-point summary rating was made across all 24 reviewed studies in order to gain a general sense of the effectiveness of supervision. A value of 2.4 for supervisees (i.e. the amount of learning for the therapist) and 2.3 for patients (clinical outcomes) indicated that these studies were generally very successful, equivalent to 80% and 77% effectiveness, respectively. Such data indicate that supervision can be associated with positive outcomes.

Measurement and the fidelity framework

Concerns about the quality of research on clinical supervision date back over 30 years, regularly featuring the problem of insensitive measurement (Hansen, Pound and Petro, 1976). To illustrate, Lambert (1980) summarised the available instruments, noting that the most reliable ones focused on the supervisee's behaviour, but that outcome data should also be gathered on the clinical effectiveness of supervision and the supervisee–client interactions. Holloway (1984) subsequently proposed that other mediating variables should also be added, so as to overcome the tendency to report findings that were based on rather global, imprecise instruments (e.g. measures of the supervisory 'alliance' or of 'leadership'). She also noted that supervision was a complex intervention, with diverse functions, subtle reciprocal interactions and alternating roles. This stepwise logic was extended in her later work (e.g. Holloway and Neufeldt, 1995) when the measurement of supervision was articulated in terms of a number of levels in the educational pyramid (i.e. consultant–supervisor–supervisee/therapist–patient). This incorporated: the supervisee's acquisition of attitudes, beliefs and skills, as relevant to therapy (i.e. competence development); the supervisee's performance in therapy related to supervision (i.e. transfer/generalisation); the interactions that such transfer promotes in the supervisee's therapy, as related to processes in

Table 9.1 A summary of the fidelity framework (based on Bellg et al., 2004; Borelli et al., 2005), with recommendations applied to supervision

Step	Recommendations
1 Treatment design	Ensure that a study can properly test its hypotheses, based on the relevant theory (i.e. hypothesis validity) and by precisely defining variables and goals so as to measure the 'active ingredients' rather than confounding variables; assess the dose (i.e. the 'effort/structure/ resource') committed to supervision; address the question: 'What is the right supervision to do?'
2 Training of supervisors	Standardise training (e.g. by using manuals) so as to meet established competence criteria and achieve the goals; monitor and boost competences; assess adherence; address the question: 'Has the right supervision been done?'
3 Delivery of supervision	Monitor whether supervision is being provided correctly (i.e. tape sessions to check adherence and goal attainment) and attempt to control for non-specific factors (e.g. credibility of the approach; interpersonal effectiveness of supervisor); aim to strengthen adherence (e.g. ensure that the content is appropriate), also known as process evaluation or a manipulation check; address the question: 'Has supervision been done right?'
4 Receipt of supervision	Attend to whether or not the supervisee (i.e. the therapist) benefits during the supervision session, as in showing signs of an improved understanding or greater proficiency (e.g. within a role-play) impacts of supervision, also known as 'mini-outcomes' or mediator/ mechanism evaluation (e.g. assessing if reflection or action-planning took place); address the question: 'Did supervision result in the right outcomes?'
5 Supervision enactment	Monitor the extent to which the supervisee benefits after supervision, by applying/demonstrating these competences in therapy, also known as generalisation/transfer; address the question: 'Did supervision result in the right impact?'

supervision; and clinical changes that can be related to supervision. This stepwise agenda for supervision research clearly makes it a complex intervention, arguably 'amongst the most complex of all activities associated with the practice of psychology' (Holloway and Wolleat, 1994: 30), or even the 'ultimate complex intervention' (Freeston, 2004). It seems to us that a priority at this stage is detailed, stepwise, small N and qualitative work, so that the initial stages of the supervision intervention are clearly demonstrated.

Based on these assumptions, Table 9.1 suggests how a stepwise, micro-analysis of process and outcome might be structured using the 'fidelity framework' (Bellg et al., 2004; Borelli et al., 2005). These authors, working in the field of health behaviour change, defined fidelity as 'the methodo-logical strategies used to monitor and enhance the reliability and validity of behavioural interventions' (Bellg et al., 2004: 443). This therefore empha-sised the need for clarity about what we are attempting to achieve in an intervention such as supervision (the model-building or conceptualisation task) and monitoring progress through systematic measurement. This is very similar to the approach outlined by Wampold and Holloway (1997: 20–22). According to this framework, there are five successive steps in implementing supervision with fidelity. We will illustrate the fidelity framework in the following section, outlining a new instrument for each step.

Fidelity is also a topical perspective to take, considering the recently implemented IAPT programme: 'supervision is a key activity which has a number of functions, not least to ensure workers deliver treatments which replicate . . . the procedures developed in those trials that underpin the evidence-base: *treatment fidelity*' (Richards and Whyte, 2008: 102; italics in original). Therefore, we will focus on the IAPT approach to supervision in the following section.

Example of tackling the measurement agenda, based on the 'Improving Access to Psychological Therapies' initiative

The design of supervision

As set out in Table 9.1, the first aspect of the fidelity framework asks us to specify and justify a model for our supervision, alongside providing information on its 'structure' (how long it takes; how frequently it should occur; what its content or constituent parts are; the qualifications of supervisors; and any other resources that are required). The IAPT literature is particularly precise about these matters, stating, for example, that one-to-one and/or group supervision should be provided for 1 hour weekly (DH, 2008c) by practitioners accredited by the British Association for Behavioural and Cognitive Psychotherapies (BABCP), and that this should amount to at least 5 hours of supervision for at least eight patients, in order to meet training standards (i.e. for the supervisee to satisfy criteria for their own accreditation as a cognitive therapist; BABCP, 2008).

In summary, the first step of the fidelity framework requires a conceptualisation of the supervision approach and an operationalisation (i.e. a specification) regarding how it should be implemented. As a result of developing soundly designed supervision, we aim to be able to answer two fundamental research questions, namely 'what is the right supervision to do?' and 'which resources are required to do it right?' Phrasing such questions in terms of what is 'right' seems appropriate, as it reflects the EBP (Roth and Fonagy, 1996) and IAPT approaches (e.g. 'right services, at the right time, delivering the right results': see the IAPT positive practice vision; DH, 2009).

We normally look to relevant theories and research findings to answer the first question, in the context of our professional standards, employer guidelines and a general understanding of how best to pursue our work. In terms of IAPT there are helpful national guidance documents (e.g. Executive summary clinical supervision principles and guidance: DH, 2008c).

The second question is often answered for us by the available resources, but there are still important choices to be made (e.g. how long to spend on a particular topic; using a particular approach). To illustrate, evidence-based clinical supervision (EBCS; Milne and James, 2002; Milne and Westerman, 2001) adopted Kolb's (1984) theory of experiential learning and then clarified how this should be implemented in supervision by drawing on research evidence (as per the IAPT example below) plus expert consensus, professional guidelines and evaluations (see Milne, 2009, for a summary). In relation to Table 9.1, this allowed us to specify what the 'active ingredients' might be (i.e. the process of experiential learning, as in the way that the supervisor facilitated the supervisee's emotional experiencing, reflection, conceptualisation, etc.). In terms of its operationalisation, a manual has been developed to support the training of novice supervisors, and there are parallel guidelines that attempt to show how the time available for supervision might best be deployed. IAPT adopts a highly congruent approach, within which the minimum 'dosage' of supervision, the credentials of the supervisor and the methods to be used are specified (as summarised above: BABCP, 2008; DH, 2008c).

Next we will try to show how the EBCS design for supervision might be measured, outlining an illustrative instrument for each step in the fidelity framework. These examples are all based on the first author's supervision of five psychology undergraduate student projects in 2006–2007, and all but one of these relates to the same clinical supervisor (the second author). The fifth and final fidelity step draws on the supervision provided by the third author.

Measuring the 'design' of supervision

REACTS (Rating of Experiential learning And Components of Teaching and Supervision; Wilson, 2007) is featured in Table 9.2 and is based on Teacher's PETS (Milne et al., 2002). However, whereas Teacher's PETS relied on direct observation, REACTS is an 11-item, one-page, supervisee-completed, paper-and-pencil rating of supervision.

It is intended to assess EBCS by considering Proctor's (1986) 'normative' and 'restorative' aspects of supervision (through items on the structure/resources, namely the frequency and duration of supervision sessions, and content that includes both management issues and the provision of emotional support). However, reflecting IAPT supervision, REACTS mainly focuses on the 'formative' aspect of supervision (i.e. educative function),

Table 9.2 REACTS: Supervisee's Feedback Form

Personal identifier: _____ *Date of supervision:* _____

Please rate the following aspects of the supervision session you have just received. Use the scale below:

1	2	3	4	5	N/A
Strongly disagree	*Disagree*	*Neither agree nor disagree*	*Agree*	*Strongly agree*	*Not applicable*

1 I am satisfied that the duration of the supervision session was appropriate (i.e. it lasted as long as it was should have).   1 2 3 4 5 N/A

2 I am satisfied with the frequency of supervision sessions (i.e. this supervision session occurred when it should have).   1 2 3 4 5 N/A

3 *Management*: The supervisor helped me with planning, managing, evaluating and problem-solving issues.   1 2 3 4 5 N/A

4 *Support*: I felt supported through the supervisor's use of 'core' relationship conditions (e.g. feeling accepted, receiving recognition and support).   1 2 3 4 5 N/A

5 *Learning*

   (a) I was able to recognise relevant feelings, becoming more self-aware (e.g. role-play helped me to express emotion).   1 2 3 4 5 N/A

   (b) I was able to reflect on events and perceive things more clearly (e.g. draw on my own experience to give events more personal meaning).   1 2 3 4 5 N/A

   (c) My understanding of my work was improved (i.e. analysing cases to gain more insight and a better grasp).   1 2 3 4 5 N/A

   (d) We agreed action/s based on this supervision session (e.g. made a plan, agreed steps, set a goal).   1 2 3 4 5 N/A

   (e) The supervisor helped me to try things out and to solve problems/practise skills (e.g. gave me corrective feedback that improved my competence).   1 2 3 4 5 N/A

6 Of the events that occurred in this supervision session, which one do you feel was the most helpful for you personally? It might be something you said or did, or something the supervisor said or did. (Continue over the page if necessary.)

7 Any other comments (e.g. unhelpful events, unresolved problems)? (Continue over the page if necessary.)

listing Kolb's (1984) learning modes (i.e. experiencing, reflecting, conceptualising, experimenting and planning). An example is item 5: 'I was able to recognise relevant feelings, becoming more self-aware (e.g. role-play helped me to express emotion)'. The 5-point rating scale ranges from 'strongly agree' to 'strongly disagree' (with a 'not applicable' option), giving a score range of 9–45 (there are nine rated items), where higher scores represent greater supervisee satisfaction and learning. REACTS also includes a 'Helpful aspects' item (Llewellyn, 1988), to collect qualitative data, and a final item inviting any further comments. It can be completed by the supervisee within 5 minutes. The psychometric details are as follows: for test–retest reliability, a highly significant correlation of $r = .96$ was obtained ($p = .0001$). Reliability between the items (i.e. 'internal consistency') was also excellent and was assessed with Cronbach's alpha ($\alpha = .94$; $p = .001$). Reliability is defined as the consistency or stability of an instrument (i.e. high reliability is indicated when changes in the results are due to parallel changes in the supervision, as opposed to changes in the instrument or changes in how it is applied).

The second conventional way to judge the psychometric status of an instrument is in terms of its validity: How well does a tool measure what it purports to measure? This is normally determined by comparing a new instrument with an established measure of the same variable (i.e. concurrent validity). Following this reasoning, ratings of the same supervision session using both REACTS and the Manchester Clinical Supervision Scale (Winstanley, 2000) were compared, but significant correlations were only obtained between the support ($r = .616$; $p = .02$) and duration items ($r = -.53$; $p \leq .05$): the overall correlation between the two instruments was disappointingly low and non-significant ($r = .36$; $p = .21$). However, on a second test of validity REACTS did better. Criterion validity concerns whether a test can predict outcomes. It was found that REACTS scores on the experiencing item (item 5) were significantly higher after a discrete supervision intervention designed to facilitate experiencing (logistical ordinal regression: $p < .001$), and that the overall REACTS values were significantly higher during the general supervision intervention phase (i.e. EBCS: $p = .036$; both comparisons calculated using the statistical program R).

In summary, REACTS illustrates how one might proceed to measure whether or not the active ingredients and dose of supervision correspond to one's theory of supervision, such as IAPT supervision. This example also illustrates the criteria that are normally used to judge whether or not an instrument is sound. On these criteria, REACTS can be regarded as a promising tool, perhaps worthy of further development (e.g. to improve its concurrent validity), not least as it is specially designed for supervision (Ellis and Ladany, 1997) and likely to be sensitive to the IAPT approach. As with all five instruments described here, an electronic copy is available from the first author, as is the original undergraduate thesis.

Training supervisors

Following Table 9.1 again, it can be seen that the second step in the fidelity framework is to train supervisors so as to ensure that the right thing is being done. This means carefully describing the nature of the given approach to supervision and then attempting to standardise the way that supervisors are trained (e.g. by means of a training manual). Evaluation of this step should also include demonstrating that competence has been acquired, in line with the design (Step 1). To illustrate, according to the policy documentation, IAPT supervision should be 'close', meaning that tape recordings of the supervisee's therapy/casework should be assessed using a suitable cognitive behavioural therapy (CBT) competence scale, together with written work and a practice log book (BABCP, 2008).

Example of measuring the 'training' of supervisors

The supervisor's adherence to the initial EBCS (Milne, 2009) two-page manual was assessed by continuous, direct observation by an independent rater, using the 'CHECK-Sup' checklist (CHECKing on SUPervision; Ramm, 2007). There were 19 items within this checklist, each credited by the observer (using tape recordings) if seen to be present at least once per supervision session (i.e. event sampling, within 60-minute supervision sessions). The items are supposed to operationalise EBCS, including educational needs assessment, setting learning objectives and the use of methods to facilitate learning (again, compatible with IAPT supervision). An illustrative example is the first item, 'Needs assessment: agree learning needs', which is defined within the manual and maps onto the IAPT emphasis of negotiating the learning contract. The score range is therefore 0–19, with higher scores representing greater adherence (competence) in this approach to supervision. Once the rater has become competent, it takes about 5 minutes to complete the checklist, following whatever is the period of the assessed tape/session.

By comparison with questionnaires such as REACTS, the convention for instruments that rely on direct observation is agreement between two or more independent observers, called 'inter-rater reliability'. Comparison between three independent coders using CHECK-Sup was $k = .84$, which indicates that the tool could be administered reliably. Criterion validity was also suggested by the finding that CHECK-Sup detected the expected changes between the use of EBCS and supervision as usual (i.e. the control condition). Adherence values for the control phases were 7.7 (41%) and 6 (32%), whilst in the intermediate EBCS phase the CHECK-Sup score was significantly higher (12 or 63%: Friedman test = 6.3, 2 degrees of freedom (df); $p \le .05$). Therefore, it seems that CHECK-Sup was able to detect this manipulation of EBCS, so it should also be able to detect competent IAPT

Table 9.3 Applying the fidelity framework to IAPT supervision, with illustrative concepts and instruments

Fidelity dimension	Conceptualisation (and principles) of IAPT supervision	Illustrative measurement of IAPT supervision
1 Design of supervision	'Case management supervision' (national supervision objectives and standards)	Supervisee's ratings of supervision dose (structure) and supervision process and outcomes (REACTS; Wilson, 2007)
2 Training in supervision	'Training in specifics' (i.e. supervisors require expertise, including manual to standardise training)	Manual plus direct observation of supervisor's competence (CHECK-Sup; Ramm, 2007)
3 Delivery of supervision	'Monitor adherence and outcomes' (including generic interpersonal competencies)	Direct observation of supervision alliance (RELATES; Procter, 2007)
4 Receipt of supervision	'Supervisee trained and demonstrates ability to use supervision' (especially reflective practice)	Direct observation of supervisee's experiential learning (RECEIPT; Weetman, 2007)
5 Enactment of supervision	'Systematic evaluation of care' (monitoring of supervisee's therapy, as feedback to supervisor)	Direct observation of transfer from supervision to therapy (ENACT; Wilkinson, 2007)

supervision (see also the summary of a subsequent and improved instrument, SAGE, below). Table 9.3 shows how the fidelity framework can clarify some key IAPT practices and principles, and how this can then be linked to measurement (i.e. it can conceptualise a particular approach to supervision). Column 2 of Table 9.3 notes defining principles, drawn from the NHS executive summary on supervision principles and guidance (DH, 2008c) and the clinical placement outcome portfolio (Newcastle University, 2009).

Delivering supervision

After training the supervisor, the next step in the fidelity framework is to assess whether the supervision has actually been conducted correctly, that is, whether it has been implemented faithfully (usually through some kind of monitoring of the supervisor's performance). As outlined in Table 9.3, this might feature an assessment of the interpersonal effectiveness of the supervisor, as per the generic supervision competences in the IAPT framework, such as alliance-building with the supervisee (Roth and Pilling, 2008d). As before, the fundamental issue is whether the training that the supervisor has received in a given approach to supervision is being implemented with fidelity. For instance, the kinds of fact-finding and Socratic questions that a supervisor might pose in high-fidelity IAPT supervision (and the aim behind them) would be expected to differ from a psychodynamic approach. The latter might not only use rather different questions, but might also give greater significance to their timing (as per the skilful interpretational question), as well as expecting them to serve rather different purposes (i.e. fostering insight, rather than simply information-gathering or awareness-raising). CHECK-Sup, the instrument that has just been described, can be viewed as a way of assessing the fidelity of such 'delivery' variables.

However, as noted in Table 9.1, part of fidelity is the complementary attempt to minimise confounding variables, such as controlling for differences in supervisors' interpersonal effectiveness or credibility. Perhaps the classic example of this is the supervisory alliance, a group of important variables that can transform the effectiveness of skills such as questioning. The following is therefore an illustration of trying to measure the role of the alliance.

The supervisory alliance can be observed directly with RELATES (Rating and Evaluation of Learner Alliance: Towards Effective Supervision; Procter, 2007), based on instructions provided within a coding manual. This was guided by the alliance tool developed by McLeod and Weisz (2005) and it operationalised Bordin's (1983) classic model of the supervisory alliance. According to Bordin (1983), the supervisory alliance consists of an emotional bond (e.g. item 3: 'supervisee appeared to be liked and accepted by the supervisor'), the supervision tasks (e.g. item 8: 'supervisor and supervisee working together equally to complete tasks') and the supervision goal (e.g. item 13: 'discussing goals collaboratively'). This formulation is consistent with the IAPT supervision competences statement (Roth and Pilling, 2008d). To operationalise the alliance there were 14 items in RELATES, each rated by an independent observer on a 5-point frequency scale, ranging from 'not at all' (score 1) to 'a great deal' (score 5). Both supervisee and supervisor are observed for the full supervision session, with all items accumulated to reach the overall frequency rating. The score range is 14–70, with higher scores representing a better alliance. The time taken to complete RELATES is as per CHECK-Sup above.

Inter-rater reliability was found to be acceptable (k = .71), but the validation work was problematic. This included assessing predictive validity (i.e. correlating the RELATES data with the corresponding CHECK-sup data), for which a negative correlation was anticipated and duly found (r = −.85). However, when we again compared data from different phases (as described above for CHECK-Sup), we found that the RELATES data from the baseline (mean = 4.21) and intervention phases (mean = 3.36) were significantly different (Wilcoxon: T = 0; p ≤ .005), indicating that the alliance was confounding this comparison between supervision as usual and

EBCS. This may have been due to the poor concurrent validity of RELATES: we had expected to obtain a positive correlation between the perceived alliance (measured by item 4 of REACTS, for the same sessions) and the RELATES, but failed to obtain this result ($r = .23$; NS). Alternatively, RELATES may have been detecting real differences in this compound, non-specific variable. Clearly, further psychometric work is needed on RELATES. In the meantime let us consider two alternative instruments with better psychometric credentials and that (like CHECK-Sup) attempt to measure the specific aspects of supervision 'delivery'.

The first is the aforementioned Teacher's PETS, which is a direct observation tool described elsewhere (Milne et al., 2002). Although it is psychometrically sound, there are other considerations to bear in mind when selecting a tool. For example, Barkham et al. (1998) have argued that there are two additional criteria of importance: factors associated with the 'implementation' of an instrument (e.g. whether it is excessively costly to use, in terms of training or to purchase) and the 'yield' (considerations about the utility of the data, given the cost of obtaining it). In these two terms, Teacher's PETS was thought to be flawed, probably as a consequence of having been designed as a research tool (e.g. it took many hours of training for the observers to achieve inter-rater reliability in the intensive, momentary time sampling of supervisor and supervisee behaviours). Secondly, we required a system that could serve the same functions as Teacher's PETS (i.e. profiling, auditing and corrective feedback) but could also offer a competence assessment. For these reasons a modified instrument was created, christened SAGE (Supervision: Adherence and Guidance Evaluation; Milne and Reiser, 2007). This built on Teacher's PETS and on an expert consensus about the measurement of effective supervision (STARS-CT, developed by colleagues in the North East of England; James et al., 2005). Based on this logic, SAGE uses a quick, 7-point rating of competence across the same kinds of variables in PETS and CHECK-Sup, and has already shown promising psychometric properties (Cliffe, 2008).

Receiving supervision

Does our approach to supervision produce the 'right' effects on the supervisee? The answer should be 'yes', if we have got the design, training and delivery steps 'right'. So, how might we measure this emergent impact, or 'receipt', to ensure that this is also right? Examples exist in both Teacher's PETS and SAGE, as these tools attempt to quantify receipt in terms of the experiential learning 'mini-outcomes' illustrated by the Teacher's PETS instrument. Therefore, this is the first fidelity step that involves outcome evaluation, as it asks: Is supervision resulting in the right (mini) outcomes?

Example of measuring the 'receipt' of supervision

Like SAGE, the Receipt scale[1] (Weetman, 2007) is an observational instrument designed to capture Kolb's (1984) model of experiential learning, and (like the fidelity model itself) it followed the taxonomy approach (Anderson and Krathwohl, 2001; Bloom, 1956). As per all the prior illustrations, it has a manual and in the case of the Receipt scale it details a four-stage taxonomy for each of Kolb's learning modes. For example, following the Experiencing Scale (Klein et al., 1969), item 1, 'experiencing', extends from the lowest level (i.e. experiencing is not observed at all) to the highest level (i.e. discussion of emotions, resulting in some transforming of the material, such as deciding how to act on it). The five items in the Receipt scale are each rated between score 0 and score 4, so the score range is 0–20, with higher scores indicative of greater supervisee learning (a criterion of more competent supervision). As above, tape recordings of entire supervision sessions were rated by an independent observer, this time using momentary time sampling. Therefore, the time taken for a competent rater to complete the Receipt scale is as per the length of the observed session, plus the time to pause/rewind the tape to consider tricky ratings. Psychometric data were again mixed: inter-rater reliability was good ($k = .75$), but when it came to criterion validity the Receipt scale values across phases did not reach significance (Kruskal-Wallis test: $H = 7.63$, 4 df, $p = .108$). However, the tool showed promise, as the obtained values for the same three phases described above were 14.7, 16.3 and 13, indicating that the instrument was at least somewhat sensitive to the assumed greater effectiveness of EBCS. Again, this would suggest that it would also prove sensitive to IAPT supervision.

Transferring supervision

It has often been suggested that clinical outcomes are the acid test of supervision (Ellis and Ladany, 1997; Stein and Lambert, 1995). However, this criterion goes beyond the scope of the original fidelity framework, so, for present purposes, fidelity stops at the assessment of whether or not 'receipt' is transferred to therapy: Do the supervisees actually enact (use) what they have learned in supervision sessions within their subsequent therapy sessions? In IAPT terms, this equates to the systematic monitoring of the care that the supervisee is providing, which can form feedback to the supervisor, potentially indicating the need for further training for the supervisor (see Table 9.3). If, however, there is high-fidelity enactment, then we can reasonably anticipate good clinical effects (this is a step or two further on than anticipated in the original fidelity framework, although it is a core facet of IAPT supervision and the augmented framework described in Milne, 2009).

---

1 The name of this instrument is not an acronym and simply reflects the fidelity category 'receipt' (Bellg et al., 2004).

Example of measuring the 'enactment' of supervision

Wilkinson's ENACT (Evaluation of New Learning And Clinical Transfer; Wilkinson, 2007) is another direct observation tool, but this time episodes are recorded, following the method described earlier (Ladany, Friedlander and Nelson, 2005). This requires the observer to identify meaningful sequences of dialogue, to label the antecedent 'marker' events for each episode and to then record which methods the supervisor uses to help the supervisee to process these issues and the effect that this has on the supervisee (both sets of behaviours drawn from Teacher's PETS, and recorded by means of a checklist), leading to the key issue of defining any specific plans to transfer this learning to therapy (goal-setting) and to the subsequent frequency with which this transfer occurs within the immediately subsequent therapy session. For example, a supervisee's (or supervisor's) concern over time management in therapy (marker) might lead to questioning by the supervisor and planning by the supervisee (e.g. to conduct agenda-setting collaboratively), and then the subsequent therapy session would be observed to see whether or not the supervisee actually enacted this agenda-setting plan in their therapy. The data were therefore the observed frequencies of supervisor and supervisee behaviours within thematically categorised episodes (expressed as the percentage of generalisation, from supervision to therapy). The time taken to complete ENACT is the length of the observed supervision session, plus approximately 5 minutes per episode.

The inter-rater reliability of ENACT was good (k = .81), which was confirmed in a subsequent observer 'drift' analysis (k = .74). In terms of criterion validity, it was found that there was considerable enactment (in the intervention phase only): the mean % observed transfer from EBCS to therapy was 50% (SD = 30.08). However, this varied by supervision method: correlations indicated that whilst goal-setting correlated significantly with transfer (r = .69; $p \leq$ .05), significant negative correlations were found between prompting and transfer (r = −.62). This reflects the complex nature of supervision, suggesting that ENACT is a sensitive instrument.

Discussion

We have tried to show how the fidelity framework (Table 9.1) can help to structure supervision research, helping to address those recurring problems of poor conceptualisation and measurement (Ellis and Ladany, 1997). The instruments presented above are all in a preliminary stage of psychometric development, but hopefully they serve to illustrate how these chronic problems might be addressed in future supervision research. To show the relevance of these tools and the utility of this framework, it was applied to the IAPT initiative. Of course, the issues of poor conceptualisation and insensitive measurement are of general relevance, going beyond IAPT supervision (and even beyond arrangements within the UK, or the profession), representing a significant concern internationally (see, for example, Watkins, 1997). Table 9.3 indicates that the fidelity framework provides a coherent and compatible way to characterise IAPT supervision (both high and low intensity versions), which helps us to formulate this approach and so helps to link it to prior supervision research (e.g. findings and methodologies that may help to guide supervision research).

But the fidelity framework is also a way of thinking generally about research in clinical supervision, given those fundamental questions that are noted in Table 9.1. This is therefore a good point at which to broaden this account and identify the implications for all forms of clinical supervision. For any approach, it is vital to: consider what constitutes the 'right' content and methods; ensure that those who use this approach are properly trained, so that the right thing is done; check whether the right thing is indeed being done right (e.g. assessing whether the approach is being applied competently); question whether, if the preceding steps are right, the intended results are being achieved in terms of the supervisee (e.g. the supervisee is engaging in experiential learning, such as reflecting); and determine whether such learning transfers into clinical benefits. This represents a significant research agenda, but it also affords numerous opportunities for the involvement of clinical psychologists in supervision research (e.g. developing manuals or guidelines that specify the approach, demonstrating that others can be trained to provide this supervision).

Although the IAPT illustration and the more general summary of its application to all supervision suggest that the fidelity framework has promise, there was also reason to develop it. As noted already, the original account omits the acid test of supervision (and the IAPT programme), namely clinical benefits (not to mention the system aspect/context in which supervision necessarily occurs, e.g. accreditation and CPD arrangements; see an extended version in Milne, 2009). Other possibilities are to vary the level of analysis (e.g. microgenetic designs; Siegler and Crowley, 1991) and to introduce additional outcome variables, for example following the Kirkpatrick (1967) taxonomy. In augmented form (based on: Alliger et al., 1997; Belfield et al., 2001; Kraiger, Ford and Salas, 1993), this taxonomy consists of five levels of outcome, ranging from attendance/participation in supervision, through simple reactions ('delivery', i.e. supervisees' satisfaction with their supervision), to learning (competence 'receipts') and ultimately the related impacts on a service system ('enactment', including clinical outcomes).

In conclusion, Tables 9.1 and 9.3 are examples of how supervision research might be encouraged to move out of its 1960s phase and be developed as a suitably 'high fidelity' part of the modern practitioner's role, whether in the context of such initiatives as the IAPT programme or as a general attempt to enhance the quality of clinical supervision.

Summary

The long-standing scientist-practitioner model was recognised as the basic foundation for clinical psychologists' involvement in supervision research, and this model is now nested in what we perceive to be the relatively comfortable environment of the NHS's research and development programme. Evidence-based practice and the recent extensions of practice-based evidence add further support for research involvement, whether this is to produce, consume or utilise research. This encouraging context is particularly valuable in relation to research on supervision, which many regard as seriously deficient in rigour and relevance (e.g. Ellis and Ladany, 1997). We have presented a more sanguine view, based on applying the 'best-evidence synthesis' (BES) approach to a series of related systematic reviews. The BES reviews were part of an evidence-based and pragmatic re-formulation of supervision, one that sought to bolster reviews with expert consensus, local audits, $N = 1$ studies and guideline development (see Milne, 2009, for a summary). A further feature of this constructive, 'evidence-based clinical supervision' (EBCS) formulation is the careful application of relevant concepts from parallel literature. In our example above we drew on the 'fidelity framework' from the health behaviour field (Bellg et al., 2004), using it to distinguish between successive criteria for analysing a complex intervention such as supervision. This addresses one major problem in the supervision field, that of weak conceptualisation. We then introduced an illustrative new instrument for each of the five fidelity levels, partly to draw attention to a second major challenge – the need to develop supervision-specific tools with adequate psychometric rigour. These instruments were linked to an exceptionally vigorous new interpretation of clinical supervision – the UK's IAPT initiative.

Acknowledgements

Thanks to the supervisees of Caroline Leck and Ian A. James for their cooperation with this work on measurement, and to Caroline's Masters students for their participation (e.g. completing REACTS forms). Mark Papworth provided helpful information from the Newcastle IAPT Certificate training programme.

Chapter 10

Formats of supervision

Linda Steen

Introduction

In much of the literature on and many of the definitions of supervision (e.g. Bernard and Goodyear, 2004; Loganbill et al., 1982), the primary focus is on supervision as a one-to-one endeavour, where an individual practitioner receives supervision from one other person who is invariably but not exclusively a more senior colleague, either from the same or another profession. In clinical psychology training in the UK for example, where the requirements for supervising trainee clinical psychologists on their clinical placements are set out in the British Psychological Society's *Standards for Doctoral Programmes in Clinical Psychology* (BPS, 2010), trainees must always receive an 'appropriate amount of individual supervision' (ibid.: 5.11.3), even in circumstances where a team or group approach to supervision is also used. Indeed, it was only in 1995 (BPS, 1995a) that the requirements for supervising clinical psychology trainees were modified to permit the use of formats such as team and group supervision, in order to supplement one-to-one arrangements. This focus on one-to-one supervision also features in much of the supervision research, particularly that carried out in the context of pre-qualification training of helping professionals (see, for example, Akhurst and Kelly, 2006). As Altfeld and Bernard (1997) point out, the emphasis on one-to-one supervision is understandable, at least in the context of psychotherapy practice, given that the majority of therapists begin their training carrying out individual psychotherapy. Thus, rightly or wrongly, the scene is set, during pre-qualification training at least, for one-to-one supervision to be considered the gold standard of supervisory arrangements, with any other arrangement falling short of this.

Even beyond the training period (i.e. for qualified practitioners, including clinical psychologists), the majority of us received one-to-one supervision when we trained and, given that one of the starting points for developing our own supervisory skills is to draw on our previous experience of being supervised (Hawkins and Shohet, 2000; Morrison, 2005), it is not surprising that we tend to carry on the tradition of one-to-one supervision (Milne and Oliver, 2000).

The importance of the one-to-one format is further reinforced by guidance such as that outlined by the British Association for Behavioural and Cognitive Psychotherapies (BABCP), which states that in order to fulfill the supervisory requirements for BABCP accreditation, in circumstances where group supervision is the main form of supervision a member receives, there must also be 'an opportunity for individual supervision should it be needed' (BABCP, 2009: 7). There are exceptions to this emphasis on one-to-one supervision, particularly where an alternative format of supervision fits more closely with the mode of therapy; as Hawkins and Shohet (2000) note, 'where possible, the supervision context should reflect the therapeutic context which is being supervised' (ibid.: 130). Practitioners receiving training or engaging in group psychotherapy, for example, are frequently required to undertake supervision within a group, and practitioners who run Webster-Stratton parenting groups engage in peer group supervision using video or DVD playback (Webster-Stratton, 2004). In a similar vein, the Association for Family Therapy and Systemic Practice in the UK (AFT) requires practitioners who are training in family therapy to engage in 'live supervised clinical practice within a small supervision group' (AFT, 2007: 1). In the main, however, one-to-one supervision remains the most popular format amongst practitioners in the helping professions, both in the UK and the USA (see, for example, Goodyear and Nelson, 1997).

As has been noted elsewhere in this book, providing and receiving supervision is now considered a key component of a clinical psychologist's role (BPS, 2005, 2006a, 2007b). Given this context, it has become increasingly impractical to ensure one-to-one clinical supervision for all and, even if this was possible, there are strong arguments for the advantages of organising supervision differently (see, for example, Milne and Oliver, 2000).

The focus of this chapter will be on different formats available for supervision, with reference to both trainee and qualified practitioners, including but not exclusive to clinical psychologists. It is worth noting that the term 'formats' is sometimes used in the supervision literature interchangeably with terms such as 'strategies', 'modalities' or 'techniques' (see, for example, Goodyear and Nelson, 1997). Additionally, some supervisory formats are both a format *and* a technique; for example, live supervision, although a format that is most frequently associated with family therapy, is also a technique that is used within a range of other formats, such as one-to-one, group or team supervision. In this chapter, in line with other writers (e.g. Milne and Oliver, 2000; Townend, Iannetta and Freeston, 2002), the term 'format' is used to refer solely to different forms that supervision can take (e.g. one-to-one or group) rather than what actually takes place during supervision, the latter being covered in Chapter 11. For this reason, live supervision will not be covered here; for a comprehensive description, the reader is referred to Liddle et al. (1997) and Scaife (2009).

What different supervision formats are there?

As the supervision literature expands, so too does the range of supervisory arrangements that are reported therein. During clinical psychology training, as previously mentioned, a variety of supervisory arrangements is now acceptable, including 'trainee to supervisor ratios of 1:1 and 2:1 and various forms of team supervision for groups of trainees' (BPS, 2010: 5.10). Similarly, in counselling training in the UK to give just one other example, 'the supervision of trainees can be provided in different ways: individually and/ or in a group' (BACP, 2004a: 4). For qualified practitioners too, a range of supervisory formats is described both in the literature (see, for example, Butterworth and Faugier, 1992) and in relevant professional and national body guidelines. The British Association for Counselling and Psychotherapy (BACP), for example, lists several forms of acceptable supervision for qualified counsellors, including one-to-one (supervisor-counsellor), one-to-one co-supervision, group supervision with an identified supervisor and peer group supervision (BACP, 2004b). For applied psychologists, including clinical psychologists, the BPS (2008a) similarly suggests one-to-one, facilitated group with a lead supervisor and peer (individual or group) supervision as options for post-qualification supervision; other professional guidelines include live supervision while the work is in progress (Division of Counselling Psychology, 2008) and telephone and email supervision (BABCP, 2009) as additional options.

Within the National Health Service (NHS) it is increasingly common to find that NHS Trusts and psychological services have policies on clinical supervision and these, together with professional body requirements, influence the supervisory practice of qualified staff. Manchester Mental Health and Social Care Trust (MMHSCT), for example, where I carry out my clinical work, has a policy on supervision within psychological services in which are listed several acceptable forms of clinical supervision, including core supervision that should 'reflect the day-to-day work of the practitioner' (MMHSCT, 2008: 8), episodic supervision when a clinician may need time-limited supervision for a specific piece of clinical or organisational work and peer supervision that could be in pairs or in groups.

There is evidence that these guidelines and policies are being applied in practice. In a survey of the supervision arrangements of BABCP-accredited therapists, for example, Townend et al. (2002) found a wide variety of supervision formats. The majority of the respondents reported making use of both informal supervision, defined as 'case discussion on an unplanned basis when a problem has occurred' (ibid.: 489), and a range of planned formal supervision, including individual supervision with the same person, individual supervision with different people, group supervision with a named supervisor, group peer supervision, pair peer supervision and supervision via telephone and email. Other writers, in both the UK and the USA, describe a similar range of formats (Gabbay, Kiemle and Maguire, 1999; Goodyear and Nelson, 1997; Milne and Oliver, 2000), with more recent texts (e.g. Milne, 2009; Scaife, 2009) including descriptions of technological developments in supervision such as the use of video-conferencing (Marrow et al., 2002), telephone and on-line supervision (Kanz, 2001).

The remainder of this chapter will describe these formats in more detail, starting with more formal supervision arrangements and ending by describing a range of informal, unplanned supervision. For each format described, the advantages and disadvantages will be considered and guidance on best practice will be given. The chapter will focus on UK clinical psychology training and practice whilst also drawing on the practice of other professional groups. Where relevant, the reader will be directed to key texts and papers for a more in-depth consideration of the issues raised.

Formal supervision formats

One-to-one supervision

One-to-one supervision, also referred to as individual or dyadic individual supervision, is described by Altfeld and Bernard (1997) as a 'time-honored form of supervision . . . the bedrock of the teaching and learning experience for individual psychotherapy' (ibid.: 382). Whilst the exact content and process of individual supervision can vary according to a number of factors such as therapeutic orientation, service context, supervisee's developmental stage and, where relevant, the training context, this form of supervision always involves one supervisor and one supervisee who, ideally, meet regularly with the aim of enhancing the supervisee's clinical practice and ultimately the clinical service provided to clients. During pre-qualification training, by definition the supervisor will be more experienced than the supervisee. In post-qualification supervision, whilst it is usual for the supervisory role to be taken by a more senior practitioner or one with greater expertise in a particular therapeutic model, this is not essential, as will be seen in the next section.

In practice, there may be circumstances where the supervisory meetings are neither regular nor with the same supervisor; in Townend et al.'s survey (op. cit.), for example, 14.1% of the sample reported receiving individual supervision with different people. In general, however, as described in Chapter 4 of this book, in order for one-to-one supervision to be most effective there is increasing evidence to suggest that the supervisor and supervisee need to establish a safe and trusting relationship, which by definition evolves over time.

In pre-qualification clinical psychology training in the UK, whilst a variety of supervision arrangements is permissible, individual supervision remains an essential component of training in order to provide 'opportunities to discuss personal issues, professional development, overall workload and organisational difficulties as well as ongoing case work' (BPS, 2010: 5.10.2). Once qualified, clinical psychologists can choose the form of clinical supervision they receive to a large extent, although this may well be dictated by service policies and service constraints. Surveys such as those carried out by Milne and Oliver in 2000 and Gabbay et al. in 1999 indicate that, at that time at least, one-to-one supervision was the format of choice amongst those clinical psychologists surveyed; over a decade later, this would still seem to be the case, particularly for newly qualified clinical psychologists (see, for example, Beinart and Clohessy, 2009).

There are many potential advantages of individual supervision, perhaps the most obvious being that it affords supervisees the opportunity for ring-fenced 'special time' (Proctor, 2000: 24) to discuss whatever they choose to bring to supervision without the need to share the supervisory stage with others; the supervisee can both set the agenda and determine the pace of the discussion, and know that they will have their supervisor's individual attention for the entire supervision session. Engagement in one-to-one supervision on a regular basis provides the opportunity for continuity in the discussion of themes arising in the course of the supervisee's work. Additionally, confidentiality is less likely to be compromised than it would be if there was more than one supervisee. A further advantage is the fact that for discussion of individual therapy this form of supervision mirrors the therapeutic dynamic, thus making it easier to reflect on therapeutic process issues played out in supervision. In contrast to supervisory formats that involve more than one supervisee, assuming that a good supervisory relationship has been established (Beinart, 2004), many argue that individual supervision is less anxiety-provoking for both the supervisee and the supervisor because it does not involve judgement by others; this, in turn, is likely to lead to the supervisee feeling safer to disclose and explore potential anxieties, vulnerabilities and mistakes (Ladany et al., 1996). Finally, at a more practical level, individual supervision is easier to organise than formats that involve more than two people.

Some of the suggested disadvantages of individual supervision include the fact that it is expensive in terms of time and resources, particularly if the supervisor has more than one person to supervise. Linked to this is the fact that it may be difficult for a supervisee to gain access to an individual supervisor as they may already have supervisory commitments. Additionally, there is the potential for the relationship to become too 'cosy' or like a 'mutual appreciation society' (van Ooijen, 2000: 32) and for the supervisee and supervisor to become dependent on the relationship. A further disadvantage is that, unlike group supervision, individual supervision affords no opportunities for either the supervisee or the supervisor to benefit from others' views. In pre-qualification supervision, as Akhurst and Kelly (2006) found in their sample of trainee psychologists, there is the additional consideration that the power differential between supervisor and supervisee has the potential to 'inhibit open and frank dialogue' (ibid.: 10).

Much has been written about the skills needed to be an effective one-to-one supervisor (see, for example, Chapters 2, 4 and 11 of this book), therefore this will not be covered in any detail here. From the supervisor's perspective, Roth and Pilling's framework (2008d) outlines the foundation skills that supervisors of all orientations need in order to supervise psychological therapies. From the supervisee's perspective too, there is an increasing literature on the active role that those receiving supervision can play to ensure they receive good quality supervision (e.g. Inskipp, 1999); for a more detailed account, the reader is referred to Chapter 4.

One-to-one peer supervision

An alternative form of one-to-one supervision is one-to-one peer supervision, also termed pair peer supervision (see, for example, Townend et al., 2002) and one-to-one co-supervision (BACP, 2004b). Here, two practitioners provide supervision for each other by alternating the roles of supervisor and supervisee either within each supervision session or at alternate sessions. The defining feature of this type of supervision is that it is individually reciprocal, with neither of the participants taking an overall lead role, hence the use of the term 'peer' within the supervisory context.

Milne (2009) makes an interesting point when he describes the term 'peer supervision' as being technically an oxymoron in that 'supervision is by definition hierarchical and hence cannot be provided within a peer relationship' (ibid.: 177). He draws the reader's attention to the ideas of Bernard and Goodyear (2004) in suggesting that it might be more accurate to consider this type of contact as 'peer consultation' rather than supervision, particularly if the supervision is a voluntary arrangement. Nonetheless, as Milne himself acknowledges, leaving aside terminology, peer supervision is very popular, be it delivered as a pair as described here, or in a group as described later. In the Townend et al. (op. cit.) survey, for example, 20.6% of respondents reported engaging in pair peer supervision and 41.8% in group peer; similar findings have been reported elsewhere (see, for example Bernard and Goodyear, 2004).

In clinical psychology it is not unusual to find pair peer supervision as a model used amongst more senior colleagues who wish to have supervision with someone at an appropriate level of seniority with whom they can share confidential information; this is particularly pertinent when supervision is used in its broadest sense to discuss non-therapeutic components of a practitioner's job, such as management. For newly qualified practitioners too, pair peer supervision can be extremely helpful in normalising the anxieties that inevitably accompany this stage in a practitioner's career. This is not to suggest that pair peer supervision can only be carried out between two practitioners from the same profession or at the same stage in their careers. On the contrary, pair peer arrangements can be made between practitioners in different organisations who are at different levels of seniority; often it is the cross-fertilisation of ideas that makes one-to-one peer supervision so valuable for its participants.

How one-to-one peer supervision is set up depends very much on the supervisory needs of the participants at any particular stage in their careers; someone who has just taken on a new role in their workplace, for example, may find it helpful to receive supervision from someone who has been in the role for some time, or may in fact prefer to pair up with someone who is similarly new in their role. What is clear from the literature is that, in order for one-to-one peer supervision to be most effective, the participants should at the very least have some aspect of their work in common, be it the nature of the work they undertake, their level of expertise or their positions within their respective organisations.

A fuller examination of the concept and practicalities of peer supervision, as well as the advantages and disadvantages, will be made in the section on peer group supervision. For the time being, it is sufficient to note that the principles outlined in the previous section pertaining to one-to-one supervision apply equally to one-to-one peer supervision.

Group supervision

In contrast to individual supervision, group supervision takes place when:

> three or more people form a fixed membership group and have planned, regular meetings in which each person gets the chance for in-depth reflection on their own practice and on the part they as individuals play in the complexities and quality of that practice, facilitated in that reflection by the other group members
>
> (Bond and Holland, 1998: 173)

It can be 'an efficient way of using supervisory resources and also helping supervisees to learn from each other' (Roth and Pilling, 2008c: 13), 'a highly valid and effective format' (Milne, 2009: 51), and a 'restorative opportunity in a pressured, often lonely, working life – for supervisor and supervisees' (Proctor and Inskipp, 2009: 137). On the other hand, if not run well, it has the potential to be an unhelpful and aversive experience for all concerned and one in which learning may be inhibited (see, for example, Hawkins and Shohet, 2000).

Much has been written about models of group supervision, particularly in the psychotherapy literature, and the reader is directed to works by Proctor (2000), Proctor and Inskipp (2009) and Altfeld and Bernard (1997) for more comprehensive reviews. As with one-to-one supervision, the way in which group supervision is organised, the style and techniques used and the structure, content and focus of the group will depend on a range of factors, including therapeutic orientation, the organisational or training context in which it is being carried out and the purposes of the supervision. To illustrate, if the supervision group forms part of a training course in cognitive therapy, then the content and process of the group are likely to mirror cognitive therapy (see, for example, Liese and Beck, 1997). By contrast, if the supervision group follows the principles of *experiential group supervision* as described by Altfeld and Bernard (1997), where the purpose is to use both primary and parallel process to explore the meaning of the issues being presented to the group, then the focus will be on identifying countertransference and group processes, drawing on participants' 'inner data' (ibid.: 38) such as bodily sensations, fantasies and images in response to the clinical material presented.

Group membership can vary widely depending on the purpose and context of the supervision. Groups may comprise trainee practitioners undertaking the same training programme or experienced practitioners either from the same or from different professions, work settings and therapeutic orientations. Whilst group diversity can encourage participants to think creatively and flexibly about their work, most writers agree that there needs to be a degree of similarity in theoretical orientation, type of client work or professional culture to make it a useful endeavour.

A distinction is frequently drawn between *group* supervision, comprising supervisees who come together solely for the purpose of supervision, and *team* supervision, where the supervisees work together outside the supervisory arena, either with the same clients (such as in a multi-disciplinary team) or with different clients within the same service or agency (such as in a primary care clinical psychology service). In clinical psychology training, the term *team supervision* is used in a slightly different way to that described above, referring to the situation where 'two trainees are allocated to one supervisor or when two or more trainees receive supervision from a team of supervisors within the same placement' (BPS, 2010, appendix 4: 3.2). Here, it is the supervisors who are likely to work within the same team or service rather than the supervisees. Group and team supervision share many of the principles and practicalities that will be outlined below, but also differ in some important respects; for example, in team supervision there will be existing team relationships and dynamics that will need to be acknowledged and negotiated when setting up the supervision contract, particularly if the supervisor works within the same team.

A review of the literature on group size reveals a variety of recommendations ranging from three (i.e. one supervisor and two supervisees) to twelve members, with some writers recommending six (Lammers, 1999), others between three and seven (Hawkins and Shohet, 2000) and others eight to ten (Akhurst and Kelly, 2006). The optimum group size depends on a number of factors, including the purpose and type of group, the time available for supervision and, importantly, whether this is the participants' only source of supervision, in which case they are likely to require more individual time than if they were receiving one-to-one supervision as well. It is worth remembering that 'dynamics of groups change with increasing membership size' (Scaife, 2009: 95) and that the larger the group, the greater the likelihood that at least some of the participants will feel inhibited about being open. As Proctor (2000) notes, group size needs to 'allow for variety and for intimacy' (ibid.: 25), with enough participants to enable the group to continue running in the event of members' annual leave or sickness absence.

Regardless of therapeutic orientation or group composition or size, much of the literature describes two broad styles of supervision group, namely those in which there is an identified supervisor who takes the lead and those in which the group members play an active part in supervising each other (e.g. Hawkins and Shohet, 2000; Lammers, 1999). Proctor (2000) and Proctor and Inskipp (2009) describe a very useful framework comprising four types of group supervision, namely authoritative, participative, cooperative and peer group supervision, which are seen as lying on a continuum on which the supervisee has an increasing role in contributing to the supervision of the other group members. In *authoritative group supervision*, there is one supervisor and several supervisees. Here, the supervisor is responsible for supervising each participant in turn as well as managing the group. The members' roles are that of supervisee and, when they are not being supervised themselves, observers of other members' supervision in which they do not participate. This form of supervision can be conceptualised as one-to-one supervision in a group or 'dyadic group supervision' (Altfeld and Bernard, 1997: 382) although, as Proctor points out, 'there is necessarily a more complex set of relationships with a group of supervisees than with one (Proctor, 2000: 41). In *participative group supervision*, the supervisor still takes the lead in supervising and managing the group but also teaches and leads the group members in co-supervising each other. All group members are expected to participate in the supervision process and one of the explicit goals of this type of group is to enable the supervisees to develop their supervisory skills. In *cooperative group supervision*, the supervisor still holds overall responsibility for the supervision and the well-being of the group but takes a much less active leadership role. Unlike the previous two groups, members agree from the outset to be active co-supervisors and one of the supervisor's central roles is to facilitate the group in sharing the group supervision tasks. Finally, in *peer group supervision*, depending on the initial agreement between group members, leadership of the group may rotate or members may decide to assign that role to one person. Members of the peer group take shared responsibility both for supervising each other and for being supervised. As this is a particularly popular supervision format amongst qualified clinical psychologists as well as other qualified and student practitioners (see, for example, Akhurst and Kelly, 2006), this will be described in more detail in the next section.

Each of the above-mentioned supervision groups has advantages and disadvantages; for a comprehensive review of these, the reader is referred to Proctor and Inskipp (2009). For the purposes of this chapter, some of the benefits and potential pitfalls of group supervision in general are described here. Beginning with the benefits, by having the opportunity to discuss their work together, supervisees have exposure to a broader range of clients and ideas than would be the case in one-to-one supervision; this, in turn, can help supervisees to gain a wider perspective on their work and gain from exposure to others' expertise, support, feedback, reassurance, validation and challenges. Additionally, group supervision provides opportunities for supervisees to develop their own supervisory skills by observing the supervisor modelling supervision with other group members and, in the more participative group formats, to have opportunities to try out some of these supervisory skills in a safe forum. Furthermore, many writers have pointed out that group supervision can minimise the potential dependency issue that can arise in individual supervision for both supervisee and supervisor. It can also increase accountability; as Proctor notes, whilst collusion is possible in any form of supervision, '. . . a group has at least four or five chances for someone to notice what is culturally unmentionable' (Proctor, 2000: 21). Finally, group supervision provides opportunities for supervisees to have exposure to and learn about group dynamics; indeed, for those practitioners who run therapeutic groups, being involved in group supervision provides opportunities 'to learn from how the supervisor runs the group and also how the dynamics of the presented groups are mirrored in the supervision group' (Hawkins and Shohet, 2000: 130).

Some of the suggested disadvantages of group supervision include the fact that joining a group may be more anxiety-provoking for all participants (including the supervisor) than beginning one-to-one supervision, as generally there is a tendency for people to feel less safe in groups. Presenting in groups too can be problematic; as Andersson (2008) notes, this is 'akin to public speaking, which for many people is more anxiety provoking than dyadic conversation' (ibid.: 38). This in turn has the potential to limit the learning that can take place in the group, as exemplified by Altfeld and Bernard's (1997) assertion that 'it . . . is not unusual for a presenting therapist to report months later that a high anxiety level prevented absorbing more than a modest amount of what was offered by the supervisory group' (ibid.: 385). A further potential disadvantage of group supervision is that in many supervision groups supervisees do not have the opportunity to present weekly or fortnightly as they would do in individual supervision and, although some supervisors organise their groups to ensure that all participants have at least a small amount of time each session, depending on the size and arrangements of the group it can be 5 to 6 weeks before a member has the chance to fully present a piece of work. Additionally, although much of the literature refers to the supposed cost effectiveness and efficiency of group methods, it is by no means 'a cheaper way of doing individual supervision more quickly' (Morrison, 2005: 247). As Milne and Oliver (2000) point out, this format may in fact require 'considerable time to implement . . . but yield few benefits due to such factors as the increased arousal or defensiveness of the supervisees in this social context' (ibid.: 293). Another potential disadvantage of group supervision is the fact that less confident individuals may be overpowered by the group and thus feel uncomfortable about being open in front of other supervisees, particularly in discussing mistakes; in training supervision, the risk here is that 'weak trainees will be overlooked' (ibid.: 297). Related to this, group supervision can allow individuals to hide behind the group or to miss supervision sessions if they know others will be there. Finally, as mentioned in relation to individual supervision, if individual client work is being discussed, group supervision is less likely to 'mirror the dynamic of individual therapy as clearly as would individual supervision' (Hawkins and Shohet, 2000: 130).

What is required of the supervisor in group supervision? Proctor and Inskipp (2009) identify a number of key roles that the group supervisor has to occupy, each with their own sets of responsibilities; in addition to group supervisor, these include group manager, facilitator and leader. Similarly, Roth and Pilling (2008d) identify four broad abilities for group supervisors, namely the abilities to induct supervisees to group supervision, to act as a group leader, to structure sessions and to manage group process. For each of these areas, key competences are described in more detail, as illustrated in Table 10.1. It is clear both from this and from the literature on group supervision (e.g. Proctor, 2000; Proctor and Inskipp, 2009) that the supervisor plays a crucial role in ensuring the group's success. Both the importance of managing and the potential dangers of ignoring the group dynamics are themes that emerge in much of the literature. Even when there is no lead supervisor, such as in peer group supervision, the importance of attending to these issues is just as important, if not more so (Hawkins and Shohet, 2000). Group supervisors need both the skills required of individual supervisors and an understanding of group dynamics in order to facilitate the group (Bond and Holland, 1998). Importantly, though, lest this should be off-putting for the novice group supervisor, Proctor and Inskipp's (2009)

Table 10.1 Supervisor competences for conducting supervision in group
formats[a] (from Roth and Pilling, 2008d)

An ability to induct supervisees to group supervision
1 An ability to help supervisees prepare for group supervision by identifying issues that enhance their capacity to be effective participants, such as:
  • expectations regarding attendance
  • considering in-group behaviours that tend to facilitate or to hinder the group's work, and the identification of group 'norms' for appropriate behaviour
  • the need to identify what they would like to gain from the group (e.g. considering in advance of a presentation what issues they would like feedback on)
  • the need to prepare and present clinical material in a manner that enables their colleagues to engage with it
  • how best to give feedback in a manner which is direct but also supportive
2 An ability to model behaviour in the group that enhances the efficacy of the group (e.g. giving feedback that is direct but also respectful and supportive, and displays appropriate empathy)

An ability to act as a group leader
1 An ability to take an active, assertive but non-authoritarian leadership role
2 An ability to listen to, and act on, feedback about group functioning from group members

An ability to structure sessions
1 An ability to clarify, and agree with group members, the way in which the group will function by identifying the mode of supervision most appropriate to the supervision task and to group membership, e.g.:
  • supervision of each member of the group in turn, with group members acting as an 'audience' (supervision *in* a group)
  • supervision of each member of the group in turn, with group members encouraged to act as active participants (supervision *with* a group)
  • supervision that encourages all group members to act as supervisors, with the group leader facilitating this process (supervision *by* the group)
2 An ability to ensure that there is a clear and transparent arrangement for allocating time to each supervisee
3 An ability to identify and agree a consistent procedure for case presentations (e.g. who presents, how cases are chosen, length and format of presentation, etc.)

An ability to manage group process
1 An ability to support and monitor the engagement of supervisees with one another (e.g. by ensuring that supervisees have the opportunity to get to know and trust one another)
2 An ability to ensure that supervisees feel supported for the work they are undertaking
3 An ability to identify (and act on) problematic interpersonal issues, especially any tensions within the group (e.g. by addressing conflict or inappropriate competitiveness)
4 An ability to address any problematic aspects of group process that reflect issues of difference and/or power (e.g. in relation to different levels of experience, or in relation to cultural issues)

---

[a] When peer supervision is carried out in a group, group members can occupy the roles of supervisor and supervisee in turn. This means that although the competences outlined here apply to this type of supervision, they would need some adaptation.

reassuring words should be borne in mind: the group supervisor needs to be 'good enough' and 'relinquish any fantasies of becoming the "perfect" group supervisor' (ibid.: 137).

From the supervisees' perspective, they need to be open to learning from others and to airing their mistakes and well as their successes, mindful of others' needs as well as their own (good group manners) and open to working cooperatively and collaboratively and giving clear, thoughtful and constructive feedback.

From the foregoing account, it should be clear that there is much to be gained from engaging in good group supervision. Careful consideration of the potential advantages and pitfalls at the outset should enable the supervisor and supervisees to decide which type of group best suits both the needs of the participants and the supervisor's supervisory style. As with all supervision, but perhaps even more importantly in group supervision where there are more participants, there needs to be a clear contracting process where supervisor and supervisees can address the purpose, focus and key tasks of the group, determine group membership, clarify the mandate and decision-making authority, define boundaries (including the issues of whether it should be an open or closed group and when to terminate the group), negotiate the facilitator's role and authority, set ground rules and agree the range of methods to be used (see Morrison, 2005, for a full description of each of these elements).

Peer group supervision

Of all the types of group supervision described in the literature, peer group supervision is the one that is most commonly cited in clinical psychology and psychological therapy service supervision guidelines, as well as in surveys of practitioners' supervision arrangements (e.g. Townend et al., 2002). A number of professions advocate the use of peer group supervision for qualified practitioners either on its own or as an adjunct to individual supervision. In counselling, for example, BACP guidance on supervision (BACP, 2004b) specifies that peer group supervision may be sufficient at times for experienced counsellors but not for trainees or newly qualified counsellors. The BPS (2008a) similarly suggests peer group supervision as an option for post-qualification supervision.

As described in the preceding section, the term *peer group supervision* refers to the supervisory arrangement that 'occurs when members supervise each other and negotiate the structure and functioning of the group' (Akhurst and Kelly, 2006: 5) and where all participants have equal status. Peer group arrangements can vary widely from very structured, where there is a nominated group facilitator and presenter for each session, through to unstructured, where any of the participants can present case material that is followed by an informal discussion about that material. As with pair peer and group supervision, the way in which a peer group is established depends on a number of factors, including the supervisory needs of the participants and the training or service context.

Many of the principles and practicalities, benefits and pitfalls of pair peer and group supervision apply equally to peer group supervision. Additional benefits of peer group supervision include the relative ease with which this type of group can be established, particularly if it comprises colleagues from the same workplace, the opportunity for supportive discussion of work in a safe, non-hierarchical forum with no explicit evaluative component and decreased dependency on expert supervisors. Moreover as peers, participants are likely to be able to identify with the issues raised, thus providing and receiving reassurance that others are experiencing the same dilemmas, issues and anxieties. It is also possible that members of the group will 'hear things better from peers than from the "authority"' (Proctor, 2000: 25).

Whilst there are a number of clear benefits to engaging in this form of supervision, potential pitfalls include the possibility that peers will find it difficult to challenge one another or to provide honest feedback, which is one of the main reasons why this might not be the best supervision format for newly qualified practitioners. Moreover, in the absence of supervisory leadership there is the potential for the group to feel unsafe, with little or no attention being paid to group dynamics. Finally, many writers point to the potential for the peer group to lapse into informal chats, becoming too 'cosy' (Bassett, 1999: 37), 'a social group rather than a work group' (Proctor and Inskipp, 2009: 143) or a 'moaning session' (Marrow et al., 2002: 278).

Despite the aforementioned pitfalls, there is evidence that, if organised well, this form of supervision is very useful throughout a practitioner's career and is particularly appropriate for trainees (Akhurst and Kelly, 2006). In clinical psychology training, the ability to understand the supervision process for both supervisee and supervisor roles is one of the core competences that trainees are expected to achieve (BPS, 2010). Whilst there are plenty of opportunities for trainees to take the role of supervisee during training, there are far fewer formal opportunities for them to take the role of supervisor, and yet this is something they are expected to undertake as soon as they qualify. In response to this, a number of clinical psychology training programmes in the UK organise peer supervision for their trainees. On the Manchester programme, for example, we have had peer supervision groups as a regular part of the third-year curriculum for 7 years, the main aims of which are to foster the development of presentation and supervision skills, provide an opportunity for discussion of and reflection on clinical work and learn about group process. It is a measure of the popularity of these groups than in response to trainee feedback, these sessions now begin in the second year of training. The sessions are timetabled for 1 hour per fortnight and trainees are randomly allocated to groups of between four and five.

Following formal teaching sessions, each group is encouraged to develop its own ground rules, to include discussion of time allocation per session, commitment, individual responsibility, openness and respect, confidentiality and boundaries. Whilst trainees are free to organise their groups in any way they choose, we suggest that there should be a group leader and that this role should rotate each session; the group leader's duties include chairing the session, identifying and naming difficulties, holding the ground rules in mind, time-keeping, recording the themes of the session and communicating with absent members. Informal feedback suggests that the group leader often is responsible for providing biscuits, which fits with Hawkins and Shohet's (2000) suggestion that there should be some informal time either at the start or end of the peer group supervision session so that group members can catch up with each other's news without this encroaching into the formal supervision time. Trainees are asked to keep a log of their discussions, from which a consistent pattern has been found over the years. Whilst initial sessions are invariably used to focus mainly on discussion of clinical work, in later sessions the focus changes to reflect the diversity of the original aims, with personal/professional issues coming to the fore: examples of these include discussion of trainee issues (placements, research, job-seeking), supervision (both receiving and giving to others), service issues (e.g. working with interpreters, working with difficult team dynamics) and ethical dilemmas. Feedback from successive cohorts of trainees has indicated many of the benefits listed above, as well as some of the pitfalls, and the programme has endeavoured to both pre-empt and respond to this in successive years. It is a measure of the groups' success that some trainees continue meeting beyond the end of training.

The clinical psychology training programme at the University of Leeds takes a different approach to peer supervision, as is demonstrated on a very enlightening DVD (Green and Akhurst, 2009). Here, trainees take part in Structured Peer Group Supervision in which the roles of presenter and facilitator rotate, session by session. There are five phases to the group. First, a group member presents a case, outlining up to three questions for personal development. This is followed by a period of questioning and identification of focus by the others in the group. There then follows a period of reflective feedback and discussion by group members using a 'round robin' approach where all members have the opportunity to contribute in turn; during this discussion, the presenter either physically leaves the circle or at least remains silent, listens to the other participants' discussion and takes notes. The presenter then returns to the group to respond to what has been discussed and, in the final phase, engages in an optional group discussion. Feedback about this type of peer group suggests a number of additional benefits to those outlined previously, including the fact that the structure helps to make the endeavour feel secure for all involved and that the round robin approach ensures that all members have the chance to contribute. Being involved in a group such as this gives the students confidence to establish similar groups once qualified.

The principles for setting up group supervision, outlined in the last paragraph of the previous section, apply equally to peer group supervision and will not be repeated here. Suffice to say, it is good practice for any peer group to be developed with as much attention to the formal aspects of supervision as any other supervision format, even though in practice peer groups often are set up on a voluntary basis.

Use of technology in supervision

In 1997, Goodyear and Nelson predicted '. . . that computer technology soon will provide new supervision formats' (ibid.: 341). Undoubtedly, the last decade has seen an increase in the range of supervisory formats available through the use of telephone, computer and other technology: these include the use of computer for electronic mail (email), Internet newsgroups or listservs, instant messaging and video-conferencing through the use of software applications such as Skype. A further example, described by Kanz (2001), involves using a computer screen positioned behind the client in the clinical session on which the supervisor can provide immediate and ongoing feedback to the supervisee.

A full review of these formats is beyond the scope of this chapter and readers are referred to Kanz (2001), Marrow et al. (2002) and Scaife (2009) for more in-depth consideration of the practical and ethical issues, advantages and disadvantages associated with each of these. To illustrate with just two examples, Yeh et al. (2008) describe an on-line peer supervision group for counselling trainees, in which the participants used a web-based bulletin board to ask questions, respond to topics posted by other participants and provide and receive support and feedback. Participants used aliases in order to remain anonymous. Having access to the system any time of day or night meant that participants could pose concerns or questions as they arose, rather than having to wait until a scheduled supervision session; the majority of messages were posted in the evening. Interestingly, given what we know about the importance of establishing a supervisory relationship, anonymity was reported to have encouraged a greater degree of openness, as participants felt less embarrassed about sharing personal issues than they would have been had their identity been known. The system was not without its pitfalls, including some technical difficulty in accessing the website. Additionally, as with any supervision format that does not involve some face-to-face contact, the authors point to the potential difficulties associated with not having access to participants' non-verbal cues, such as misinterpretation of messages.

Marrow et al. (2002) describe the use of video-conferencing technology to enable long-distance supervision for 40 qualified nurses, many of whom worked in rural areas. Unlike the study described above, the participants either arranged to meet each other beforehand or, at the very least, could see each other through the use of video technology; indeed, establishing a face-to-face relationship prior to the video sessions was reported to have been important in aiding the disclosure of information. Of several benefits described in the article, one of the most important was the fact that it gave the nurses access to peer or one-to-one supervision when they would not have otherwise had access to this in their respective workplaces, either because of their rural locations or specialist work. As in the Yeh et al. (2008) study, however, some technical difficulties were encountered, including broken sound and no picture at times, which resulted in 'some anxious and distracting experiences' (Marrow et al., 2002: 279).

Technological formats have clear advantages in making supervision more accessible, particularly for practitioners to receive expert supervision from colleagues around the world or, as described by Marrow et al. (2002), for those practitioners who work in isolated locations. Some studies have indicated an additional advantage to the participants not being in the same location as each other, namely that it is easier to get to the heart of the issue more quickly. Whether the format is cost effective depends very much on individual circumstances; a local telephone call, for example, will be far less expensive than setting up video-conferencing equipment for a group of supervisees.

Kanz (2001) ended his review of on-line supervision in 2001 by stating 'with continued research, improved encryption techniques and legislative action, on-line supervision is likely to become a freely accepted and widely used method for supervision' (ibid.: 419). A review of the literature suggests that technological formats have had an increasingly important part to play in both training and post-qualification supervision over the past decade. Currently, however, most professional body supervision guidelines, at least in the UK, either do not include mention of these formats or suggest that they should be used only in conjunction with other formats; BABCP (2009), for example, permits telephone or email supervision for accredited practitioners with the caveat that 'there must be some direct personal contact on occasions' (ibid.: 7).

Informal supervision formats

Whatever formal supervision arrangements we may have in place, undoubtedly there will be times when we need to seek informal advice about a thorny clinical or ethical issue that cannot easily wait until our next scheduled supervision session. Leaving aside for the time being the issue of whether this supervisory support comes from our own supervisor or from another colleague, the question remains: How does this informal arrangement fit with the supervisory frameworks that are described both in the general supervision literature and elsewhere in this book?

In the opening paragraph of their chapter in this book (Chapter 2), Wheeler and Cushway note that supervision has developed from an informal to a strictly formal process. Certainly many of the recognised definitions of supervision refer to supervision as being a formal process (BACP, 2004b; DH, 1993; Milne, 2009) that, moreover, is conducted in a boundaried space (DCoP, 2008), guided by some form of contract (DH, 2000; Roth and Pilling, 2008c), carried out on a regular basis (Bond and Holland, 1998) within a facilitative relationship (Beinart, 2004; Bernard and Goodyear, 2004; DCoP, 2008; Milne, 2009). Given these defining features and particularly the centrality of the formal nature of the activity, one could question whether the concept of informal supervision is a valid one or whether it is yet another oxymoron, in a similar vein to the concept of peer supervision (Milne, 2009: 177). Regardless of whether this type of supervisory contact constitutes supervision as formally defined, however, it is a very frequent occurrence in the workplace; as Hawkins and Shohet (2000) note, 'a great deal of supervision happens in times and places other than those officially designated for supervision' (ibid.: 57). Often occurring amongst practitioners who work in teams, perhaps because of the ease with which colleagues can consult with each other, informal supervision occurs most commonly as an adjunct to formal supervision but can sometimes be an alternative. In the Townend et al. (2002) survey described previously, for example, 47.8% of their sample of 170 cognitive behavioural psychotherapists reported making use of informal supervision 'sometimes' and 38.5% 'often', this being in addition to formal, planned supervision. Similarly other writers have noted the importance for practitioners of having access to informal supervisory support outside the formal supervisory space (see, for example, Hawkins and Shohet, 2000; Scaife, 2009). For some professional groups, particularly where supervision is not mandatory, informal discussion may be the sole means by which a practitioner obtains support for their work. In general practice in the UK, for example, 'most GPs do not receive clinical supervision' (Launer, 2007: 182) as formally defined but discussion of clinical work still takes place, 'most commonly in the corridor, over coffee, or in phone calls to local specialists' (ibid.: 182). Similarly in nursing, the 'tea break/tear break' (Butterworth and Faugier, 1992: 9) is a well-recognised form of peer support where colleagues share and receive feedback on their management of stressful clinical experiences.

As with other supervision formats, for clinical psychologists in the UK the scene is very clearly set for the importance of informal supervision during pre-qualification training, where an essential component of training is that trainee clinical psychologists have opportunities for informal contact with their supervisors as well as scheduled formal supervision (BPS, 2010). For qualified clinical psychologists too, professional practice guidelines (e.g.

BPS, 2005) add yet further weight to the importance of informal supervision by reminding us that we can make use of 'the many modes of less
formal supervisory discussions' (ibid.: 6), which include informal
discussions with a colleague.

If we recognise informal supervision as being acceptable and standard
practice, what forms can this take? Drawing on both my own experience
and the extant literature, it would seem there are a number of possible
informal supervision scenarios, many of which are likely to be preceded by
the question 'can I have a quick word with you?' and fall into one of two
categories, namely:

- ad hoc requests for either urgent or non-urgent supervision; this could
  be with one's own supervisor outside the normal supervision time and
  place or with another colleague;
- informal supervisory discussion (or chats) about clinical or other work
  with peers or others within, or sometimes outside (Scaife, 2009), the
  workplace.

A third example has already been described in the section on peer supervision and therefore will not be covered here. This is where a formal
supervisory format such as peer group or pair peer supervision is set up
on a voluntary basis, with no formal supervision contract or structure;
participants simply meet together for informal discussion of work. Here,
whilst the supervision is planned rather than ad hoc, the arrangements are
informal.

The remainder of this section will consider informal supervision formats
in more detail, including guidance for good practice.

Ad hoc requests for urgent or non-urgent supervision

The most common type of informal supervision is the urgent request for ad
hoc supervision when a practitioner needs immediate supervisory advice.
Good practice would dictate that, where possible, this ad hoc supervision
should be delivered by the practitioner's own supervisor, as there already
exists an established supervisory relationship and there is likely to be a
supervision contract in place. If the supervisor is not available, however, or
if the practitioner doe not have a supervisor, it is not unusual for another
appropriately qualified colleague to be approached.

If it is the practitioner's own supervisor, the urgent and informal nature
of this type of request should not detract from the fact that this is still
taking place within a supervisory contract and that any advice and actions
should be as accountable as if the discussion was being held within a formal
supervisory context (Morrison, 2005). If it is not the practitioner's supervisor who has been contacted but rather another colleague, then it is

important to remember that, as with all supervision, 'once information is shared, so is responsibility' (BPS, 2005: 4). In the absence of a supervision contract, there is likely to be far less clarity about the issues of responsibility and accountability, and this will be further complicated if the supervisee and supervisor are from different professional groups as their work will be guided by different codes of practice. This is not to say that this type of supervision should never take place but rather to alert the reader to these issues so that they can be considered in advance.

Morrison (2005) provides a very helpful list of suggestions for supervisors to manage such ad hoc requests, all of which apply to any form of supervision but are all the more important to bear in mind when faced with an urgent situation, not least because there is the potential for both the supervisee and the supervisor to be more anxious in this situation. A full list of suggestions can be found in Morrison (2005) but examples include: advice to the supervisor to clarify exactly what the practitioner wants from supervision and the reason for it being urgent; be clear about and frame positively the amount of time available for discussion; reassure, normalise and remain calm; listen to all the key facts; make clear decisions and conclusions; agree actions; record the outcome of the discussion; and decide when and how the supervision will be followed up.

If the request for urgent supervision has been made by telephone rather than face to face, then in addition to the suggestions listed above Morrison (2005) reminds the supervisor to consider whether the supervisee is in a location where they can talk freely and confidentially, to be aware of the significance of not having access to non-verbal cues and the resultant need to probe more carefully for feelings, and to summarise back to the supervisee what is clear, what is not clear and what aspect is urgent.

There may be times when an ad hoc request arises not from an urgent situation but rather from a need for expert advice, for example from a practitioner who works within a particular therapeutic orientation or has specialist knowledge of a clinical or professional issue. Here, as in the urgent situation described above, whilst it is all too easy for the person being asked for advice to launch into giving an opinion, it is well worth both parties taking time at the outset to discuss the nature and status of the advice; this may not involve drawing up a formal supervisory contract but at the very least could involve a simple contract that enables discussion of accountability and, importantly, follow-up. As will be discussed in the conclusions, it may be more appropriate to refer to this type of arrangement as consultation rather than supervision.

Informal supervisory discussion

Be it the aforementioned discussions with colleagues in the coffee room (Launer, 2007) or informal case discussion amongst students working together within the same clinical placement, this very common form of informal support and supervision often takes place without the participants necessarily realising that they are engaging in supervision. From my experience of working with trainee clinical psychologists, there are mutual benefits to engaging in informal supervision of this type, as this is one of the ways in which trainees hone their skills in supporting and supervising others. Aston and Molassiotis (2003) report similar findings in their description of a structured peer support scheme for nursing students on placement. Whether the need is for an opportunity to debrief after a particularly challenging clinical session or to seek specific advice about a piece of work, this type of informal contact with seniors or peers is no less important post-qualification.

Helpful though they may be, informal supervision arrangements carry with them a number of potential dangers, particularly where this is the only form of supervision a practitioner receives, in which case it could be used by both the supervisee and supervisor as a way of avoiding having their work scrutinised within the structure of regular supervision sessions (Hawkins and Shohet, 2000). It is one thing to need 'quickly available alternative supervision, e.g. advice in a crisis situation' (BABCP, 2009: 7) but quite another to have informal supervision as one's only source of support, particularly as it is highly likely that this supervision will only be sought when things are going wrong. Not only does this give the message that practitioners have to be seen to be working well and that by having to seek supervision they are falling short in some way, but it also deprives them of invaluable opportunities for a restorative space in which to develop their skills by reflecting on their achievements as well as discussing areas of difficulty.

In the opening pages of her book, *Supervision in Clinical Practice*, Scaife (2009) describes some very interesting research showing how widespread the practice of discussing client-related issues is outside a formal supervision setting. Whilst this is generally reported to occur with due attention to client confidentiality, undoubtedly 'a formal and effective supervision arrangement can obviate this threat to professional integrity' (ibid.: 2). This is not to deny the value of informal support and supervision but simply to suggest, as do Hawkins and Shohet (2000), that if practitioners recognise that regular 'informal chats' are a form of supervision, then this can be 'negotiated and improved' (ibid.: 57), leading to better quality supervision.

Conclusions

It is interesting to reflect on whether we have moved any further from the position outlined by Milne and Oliver (2000) over a decade ago, when they reported 'a marked preference for one-to-one supervision' (ibid.: 293). Professional guidelines and service policies certainly encourage the use of other supervisory formats, and evidence from literature and personal experience suggests that these are being put into practice, both during training (e.g. Akhurst and Kelly, 2006; Green and Akhurst, 2009) and post-qualification.

A wide range of supervision formats exists, including formats that have not been described in detail in this chapter, such as live supervision and co-therapy (Goodyear and Nelson, 1997), the latter being particularly useful during training as it enables the supervisor to both observe the trainee's work and act as a role model within the context of joint working. For the supervisee, the choice of format will depend upon a number of factors, including personal choice, access to different supervisory formats, career stage, qualifications, the theoretical model and therapeutic modality within which they work, professional requirements, service setting and service policies (Roth and Pilling, 2008c). For the supervisor too, the format used to deliver supervision will depend on a number of similar factors, including additionally the supervisor's confidence and competence in delivering supervision in a range of formats. As Scaife (2009) points out, new supervisors may well find it easier to start by offering individual supervision, as the one-to-one format does not require the supervisor to consider the complex dynamics that accompany group supervision. If group supervision is the format of choice, there may be some advantage for new supervisors to begin by running an authoritative group (Proctor, 2000) in order to gain confidence of working within a group, before moving on to include the participants in a more active manner as the group develops.

For qualified practitioners, ideally the supervisee (and supervisor) should have the opportunity to choose a supervisory format rather than have one imposed and this choice should be made for positive reasons rather than negative, such as perceived cost effectiveness, bearing in mind the advantages and potential pitfalls of each format. The literature would suggest that different formats may be useful at different stages of one's career (BPS, 2005) or for different purposes, and it is not unusual for practitioners to experience a range of supervision formats alongside each other (e.g. BPS, 2005; Durham, Swan and Fisher, 2000; Gilbert and Evans, 2000; Proctor, 2000; Townend et al., 2002). Engaging in a range of formats has the advantage of enabling ideas from one format to be applied in another (Milne and Oliver, 2000; Proctor, 2000): for example, the principles of group supervision can be applied when there is one supervisor with two supervisees.

Different supervision formats may fulfil different supervisory functions (Carroll, 1996) or roles, with some peer group supervision, for example, having a supportive function (BPS, 2005; Marrow et al., 2002) and other, more structured peer groups providing both support and education (Green and Akhurst, 2009) but with little, if any, evaluative function. In contrast, some forms of on-line supervision may fulfil more of an educative role. For this reason, some formats such as peer group supervision are not thought to be suitable as one's only source of supervision or professional support (Akhurst and Kelly, 2006; Proctor, 2000) but can be a good supplement to another format, such as one-to-one supervision. It is important to remember, however, that many practitioners do not receive any supervision let alone have a choice of format; choice is not always going to be possible and may well be limited by the constraints and professional culture of the service or agency within which the supervisee and supervisor work.

The advantages of receiving formal and regular supervision that is boundaried, relationship-based, structured and bound by a supervisory contract are well documented both elsewhere in this book and in the general supervision literature. Informal supervision has its place but only as an adjunct to formal supervision. Over-use of informal supervision is likely to indicate that a practitioner needs more appropriate professional support or training; the recognition of this has led some services to set up regular consultation clinics, where practitioners (often members of a multi-disciplinary team) can consult about client- or service-related issues in a planned manner rather than having to engage in snatched informal conversations in the coffee room or corridor, which is invariably unsatisfactory for both parties.

One of the themes to emerge in this chapter, as in the more general supervision literature, is the way in which terms are often used interchangeably and, at times, inaccurately. In the European and American literature, the terms *supervision, consultation, coaching* and *mentoring* are all used in slightly different ways to describe similar yet distinct activities (see Scaife, 2009, for a fuller description). There are times when we think we are engaging in supervision when, strictly speaking, we are not; this is particularly applicable to the type of voluntary peer supervision that provides support but does not adhere to a clear structure or involve an evaluative or feedback component (Milne, 2009). The supportive role is one of the three main supervisory roles identified by many writers (e.g. Carroll, 1996), but in the absence of educative and managerial/evaluative components the activity is not supervision as formally defined but rather peer support, peer consultation or group discussion (Proctor, 2000). With regard to informal conversations about clinical work, Marrow et al. (2000) point out that it is easy for practitioners to 'delude' themselves that 'the almost daily discussions . . . about patient care, ward management or staff development could be classed as supervision' (ibid.: 278), suggesting that this might be better regarded as 'incidental reflection' (ibid.: 278). In a similar vein, although many writers describe one-off requests for advice as informal supervision, this is probably more accurately termed consultation or consultative support.

To add to this somewhat confusing picture, the term *consultation* also means different things to different professional groups, the commonly acknowledged difference between consultation and supervision being the issue of responsibility (Brunning and Huffington, 1994). The importance of using accurate terminology in this context is to ensure that all participants share an understanding of the activity in which they are engaged, particularly with regard to issues of accountability and responsibility. It is widely acknowledged, however, that different terms sometimes have very different connotations for different professional groups. For this reason, provided the activity has a very clear contract, there may be times when using the correct term is less important than finding a name that has a familiar and positive connotation for the participants so that the process can be supported at an organisational level, 'especially in a corporate context where asking for help may equate with admitting one's incompetence' (Lammers, 1999: 115).

Different supervision formats may be growing in popularity but what is known about their effectiveness? There is some evidence for the relative effectiveness of different formats but, in keeping with much of the supervision research to date, this is based mainly on supervisee and supervisor reports of satisfaction or increased confidence rather than on outcomes such as supervisees' competence or client outcomes. Despite a wealth of anecdotal evidence for the popularity (as well as the pitfalls) of various formats, as Goodyear and Nelson stated in 1997 'there have been curiously few investigations to determine . . . the efficacy supervisors perceive (different formats) to have' (ibid.: 328). As stated in the introduction, the majority of empirical research to date has focused on one-to-one supervision (Akhurst and Kelly, 2006); the challenge now is to apply this to other formats.

Milne and Oliver (2000) conclude their review of flexible supervision formats within clinical psychology by stating that more training is needed in formats other than one-to-one. Beyond clinical psychology, other writers similarly describe the need for training in a range of formats, particularly in preparation for group supervision, which is not 'a process at which good individual supervisors will necessarily be competent' (Morrison, 2005: 247). As Hawkins and Shohet (2000) note: 'all those who consider supervising in groups should have some training in this field . . . (which) should include understanding the basic stages that groups go through and how to facilitate the group development in the various stages' (ibid.: 143). In pre-qualification clinical psychology training, guidance for those organising clinical placements includes the statement: 'where the ratio of trainee to supervisor is other than 1:1, the programme must ensure that appropriate guidance is given to supervisors and trainees on the procedures which are necessary for good team supervision. It will probably be necessary to establish supervisor workshops related specifically to team supervision' (BPS, 2010, appendix 4: 2.1). Despite this guidance, whilst initial supervisor training provided by clinical psychology programmes covers some aspects of other formats, it focuses predominantly on one-to-one supervision; indeed, the Supervisor Training and Recognition (STAR) criteria for supervisor training within clinical psychology (described in Chapter 6), make no explicit reference to formats other than one-to-one. The work of Roth and Pilling (2008d), whose framework for group supervision is presented in Table 10.1, is a very helpful development in shaping a curriculum for supervisor training. Moreover, there are many texts (e.g. Lammers, 1999) and external courses on specific supervision models and formats, including group supervision.

Whilst it seems unlikely that pre-qualification clinical psychology programmes will have the resources to deliver extensive training in a range of formats, either in addition to or as part of the initial supervisor training already offered (see Chapter 6), there are other ways of acquiring skills in supervising using different formats. As Milne and Oliver (2000) suggest, these include co-supervising with someone from another discipline who has experience of different formats. Moreover, as has been noted throughout this chapter, receiving supervision in a variety of formats can be a very good starting point for developing one's own supervision skills. Clinical psychology trainees now get exposure to a range of supervision formats, both on placement and in the classroom, and this will undoubtedly shape their future practice as supervisors.

Summary

This chapter began by considering the popularity of one-to-one supervision amongst practitioners in the helping professions and went on to describe the features of both this form of supervision and a range of alternative formal and informal supervision formats. These include pair peer supervision, group supervision with a lead supervisor, peer group supervision and use of technology in supervision, as well as ad hoc requests for supervision. Consideration has been given to the practicalities as well as the potential benefits and pitfalls of each supervision format. What emerges is that different supervision formats are likely to be more useful at different stages of one's career or for different purposes, and that there are some benefits to engaging in a range of formats alongside each other. The chapter concludes by advising that, whichever format is used, it is important to set a clear supervision contract that takes account of the potential benefits and pitfalls of that format. Further research and training in formats other than one-to-one are needed.

Chapter 11

Practical aspects of supervision: All you ever wanted to know but were too afraid to ask

Jan Hughes

Introduction

What are the fundamental elements of practising supervision and how does this differ across models of therapy, models of supervision and professional groups? This chapter aims to outline a trans-theoretical approach to delivering supervision and to consider the elements that are essential to effective delivery of supervision in order to aid service delivery. The focus of the chapter is on clinical supervision but, where appropriate, issues relating to other forms of supervision (e.g. managerial supervision) will also be considered. The aim is to cover elements of supervision that are relevant to both pre-qualification and post-qualification supervisory processes. The chapter is divided into four areas, namely: before starting supervision, beginning supervision, the supervisory process and ending supervision. Whilst a chapter on practical aspects of supervision will inevitably read as somewhat of a list, I have tried to include some personal observations where appropriate.

Before starting supervision

In this first section elements to consider before starting supervision are described, for both the supervisee and the supervisor. It really is worth taking time to consider these elements before you start. As the saying goes – act in haste, repent at leisure.

The organisational context

There are a number of guidance documents to help new supervisors and supervisees, including the Division of Clinical Psychology (DCP) *Policy on Continued Supervision* (BPS, 2005) and the BPS *Guidelines on Clinical Supervision* (BPS, 1995b). Before agreeing to enter into a supervisor relationship it is important to consider the organisational context and raise a number of questions:

- Is the potential supervisor the best person in this organisation to provide this supervision, that is, is the supervisor appropriately trained?
- What are the clinical governance arrangements regarding supervision in this organisation and can these be met through this arrangement?
- Who holds managerial responsibility for this supervisee and can the supervisor communicate about this person if the need arises?

Supervisor competences

There are a number of competence frameworks that supervisors can use to help them consider whether they are competent enough to start a supervisory process. For clinical psychologists there are learning objectives within the Committee on Training in Clinical Psychology accreditation criteria (BPS, 2008b). Closely linked to this is the Improving Access to Psychological Therapies (IAPT) supervision competence framework, designed from a multi-professional perspective and with application to a number of theoretical models (Roth and Pilling, 2008a). Other competence frameworks are also available, for example that of Falender and Shafranske (2004). There are also some self-evaluation tools that supervisors can use to assess their supervision (e.g. the self-assessment questionnaire for supervisors: Hawkins and Shohet, 2006). I have used the Supervisor Training and Recognition (STAR) learning objectives questionnaire developed by the Hull Doctor in Clinical Psychology programme, combined with elements from the Roth and Pilling framework, to devise a self-evaluation questionnaire for those undertaking supervisor training within the IAPT model. It seems that having some framework that helps to define aspects of the skills needed and provides a marker point for further development has been very useful. In assessing their own competence it may be that supervisors make a decision to engage in further training before embarking on a particular supervisory process. This may be linked to developing their knowledge and skills further in the particular model of therapy being utilised by the supervisee or it may focus on generic or applied supervisory knowledge and skills.

There are a number of different frameworks that can help provide guidance for a new supervisor or supervisee. Some are linked to generic processes: an example is the Developmental Model (Stoltenberg and Delworth, 1987), which suggests that supervisees will need different approaches depending on the developmental stage of their training. So, for example, those who are novice therapists may need a more prescriptive approach with more direct advice. Other models can be helpful to structure sessions for new supervisors and supervisees: an example is the Process Model (Hawkins and Shohet, 2006), which states that there are seven modes of supervision that can be utilised within and across supervision sessions. The focus within the different modes is as follows:

- Mode 1: The client.
- Mode 2: The strategies and interventions.
- Mode 3: The relationship between the client and the supervisee.
- Mode 4: The supervisee.
- Mode 5: The supervisory relationship.
- Mode 6: The supervisor's process.
- Mode 7: The wider context.

Other models can also help supervisors to develop within a particular area of therapy supervision, such as cognitive behavioural therapy (Armstrong and Freeston, 2006).

Training for supervisors

It is recommended that before embarking on a supervisory process serious consideration should be given by supervisors to training in supervision, to ensure competence as discussed above. The process of being trained as a supervisor is now beginning within pre-qualification training, with trainee clinical psychologists being taught within doctoral programmes about 'becoming a supervisor'. For qualified clinical psychologists a STAR-compliant course should be provided within the local area. It is recommended that this should be a minimum requirement for clinical psychologists engaging in supervision. There are also supervision courses that can be accessed for supervision within a particular context (e.g. IAPT supervisor training). For those who wish to study further, institutions around the country also offer academic qualifications at certificate, diploma or masters level. I can clearly remember the embarrassment of recognising (after many years of practice) how limited my supervisory practice was during supervision training and would highly recommend that any supervisor avoids this.

Support for supervision

A number of structures need to be in place to support the provision of supervision. The supervisor needs to have managerial support to provide supervision, particularly in the context of organisations engaged in performance-related pay contracts, where the emphasis may be on face-to-face service user contacts. For a new supervisor it is recommended that supervision for supervision is organised, either within the clinician's current supervisor arrangements or ideally as a separate process. Supervisors should also have regular access to Continuing Professional Development (CPD) events related to supervision.

Roles and responsibilities in supervision

It is important that the roles and responsibilities are discussed between supervisor and supervisee before embarking on supervision. These include but are not limited to: clinical responsibility of cases, confidentiality, boundaries, discussion of personal and professional development issues, evaluation and the supervisor's and supervisee's requirements. In a training placement the evaluation role is clear. However, within any supervisory relationship it is the supervisor's responsibility to ensure that the supervisee is fit to practise and to take active measures if this is not the case. It is important that it is emphasised that supervision is a two-way process, with both having responsibility to try to make it work effectively. In my own practice as a supervisor I do this in two ways: by having explicit clear conversations about responsibility within the contracting process, and implicitly through the modelling of shared responsibility in the relationship.

The goals of supervision

It is clear that before starting supervision there needs to be an agreement on the goals of supervision. This may be within a professional framework, such as clinical psychology training. They may include goals relating to knowledge and skills, to insight and awareness and to personal development issues.

Group or individual supervision?

One of the considerations to make before starting supervision is whether the supervisee would benefit from individual or group supervision. The supervisor may need to offer advice about how to access one or the other. There are advantages to group supervision in that it is more cost effective, supervisees can see the supervisor modelling the supervision with more than one person and they can learn from their colleagues.

Summary

The main theme to emerge from this section is how much work needs to be done before you even start. It is invaluable to do this preparation and to be clear that is acceptable for either the supervisee or the supervisor to say 'no'.

Beginning supervision – the contracting process

The first few sessions should focus clearly on the contracting process. Prior to engaging in a contracting process it is important for both supervisees and supervisors to give some thought to what it might be important to cover. Implicit throughout this process is a respect for individual development and the need to modify the contracting process depending on the needs of the supervisee. The following is not an exhaustive list but they are all issues that could be considered.

Developmental stage of the supervisee

As discussed above, the Stoltenberg and Delworth (1987) approach can be a helpful starting point to consider the developmental stage of each supervisee. Assumptions should not be made; rather, an explicit discussion should be had about the supervisee's previous experience, knowledge and skills.

Learning style of the supervisee

Two theories are helpful in considering the learning style of the supervisee and the supervisor, and the impact this may have on supervision. The first is Kolb's (1984) experiential learning cycle, which describes how learning needs to move through a cycle of experiencing, reflecting, abstract conceptualisation and active experimentation. Linked to this are models of learning style, such as Honey and Mumford's (1984) classification of four learning styles: activist, reflector, theorist and pragmatist. Although the concept of learning styles is used extensively in the literature on education and learning, there is little evidence of a fixed learning style that does not adapt across contexts (Scaife, 2009), leading some to ask 'when will learning style go out of style?' (Norman, 2009). Bearing this in mind it is useful as a starting point to consider that if a supervisee (or supervisor) has a particular learning style that is being activated in this particular context, this may affect both the point of the Kolb cycle where learning starts for this individual and also where they may become 'stuck'. For example, if the supervisee has a primary learning style of theorist in this context, they may tend to start their learning process with needing to be aware of the particular research and theories linked to this clinical issue. While this can be a positive starting point in the cycle, problems can occur if the supervisee struggles to move through every element of the cycle (e.g. if it is difficult to move into active experimentation and put the theory into action). Discussion with a supervisee about their particular learning style in this context as part of the contracting process can be beneficial in helping them get the most out of supervision. Supervisors may also want to divulge their own particular style within this role and how they may also get stuck. It is also important to remember that this is a dyad and learning styles are on a continuum, so whilst my perception of myself is as a pragmatist who can struggle at times to think 'theory', in some dyads with certain colleagues I can find myself clearly the theorist!

Supervisee's needs within supervision

It is important within the contracting process to focus on the needs of the supervisee, for example what has brought them to supervision, what are their objectives and what do they want to get out of it? The supervisee needs to feel heard and to have the opportunity to discuss any fears and anxieties, and also hopes, for supervision.

The supervisee's and supervisor's previous experience

Linking to the previous point it is also important to explore the supervisee's previous experience of supervision. In particular, hearing the supervisee's experience of what has been helpful and what has been unhelpful can be very enlightening and increases the likelihood of it being possible to address this within the current supervision. The supervisor can also share their experience of giving and receiving supervision. A helpful question that has been asked within the contracting process for trainees within the Sheffield Doctorate in Clinical Psychology for many years is: What are the 'unsaid' elements of supervision (i.e. the unwritten rules, the 'things that really annoy me') that both supervisee and supervisor have developed from their previous experience? This can be a powerful question to get to the fundamentals of what is important for each person (e.g. 'please always come with something written down' or 'please let the silence remain when I need to reflect').

The practicalities

It is obviously important at some point during the contracting process to negotiate the practicalities of supervision. Issues to consider are the following:

- How often will we meet?
- Where will we meet?
- How long will our sessions be?
- Over what time period will we meet and how will we review this?
- What resources will we use (e.g. process notes, audio/videotapes)?
- What methods might we use?
- How can we let each other know if we need to cancel a session?

Individual session contracting

It is also helpful to have clarified issues around how each session will be contracted. Again, there are a number of issues to be negotiated:

- Will we have an agenda every time we meet?
- Whose responsibility is it to devise this?
- What will be the focus of each session? (e.g. will we have a maximum number of service users or carers? Can more general issues be raised?)
- Who is responsible for time keeping within each session?
- How do we give and receive feedback?

Evaluative or managerial role

In terms of trying to create a clarity and security in supervision, it is important to be open about any other roles the supervisor may have with the supervisee. If an evaluative role is involved, the supervisee must be clear about how and when they are to be evaluated and using which process. If it is a fixed term placement, for example, the supervisee must be aware of when they will be evaluated within this and on what criteria, so there is clarity around expectations. It is not recommended that supervisors should also have a managerial role with their supervisee, but sometimes this is unavoidable and in this situation it is imperative to be open about the dual relationship and how this may be managed.

Clarity about professional guidelines, clinical responsibility and philosophical underpinnings (including theoretical orientation)

It is necessary within the contracting process for supervisees to be aware of the professional practice guidelines within which the supervisor is working, particularly if two different professions are involved. The DCP have produced some very useful guidelines for continued supervision (as mentioned in the previous section) and The Committee on Training in Clinical Psychology has also produced helpful guidance for training supervision (BPS, 1995b). It is helpful to have an open discussion around the philosophical underpinnings within which we all work, in particular that reduction of harm to the service user or carer (and the supervisee) is paramount. Linked to this is the need to be clear about the supervisor's responsibility to act if this principle is not being adhered to, if necessary without the supervisee's permission (although any action should be made explicit to the supervisee). Part of the discussion around philosophical underpinnings may also need to include theoretical orientation of both supervisee and supervisor, particularly where there is some divergence. Open discussion around how this can be managed is imperative.

Ways of developing mutual trust

The development of a clear and negotiated contract begins the process of developing mutual trust between the supervisee and supervisor. Many of the above conversations can engender a sense of mutual trust, as there is clarity around the role and expectations of the supervisee and supervisor. Other ways of developing the supervisory alliance include the use of *appropriate* humour. Appropriate self-disclosure may also help to develop the alliance. Questions that could be asked to facilitate the alliance further include: 'my image of successful supervision is . . .' or 'what I fear happening in supervision is . . .'.

Ways of constructively challenging when appropriate

It can be helpful to have a discussion in the contracting process about the need to challenge and give feedback. There are a number of principles to be borne in mind, for example that feedback should be specific and perceived as genuine (Scaife, 2009). The supervisee may have suggestions about how they prefer to be challenged and it can be helpful for the supervisor to provide a model of being open to challenge.

Negotiation regarding the use of the parallel process

The parallel process is a term coined by Harold Searles and has been integrated into the Hawkins and Shohet model of supervision (Hawkins and Shohet, 2006). The supervisor's reactions within the supervision are explored as potentially helpful information that may be paralleling the therapeutic process. An example of this could be the supervisor consistently finding it hard to focus on the supervisee when one particular service user or carer is being discussed (despite being fully alert and attuned during the rest of the supervision session). It may be helpful to explore this reaction to see if this resonates with the supervisee's experience of being with this person in session. It may be that this is important information about the supervisor's difficulty in connecting with the supervisee that parallels the supervisee's difficulty in connecting with the service user. This may also parallel the person's difficulty in connecting with others in their life and may provide useful information for the therapeutic aims. It is also important to be very aware of your own issues as a supervisor when using the parallel process and that this reaction is not just because you are tired!

It is important to be explicit about the use of the supervisor's feelings about the work being discussed in supervision from the start. If this is to be one of the pieces of information to be used in understanding the therapeutic process, then this needs to be negotiated rather than assumed. One of my biggest mistakes as a supervisor was to begin to use the parallel process with a qualified colleague in supervision without having agreed this first. The discomfort the supervisee felt quickly became apparent and we were able to stop and openly address this. But this was a good lesson in clarity around contracting and what will and will not be the focus in supervision.

Although the use of the parallel process may have been made explicit at the start it may be important to be tentative (at least initially) about its use, particularly for those who have not experienced it before. The use of the parallel process can help the development of the supervisory relationship over time as it models mutual disclosure.

The issue of how to deal with personal issues that arise for either supervisee or supervisor links to the use of the parallel process. Working in this way is inherently about using one's own intuition and self and, as such, discussing personal issues is part of the work. It is perhaps important to reflect on the focus of the work being the service user or carer and the difference between therapy and supervision. This is something that I have found particularly helpful to reflect on during my own supervision process.

Confidentiality boundaries

Confidentiality boundaries are important on many levels:

- Service user/carer information.
- Contextual information.
- Therapist (supervisee) information.
- Supervisor information.

It is important to have clarity around what information will be brought to supervision and that this fits with any clinical governance arrangements: for example, some services make it clear that supervisees must not divulge the name or other identifying features of the service user or carer within supervision. Personally for me it is important to know a name because this can help me connect more fully with the therapeutic process.

At times it may be important that the supervisee keeps confidential contextual information about where they are working. The limits of what can be brought and what will be done with any information that is brought need discussion. Similarly the supervisee may wish to bring personal issues that affect their work into supervision, and this again needs to be negotiated. The supervisor must bear in mind their duty of care if the supervisee divulges any information that may put themselves or any service user or carer at risk, and the responsibility to act on this information (in collaboration with the supervisee) that the supervisor holds. At times it may be highly beneficial for the supervisor to divulge aspects of their work or themselves, and again having clear boundaries about the confidentiality of this information is important. If the supervision work is to be taken into any other arena by the supervisor (e.g. own supervision of supervision or peer supervision) then this needs to identified as part of the contracting process. As part of this (if appropriate), the name of the supervisor's supervisor should be divulged. This is always part of my practice as there may be potential conflicts of interest. These boundaries can sometimes be difficult to manage: for example, I was working in a peer supervision group when it became clear that I knew the supervisee that a colleague was discussing. The conversation was stopped and we discussed the appropriateness of continuing, and at what level the supervision work could be discussed.

Working with difference

It is important to bear in mind the socio-political context of the service users with whom the therapist is working and also of the therapist/supervisee and the supervisor. There are a number of ways in which difference may occur, including ethnicity, gender, sexuality, age, religion, social class and dis/ability. The difference may be between the service user or carer and the supervisee or between the supervisee and the supervisor, or the issues of difference may emerge as a contextual factor. There may also be assumptions made about 'sameness' – exploring these issues in supervision can be very enlightening and can help us all to continue to work on our own prejudices, biases and assumptions. To have had an open discussion about difference and sameness in the initial contracting stages can make it much more possible to work with this, rather than avoiding it. I have had conversations within contracting meetings about 'visible' differences (e.g. age) and the assumptions we might both make, but while also acknowledging less 'visible' differences (e.g. class) and why this may become important within the work. Within the training I have been doing for a number of years for both supervisees and supervisors, exploring working with difference is a key element. This starts with exploring how people define and understand themselves in terms of difference and how this may impact on the supervisor–supervisee dyad. There is an emphasis on the importance of developing a supervisory relationship where difference can be discussed, and on keeping a watchful eye within the supervisory process for any ways in which difference might have an impact.

System for review and feedback

Part of any supervision contract should include the need to review the process. This involves a system of ensuring that there can be regular feedback from both sides. Within some models of supervision, actively gaining feedback from both parties on the supervision session can be built into every session. Taking additional time on a regular basis can also ensure that both supervisee and supervisor take time to reflect at a deeper level.

Summary

A number of themes emerge when considering contracting for supervision and it is very important to cover a multitude of issues. It is worth taking the time now to highlight these issues and discuss and get agreement, as this potentially can save so much time in the long run. My method of approaching contracting as a supervisor is, in the first meeting, to very much focus on the supervisee's issues regarding beginning supervision. Often many of the above issues will emerge naturally as part of this conversation. Between the first and the second meeting I will go back to my 'list' to check what has been covered and what has been missed, so I can then raise this at the second meeting. I also focus on checking that we have a *shared* understanding of what has been discussed and agreed and, if necessary, I will revisit any of the issues in later sessions. It is hugely important to 'set the tone' for supervision from the start. This will help to foster an open and reflective relationship so that, whatever happens in the supervisory process, this can be faced between the two (or more) of you together.

The supervisory process

This section will cover the key issues to consider during the process of supervision. Many of the issues discussed within the previous section may of course emerge throughout the ongoing process of supervision.

In-session structure

An important element of supervisory process is the structure of each session. This will vary between models of therapy and supervision. Some models have clarity around the beginning, middle and end of each session. For example, in CBT supervision there are tasks to be completed at the start (e.g. checking in, reviewing homework, setting an agenda), those that occur in the main part of supervision (e.g. reviewing progress, reviewing agenda, summarising) and those that occur at the end (e.g. review of learning, setting of homework, feedback). For other models an informal agenda may be discussed and agreed at the start and reviewed throughout, but no further structures are set in place, such as when using an inter-personal approach. For other models, for example within a person-centred approach, no agenda is set as it is important to allow for issues to emerge as part of the supervisory process.

Across-session structure, including preparation

Some models of supervision can be helpful for supervisees and supervisors across supervision sessions to monitor if all elements of supervision are being considered. The Hawkins and Shohet (2006) model discussed previously can be used for this purpose, to check that all seven modes are being used where appropriate. Similarly, the Systems Approach (Holloway, 1995) provides helpful structures to monitor that supervision is covering a wide range of tasks and functions.

It is also important in the process for both supervisees and supervisors to remember to prepare! Depending on the model of therapy and supervision, preparation may take different forms: from active reviewing of notes and planning potential agendas, to quiet contemplation on the previous session(s). Building in the time around supervision to prepare will benefit both the supervisee and supervisor.

The supervisory relationship

It is widely acknowledged that the supervisory relationship is an important influence on the effectiveness of supervision and on the satisfaction of supervisees (e.g. Ladany, Ellis and Friedlander, 1999; also see Chapter 4 of this book). There are three domains of the supervisory alliance (linked to the therapeutic alliance), namely: the bond between the supervisor and supervisee, the agreement on the supervisory tasks and the agreement on the overall goals and aims of supervision (Bordin, 1983). In a study to address this, Beinart (2004) found that satisfaction with supervision from a supervisee perspective was the strongest predictor of effective supervision, followed by rapport. Clohessy (2008) examined the supervisory relationship from the supervisor's perspective and found that the quality of the relationship was linked to three factors: contextual influences, the flow of supervision and core relational factors. Other studies have also looked at what is helpful in supervision (e.g. Cushway and Knibbs, 2004) and a positive supervisory relationship is one of the most important factors.

As we gain a greater insight into the elements of the supervisory relationship, how can this help supervisors to facilitate better relationships? Some key themes emerge:

- being boundaried;
- being clear;
- being consistent;
- acknowledging contextual factors;
- creating an environment of mutual trust;
- being curious.

Clohessy (2008) gives some interesting ideas about how to resolve problems in the supervisory relationship, starting with exploring the problem collaboratively and clarifying any misunderstandings that may have occurred. It is important then to re-establish boundaries and put time and effort into spending more time together. Clohessy states that it is important to focus and build on positive experiences whilst maintaining a positive, non-blaming stance. There is also a balance to be struck around wanting a resolution versus remaining concerned about any on-going issues. The issue of what happens when things go wrong is discussed further below.

What happens when things go wrong?

It is important to explore the issue collaboratively when things start to go wrong in supervision. There are a number of models and approaches that could be used. Having discussed, as part of contracting, the issues of difference and sameness this could then be something to turn to and explore further. Are the problems in the supervisory relationship linked to differences in approach associated with issues of diversity? Are they linked to differences in learning style and therefore a fundamentally different approach to learning and supervision?

A useful model to help explore what has happened when things go wrong in supervision is the Core Qualities Model (Ofman, 2001). This was introduced to me in some training I attended by Michael Carroll and I have found it immensely useful.

The model states that we all have our *core qualities*. For example, one of my core qualities is a sense of responsibility. This is an essential part of my life – if I commit to something, then I am responsible. On many occasions this is a helpful core quality as it means that things get done and it allows people to trust in my commitment. The model states, however, that if we engage in our core quality too much then this can become our *pitfall*. So, if I take too much responsibility too much of the time then this can have a negative impact on many levels. It may have a negative impact on me – if I cannot let go of my sense of responsibility where appropriate, then I may risk becoming over-burdened and burnt out. It may have an impact of those around me – if I am always the one taking the responsibility it may not allow others to do so, thus potentially affecting their ability to develop and progress. It could also have an impact at an organisational level if I am seen as taking too much responsibility. The *challenge* to avoid our pitfall is to balance our core quality. So the balance for me is to monitor whether I need to take responsibility for an issue, and to consider whether this is someone else's responsibility. The model states that our *allergy* is the thing in other people that we cannot stand, and the opposite to our core quality. I am aware that I find it difficult to relate to people who appear to have a lack of commitment and sense of responsibility.

A common core quality that people working in the health profession may have is helping others. While this is obviously a positive core quality, the pitfall to this is that people may help too much – again to the detriment of themselves resulting in burnout, or to the detriment of those in their care leading to a potential lack of developing independence. This is a core quality that could emerge for the supervisor, the supervisee or both.

A common core quality that can emerge in supervision, particularly within a training supervision where a supervisee may have spent many years trying to access that training, is perfectionism. Again this is a very positive core quality – to want to do well and have high standards – but the pitfall if this is used too much (particularly within a highly stressful training situation with multiple demands) is that it may have a detrimental effect on the supervisee in a number of ways. Again there is the potential for burnout if every piece of work has to be perfect. There is also the risk that the supervisee misses out on some real opportunities for learning, in terms of experimenting and taking risks to show mistakes in supervision. The challenge for the supervisee is to hold on to the positive aspect of having healthy perfectionism whilst balancing this with the need to be 'good enough' at times. It is worth bearing in mind that a supervisor may become the supervisee's allergy if they do not have the same perfectionist tendencies!

This model can be helpful to explore in supervision. It could be done as part of the contracting process, so that it is within the dialogue of supervision from the start, or it could be utilised when there seems to be some 'stuckness'. It can also be just a helpful way of exploring what we need to do to work the most effectively together. For example, I have had a conversation with one of my supervisees recently where we recognised that their core quality is that of calmness, and given that my style of working is in quite a fast-paced manner I could easily become their allergy. This allowed me to see how slowing my pace in our meetings is helpful for this particular person.

When supervision starts to go wrong it is important to begin to tackle this as soon as possible. It may be that feedback is needed on both sides, utilising the ideas described below. It may be that giving someone feedback helps to move the person and the supervisory process forward. In giving feedback it is important to listen to the person, not make any assumptions and to hear their perspective. It is important also to watch for the emotional reaction that this may evoke and to be aware of any emerging sense of shame that needs to be discussed. It may also be that the best outcome for both parties is that the supervisory relationship is ended.

Giving feedback

Giving feedback is linked but does not equate to evaluation. At its best, feedback is an integrated and mutual process in supervision. One model developed by Hawkins and Shohet (2006) that is often used to highlight issues in feedback includes the following elements:

- *Clear*: There should be no ambiguity about feedback that is being given, particularly when it is negative feedback. The supervisee (or supervisor) should not be left in any doubt as to what the issue is and what needs to be done about it.

- *Owned*: The individual must be clear that this is their own opinion and that they are not being swayed by other (e.g. contextual) factors.
- *Regular*: Feedback should be part and parcel of the supervision process.
- *Balanced*: Supervision should include both positive and negative feedback. The singularly most often used complaint that I hear from supervisees is that the feedback they have had from their supervisors is 'everything is fine' and they are doing well. This gives no scope for development in the supervisee as they have no sense of what they need to work on to improve their practice.
- *Specific*: This is linked to the point above – unless the supervisee (or supervisor) is given specific feedback about how they can improve their work, the time given to feedback is wasted.

I would also add two other elements:

- *Mutual*: Feedback should be both ways. In order to foster a learning environment where it is clear that both the supervisee and the supervisor are learning (which I believe to be the case), both need feedback. The supervisor must model to the trainee that they welcome receiving feedback on a regular basis.
- *Respectful*: There are ways to consider how feedback is given in order to be as respectful to the supervisee (or supervisor) as possible. One way to do this might be to let the supervisee know that there is a need to give some feedback and to negotiate how and when (not if) this could be given.

Evaluation

The following has emerged from the work I have done with colleagues over the last few years, in supervision and in supervisor training, as a model of good practice for supervisors regarding evaluation:

- Contract with the supervisee about any evaluative process within the first 2 to 3 weeks of the supervision. If this is a training placement be specific about what is expected using the programme documentation as guidance. Familiarise yourself with the assessment paperwork and the competencies that are to be assessed.
- Be explicit about your own model of learning and your own model of competence.
- Negotiate the need to 'challenge' what the supervisee feels comfortable with in terms of getting constructive criticism.

- Use direct observation (sitting in, audio or videotapes, live supervision) on which to form your opinion and be explicit about which aspect of the supervisee's work you are assessing.
- Use objective measures if applicable.
- Consider if there are any barriers, from either you or the supervisee, that may affect the possibility of open reflecting on skills.
- Be open throughout (there should be no surprises at formal evaluation points).
- Consider the need for your supervision on being a supervisor. Consider the individual(s) you can contact within your own system to discuss any concerns.

Within a training placement, in addition:

- Use the university tutor for advice. It does not have to be a major problem to contact tutors, and part of their job is to help train and support supervisors.
- If there are major areas of concern that continue despite regular feedback, make sure everything is documented and utilise the tutors to follow the programme guidelines and due process.

Observation

It is essential within any training supervision that the supervisee is observed. This could be either by joint working, direct observation, audio or videotapes or a combination. Scaife (2009) states that there are a number of advantages to using observation in supervision, including the supervisee getting an enhanced empathy for the therapeutic process, that it can remove doubts about competence and that it can be an adjunct to therapy if, for example, tapes are used as part of the therapy and given to the service user as well. It is also clear from the literature that we all tend to have selection biases in self-reporting (often an unrealistically negative self appraisal, but can also be an unrealistic positive self-appraisal; Collins, 2002) and it is important to balance this with an objective opinion. The practical considerations of taping include the technical aspects of how this will be done and also obtaining consent. It is suggested that a specific process should be followed by the supervisee to gain consent:

- Discuss the purpose of taping with the service user.
- Give the opportunities for the service user to discuss any concerns.
- Gain consent without coercion – the service user is entitled to refuse consent at the outset of therapy or at any point.
- Ensure that the service user knows who will be listening to the tapes.
- Obtain formal written consent for taping.

How and when observation is done can be negotiated between the supervisee and the supervisor. There are also a number of other dimensions that need to be considered, for example who listens to the tape (supervisee, supervisor or both), when (in or outside supervision), full or part tape, focus (supervisee skill, therapeutic relationship), macro or micro skill (e.g. alliance building, ending sessions) and control (supervisee or supervisor).

The paperwork

An important practical element to consider in supervision is what paperwork needs to be completed and when. This needs to relate to any clinical governance arrangements and, in the case of training supervision, any university requirements. The DCP Policy (BPS, 2005) offers minimum professional guidance regarding continued supervision:

- Keep copies of all supervisory contracts and any updates.
- Record the date and duration of each session.
- Keep a supervision log book and enter notes on the content of each session, the decisions reached and the agreed actions.
- Record in writing all reviews of supervision.

There are additional paperwork requirements within a training placement: to complete a placement plan within the first 2 to 3 weeks of placement, to complete paperwork around the mid-placement mark and to review the paperwork at the end of placement. Individual training programmes have differing paperwork and guidance around their completion (the who, what and when) should be available. If there are more than two supervisors involved in a placement it is important to negotiate if one or both will take responsibility for completing the evaluation paperwork.

Methods in supervision

Creative approaches to supervision

Reflective practice exercises can be used in supervision to help deepen understanding and find new ways forward. I have used one exercise to explore the therapeutic relationship, particularly when it feels as if supervision (and possibly therapy) has become stuck in some way. This could be used in various ways regarding relationships – with service users/carers, with colleagues, with managers – and involves the following process:

Suggest the supervisee closes their eyes to focus on a particular image (this is not necessary if the supervisee feels uncomfortable doing this). Let the supervisee know that you are going to ask them to focus on a particular image, that you will firstly ask them to picture a scene and then spend a few minutes exploring that image. Then ask them to picture the following scene:

> 'You and the service user (colleague, manager) are standing in front of a lift and the lift arrives – what happens next? '

Allow the supervisee to imagine the scene quietly for a few moments and then ask some of the following questions, staying with the image they have in their mind:

- Allow the image to develop . . . what happens next . . .
- What can you see . . . hear . . . feel . . . smell?
- What do you notice about the lift – is it small and cramped or spacious and open?
- Who presses the button?
- Does the lift go up or down . . . fast or slow . . .?
- Where are you standing in relation to the other person?
- Where does the lift take you?

The next step in the process is 'reflecting on reflecting', where the supervisee and supervisor consider what emerged from engaging in this process. Were there any new insights gained into this dyad that might help find a way forward? How might this influence how the supervisee approaches the next session?

Hawkins and Shohet (2006) offer exercises that can be done exploring every mode of supervision. For example, if the focus is on Mode 1 (the service user) the supervisor could ask the supervisee to close their eyes and picture the last time they saw a particular service user – what do they notice about this person that is different? This can then be explored in more detail to enhance insight into the service user.

Other creative approaches include the use of metaphors and stories in supervision. Creative materials such as art or collages can be used, or more physical approaches such as sculpts or empty chair work. Mooli Lahad provides some interesting ideas to creative approaches for the interested reader (Lahad, 2000). In my most effective supervision my supervisor has helped me move between various different approaches in a fluid and playful manner, experimenting with methods that have not always felt comfortable (e.g. empty chair) but nearly always resulting in some new insight and way forward.

Interpersonal process recall (IPR)

Interpersonal process recall (IPR) is a method used in supervision through the medium of tapes. It is a process that was developed by Kagan and colleagues (e.g. Kagan-Klein and Kagan, 1997), where the supervisor takes the role of enquirer. It is a method of using tapes in supervision where the supervisee has complete control over the tape. The supervisee reviews the tape beforehand and decides where it would be useful to start. The supervisee starts the tape in supervision and decides when to stop. The supervisor then uses a number of facilitative questions to help explore the issues raised for the supervisee within the material presented: for example, 'what thoughts were going through your mind at this point' or 'how did you think the other person was feeling'. The aim of this approach is to help the supervisee access aspects of the session that they had been previously unaware.

Role-playing and modelling

Aspects of the therapy can be explored in supervision through the use of role-playing, where the supervisee can take a number of roles. They may take the role of the service user and recreate an aspect of the therapy with the supervisor acting as therapist. This can often provide useful insights into the service user's position. The supervisee could also role-play themselves, with the supervisor acting as the service user. It is possible here to create different scenarios where different interventions are used and the supervisee can be creative about their approach. Certain techniques may also be modelled by the supervisor in supervision: for example, it may be helpful for the supervisor to model exposure work with the supervisee so they understand the impact of this.

Ethical issues in supervision

There are a number of ethical principles related to supervision that have been helpfully summarised by Scaife (2009):

- *Autonomy:* individuals have the right to freedom of action and choice.
- *Beneficence:* actions should do good, using knowledge to promote human welfare.
- *Fidelity:* being faithful to promises made, and to 'right'/proper practices.
- *Justice:* ensuring that people are treated fairly – equitably and appropriately – in light of what is due to them.
- *Non-maleficence*: striving to prevent harm.

There are also a number of major ethical issues that can emerge in supervision:

- *Confidentiality:* The many levels of confidentiality (service user/carer information, contextual information, therapist (supervisee) information and supervisor information) were discussed previously. It is important that confidentiality is maintained across all levels throughout the supervision process.

- *Ensuring standards:* The supervisor (and the supervisee) has a gate-keeping role to ensure standards are maintained and that the public is protected.
- *Accountability:* The supervisor and the supervisee are accountable on a number of levels – to each other, the NHS and the public.
- *Following due process:* It is important ethically to follow due process whenever there are any concerns raised in supervision. This is to ensure that all supervisees are treated fairly and given the opportunity to develop any skills that are needed.
- *Awareness of issues related to difference and diversity:* Another ethical issue in supervision is being aware of any issues of difference and diversity – to be able to actively address any difficulties that emerge and to pro-actively utilise any positive impact of diversity.
- *Dual relationships:* There are guidelines for clinical psychology training around not having sexual relationships between supervisor and supervisee. There can also clearly be difficulties if there is a friendship between supervisee and supervisor. Other difficulties may emerge if the supervisor is also the manager of the supervisee. The crucial question is how does this dual relationship affect the supervision? Is it possible, given this relationship, that supervision will be open, free, able to focus on all elements of the work and able to engage in challenge? What would happen if the supervisor had serious concerns about the super-visee's work? Could they follow, objectively, other ethical principles (e.g. accountability, following due process)?
- *Power:* Many of these issues above link to an over-arching theme of power. It is important to recognise the power a supervisor holds, often to the point of influencing whether a supervisee continues to work in their chosen profession. This power should be openly acknowledged and not hidden. Power can be used in positive ways to help influence and develop supervisees, but is it also important to acknowledge that with power comes responsibility and the potential to do harm.
- *Codes of conduct:* To help supervisors and supervisees around any ethical and professional issues there are codes of conduct. For clinical psychologists these include guidance from the BPS (2009) and the Health Professions Council (2008b).

Helping supervisees to develop professionally and personally

Considering the links between personal and professional development is one of the foci in *Personal Development and Clinical Psychology* (Hughes and Youngson, 2009). This book considers how important it is to consider developing personally within the role of the clinical psychologist and how this can be approached in supervision; in Chapter 7 Joyce Scaife addresses this issue directly and suggests a number of approaches to help supervisees develop personally, including constructive challenge and reflective writing.

Ending a supervisory relationship

When does ending start? It is perhaps a cliché to say the ending starts at the beginning, or the beginning is the start of the end. But I would argue that it is important to consider the ending at the start, as part of the contracting process. The issues to consider regarding ending are obviously different if it is a fixed term supervisory arrangement (e.g. training placement) or an on-going arrangement. Additional issues need to be considered for the latter:

- Who will make the decision to end?
- How will this be done?
- What will be the ending period (i.e. the number of supervision sessions left)?
- What are the review points?

The decision to end may be forced, for example if the supervisor or supervisee leave their jobs or change their role. The decision may be made for positive reasons, for example if it is considered that the supervisee has made much progress within their work and it is timely to move on to another supervisor. It may be, however, that the decision is made because of negative reasons, for example the supervision is no longer beneficial for the supervisee. In this situation the supervision may have become stuck and it has not been possible to find a solution. It is the best option for both parties that this is accepted and the supervision is ended.

Making the best ending possible

There are a number of factors to consider in trying to make the best ending possible:

- *Timing*: Clarity around when the ending will be, and the date of the last session.
- *Clinical responsibilities and the ending for service users/carers*: Clarity around who will be discharged and who will need further input.
- *Evaluation*: Allowing time to discuss, in a sensitive and detailed way, the assessments the supervisor has made.
- *Feedback from the supervisee*: Allowing time for the supervisee to also give feedback on the supervision.

- *Completion of paperwork*: Time must be allowed for the completion of any paperwork that needs to be done. As this is often a summary of the work the supervisee has done over an extended period of time, it is important this is given the time it deserves.
- *The impact of ending*: The ending of supervision (particularly linked to the ending of a training placement) can often be a difficult time for supervisees. They are dealing with the impact on the service users of the ending of their work together, which may evoke past endings for many people. They are also dealing with their own feelings about ending both the therapeutic work and the supervisory process. It is important that time is allowed to discuss and acknowledge these feelings. In conjunction with this the supervisor may wish to openly acknowledge their feelings regarding the ending.
- *The supervisory relationship*: Considering the supervisor relationship during ending can be helpful, including: Where do we go from here? What will be the impact of any new working relationships and potentially having different roles in the future?
- *Unfinished business*: At the end of any supervisory relationship I try to determine whether there is any unfinished business between us by asking: Is there anything that we need to say to each other before we end?

Summary

The aim of this chapter was to provide a whistle-stop tour of the practical aspects of supervision and highlight the many issues to consider as a supervisee or supervisor throughout the process of supervision. Whilst some topics have been the focus of one section (e.g. beginning supervision) it may be that this also needs to be taken into consideration at other times during supervision. Taking these practical issues seriously and giving them consideration and time in supervision is important in providing the best possible service to services users and carers. It can also make this a hugely rewarding experience for both supervisees and supervisors.

In considering all of these practical elements, there are some key themes that emerge for me in providing supervision:

- The importance of *contracting* – at the start of supervision, within regular reviews and as a way of responding to any difficulties that emerge.
- Being *responsive* to the supervisee's needs, and having a range of methods/tools that can help with this process.

- Developing an effective *supervisory relationship*. Creating a safe base from which the supervisee can experiment with their work, take some risks and 'play' is, in my opinion, the bedrock of effective supervision. Although there are many practical elements to consider in supervision my advice would be: if in doubt, go back to the relationship.

I have worked as a clinical psychologist in a number of roles over the years (including therapist, team worker, supervisor, trainer and manager) and I have always argued for, and been fortunate to receive, supervision in every role. The value of having the reflective space to consider your work is immense and I hope that this chapter will help to guide the reader through the practical elements of planning, starting, engaging in and ending supervision.

Chapter 12

Conclusions

Ian Fleming and Linda Steen

We concluded the first edition of this book by reflecting on the status of supervision within clinical psychology and making a number of recommendations about the priorities for the immediate future. These included the suggestions to: carry out more research in order to evaluate both supervision and supervisor training; consider the most important tasks in pre-qualification and post-qualification supervision; consider the content of supervisor training for clinical psychologists and the question of who should deliver that training; attend to the issue of supervisor accreditation; further our knowledge about and understanding of the supervisory relationship; address issues of diversity and power within supervision.

This book has provided an overview of the issues directly relevant to supervision within the profession of clinical psychology, and in doing so has incorporated all those recommendations mentioned above. This has been achieved by contributions both by leading figures in the field of clinical psychology training in the UK and by experienced clinicians and supervisors, who have drawn on current research and practice and, where relevant, NHS policy. Whilst the focus has been on clinical psychology within the UK, many of the chapters have covered topics that apply equally to any professional group engaged in the practice of supervision.

At the beginning of this book we identified some of the changes that have taken place since the first edition was published in 2004. We asked a number of questions about the effect that external factors might have had on supervision in clinical psychology. These have been covered in a number of chapters and will be reviewed here, together with more general themes. We will end by considering future issues for supervision within clinical psychology.

Service issues and external influences

If we start from the outside and work in, our priority should be to consider the impact of service changes and policies on the practice of supervision in clinical psychology. In Chapter 3 Graham Turpin stated that the most significant change since the first edition of this book has concerned applied psychology rather than clinical psychology alone. He went on to say that 'Despite the obvious interdivisional rivalries, applied psychology has been accepted as an overarching construct both within and outwith the profession' (p. 25).

Whatever the accuracy and application of this remark overall, clinical psychology continues to exert a particular identity. The strengths and breadth of clinical psychologists' work clearly remain attractive, as evidenced by the ever increasing demand for places on training programmes. Strategic Health Authorities (SHAs) remain convinced of the need to fund this training, and policy documents retain the use of the descriptor 'clinical' rather than 'applied'. These are some of the reasons why we felt it important to continue to focus on clinical psychology in this second edition.

One particularly influential service model that considers the contributions of a broader group of practitioners, including applied psychologists, and that has been discussed by several of the contributors to this book is the Increasing Access to Psychological Therapies (IAPT) programme in England. The impact of this programme on the development of supervision will be considered later in this chapter.

Different paths in the development of supervisor training and supervisory competence

'In the UK, the art and craft of supervision has not traditionally been learned through formal training but has passed from supervisor to supervisee' (Proctor, 2000: 20). As Proctor herself acknowledges, this system of 'handing on' supervision skills is now being challenged in a variety of ways and no more so than in the clinical psychology arena. Perhaps more than in any other area of supervision there have been significant developments in supervisor training, both within and outside clinical psychology, since the publication of the first edition of this book.

All the contributors to this book share an important role in developing good practice. It is interesting that within a small profession in a small country there are divergences. In Chapter 3, although there is an extensive discussion of supervision and a reference to the development of agreed competences with respect to IAPT, there is limited mention of the Supervisor Training and Recognition (STAR) initiative. On first reading, it might seem as if these two developments have taken place in isolation from each other. In reality there has been a lot of contact between individuals involved in the two initiatives and their inclusion in this book is representative of this. Furthermore, Jan Hughes has been involved in developing a form of supervisor training for IAPT staff that is derived from the established training programme for clinical psychology supervisors at Sheffield, itself based on the STAR criteria.

However, any suggestion that there is a complete correspondence between the perceptions of supervisory competences within the two developments should be accompanied by a note of caution. Despite a lot of common ground, there are differences: for instance, in the differing views of the range of tasks and the learning models within supervision, and the importance of the supervisory relationship, some of which are discussed in David Green's discussion of different models of supervisor training. Arguably some of these differences can be traced to the different emphases in the psychological models underpinning supervision. Of course, another factor has been the different requirements and demands of supervision within specific services. In this way supervision can be seen to be flexible and able to adapt to the particular needs of different service contexts. Whether there are losses or gains in the quality of that offered remains to be seen and is a fruitful area for further research. The different interpretations made of supervision are discussed in more detail later on, as is the general increasing demand in health services for 'supervision'; this single example points to the need for greater clarity and agreement about what is required of and from supervision in the future. It is interesting now to reflect on how this issue was discussed in the first edition of this book.

Similarities between clinical psychology and other health professions

A number of the important developments concerning supervision and clinical psychology have incorporated the experience gained by other UK health professions. In the first edition of this book it was suggested that clinical psychology was engaged in 'catching up' with other health and care professions. How much has been achieved in the intervening years and how much can we learn from the experience of other professions?

This book contains some discussion of the supervisory arrangements that exist for other UK health professions. Real comparisons are hindered by, for example, the lack of details concerning the form and content of training of supervisors. On occasions, as was discussed in Chapter 10, there can also appear to be a blurring between the concepts of supervision, mentoring, consultation and coaching, with different professions either using different terms to refer to the same activity or using the same term to mean different things.

Developments in assuring the quality of supervision have incorporated learning from other professions. The model in which the professional body is responsible for accrediting supervisors was developed for other health professions, as was the role of the Higher Education Institution (HEI) as the 'gatekeeper' within this process. (This is discussed further in a later section below concerning accreditation of supervisors.) The previous experience of other professions, however, was less influential in the development of the content and process of supervisor training.

Learning from research

One of the concluding comments of the first edition referred to the relative paucity of research dedicated to both supervision within clinical psychology and supervision practice in the UK. We stated that the book would have been considerably slimmer had we not drawn on literature from counselling and psychotherapy and on research carried out in the USA. Whilst several of the contributors to the current book (e.g. Wheeler and Cushway, Chapter 2 and Beinart, Chapter 4) have noted the continued preponderance of American research (see, for example, Wheeler and Richards, 2007), which often uses either trainee populations or analogue situations, in the intervening years there have been significant developments in this area, many of which have been both carried out and reported by contributors to this book. Given our status as scientist-practitioners, it is important that we keep abreast of these developments and incorporate into our learning new knowledge from research and practice.

What has been learned from research?

Taking as their starting point both the methodological flaws of some of the earlier supervision research (see, for example, Ellis et al., 1996) and the dearth of research using UK clinical psychology populations, two particularly influential developments in supervision research that have been reported in the current book are those undertaken by Helen Beinart and colleagues in Oxford and by Derek Milne and colleagues in Newcastle.

For the past decade, Helen Beinart and colleagues have been undertaking a programme of research to examine in detail the factors that predict the quality of the supervisory relationship. This has led to the development of a valid and reliable measure of the supervisory relationship from the *supervisee's* perspective, namely the Supervisory Relationship Questionnaire (SRQ; Beinart, 2002; Palomo, 2004) and work is currently underway to develop a measure from the *supervisor's* perspective (Clohessy, 2008). Through this, we now have a much clearer picture about what needs to be in place to aid the development of a 'good enough' supervisory relationship, which includes establishing a clear contract, creating a safe, boundaried space and establishing opportunities for regular, mutual and open feedback.

Derek Milne and colleagues' work has similarly been in response to recurring problems of poor conceptualisation and measurement in supervision research carried out over the past 30 years. They have drawn on the 'fidelity framework' (Bellg et al., 2004) to structure a programme of 'small N' qualitative research, through which they have developed a series of new supervision-specific measures, each linked to one of the five fidelity levels, namely treatment design, training of supervisors, delivery of supervision, receipt of supervision and supervision enactment. This work is reported upon in detail in Chapter 9.

Both of these developments have important implications for the assessment and enhancement of the quality of supervision and for supervisor training, both within UK clinical psychology and more generally, and this will be returned to in later sections of the chapter. Worthy of note here is the fact that both programmes of research have provided opportunities for trainee clinical psychologists and undergraduates to carry out research projects in the field of supervision, reflecting the growing interest in and acceptance of supervision research within both the NHS and HEIs.

Training clinical psychologists to be supervisors

In developing supervision what are the most important issues concerning training of supervisors? Within this book a number of key issues have been identified.

Providers of supervisor training

There appears to have been little change since 2004 in who are the main providers of supervisor training for clinical psychologists. If anything, a greater proportion of training is now provided by clinical psychology training programmes based in universities across the UK and funded by the local NHS. HEIs continue to be best placed to articulate and deliver supervisor training, and to take on associated roles connected to developments in supervisory provision.

Staff members of clinical psychology training programmes are well placed to continue to have the lead role in providing training for supervisors. They already have a close working relationship with large numbers of local clinical psychologists and, for a significant proportion, these relationships date back to their qualification through these training programmes.

The relationship between clinical tutor and clinical psychologist necessitates clarity, honesty and an appreciation of the tasks of supervision. Clinical training staff members are also likely to work as clinicians in the NHS and other healthcare settings and thus will appreciate the pressures that can impinge on supervision.

The costs of providing high quality supervisor training are not insignificant, and the amount of training recommended by the BPS may exceed that provided for other professional groups. Furthermore, if the issue of evaluating training is to be seriously addressed (see below), this will require the allocation of resources. Another factor that is likely to support ongoing provision of training for supervisors is the fact that it is provided free of charge. In contrast, the significant costs attached to alternative training will continue to act as a dis-incentive to those seeking training. Finally the provision of excellent supervision on clinical placements (which correspond to approximately 50% of the 3 years of doctoral training for clinical psychologists) is a necessity, and should be seen as part of the contract for training.

On the Manchester clinical psychology programme the costs incurred in our annual 5-day supervisor training programme have been calculated and are modest and manageable, but without access to 'free' teachers and venue they would be considerable. The training is provided free of charge, and it is acknowledged that this is a constituent of the partnership between the university and local NHS, with mutual benefits: trainees become qualified and clinicians gain Continuing Professional Development (CPD) skills that are of benefit to their employers, especially in the current era of increased demands on clinical psychologists for supervision and management. In this way, there is a clear feedback loop for the SHA in funding supervisor training on behalf of local NHS Trusts.

Wheeler and Cushway (Chapter 2) refer to earlier difficulties in attracting clinicians to supervisor training. In Manchester there has been regular supervisor training for over 15 years, and it has been our experience that the training is increasingly popular and we are regularly oversubscribed. Fortunately, our two neighbouring training programmes provide supervisor training and between us we can usually meet the demand. It is our impression that there has been a culture change over the last 20 years in that clinical psychologists now expect to supervise and look forward to supervising. In turn, they want to receive training in how to supervise, they understand the need to evaluate their supervisory practice and they want support to maintain these skills. Although historically the focus has been on supervising other clinical psychologists (especially those in training), there is an increasing recognition of the role of supervising members of other professions, and the need to understand the attendant complexities.

Interprofessional learning

Are there advantages to interprofessional (or multi-disciplinary) training in supervision skills? Within the NHS there are repeated calls for interprofessional working and learning (and by implication supervision), therefore should clinical psychologists be developing training with members of other professions? Although there is little existing practice to consider, Butler has described such a scheme in Plymouth that is open to placement supervisors from Clinical Psychology, Social Work, Nursing and Occupational Therapy (Butler, 2007). Feedback from participants was positive, and there are plans for the training to be continued and for better evaluation of this to take place.

Consistent with policy developments such as those described in Chapter 3, it would seem that the greater advantage may lie within the requirements for cross-specialism supervision across the family of applied psychology.

Training methodologies

Scaife (2008) has offered some interesting advice for trainers from a constructivist perspective that reminds us of the need to develop an environment in which learning through reflection can take place, and Milne and Scaife (2008) utilise a framework of evidence-based practice to highlight the disparity between desired and actual methods employed in training in supervisory skills. Their conclusions encouraged a strong consensus on what trainers might do, with some indications towards 'an integrative/ pluralistic/reflexive (i.e. socially valid) device for defining a supervisor training system', and suggested that trainers employ a range of 'critical instructional strategies' (Kaslow et al., 2004), including modelling, role-play, the use of vignettes, in vivo experiences, supervised experiences and 'other real-world experiences'.

Content of training

Learning outcomes for introductory supervisor training have been adopted by the BPS, most recently as an Appendix to the *Standards for Doctoral Programmes in Clinical Psychology* (BPS, 2010). By implication, this content is suitable for all Divisions of the BPS. Given the concerns expressed in Chapters 7 and 8 of this book, it is important to note the inclusion of content concerning difference and diversity. Other important elements of supervision discussed in this volume are reflected in these competences, for example that of establishing an effective supervisory relationship (see Chapter 4).

Coincidentally an alternative development for supervision, associated with the IAPT service development, has constructed a list of competences for supervisors (see Roth and Pilling, 2008d). Although there are certain divergences from the BPS competences, there is a lot of similarity in defining necessary supervisor competences between these two approaches. This is not surprising in view of the overlap of personnel involved, and the close communication about supervisory developments within the profession of clinical psychology. Finally, the lead in this has come from trainers who are members of the Group of Trainers in Clinical Psychology (GTiCP) and in recent years supervisory developments have been regularly discussed at meetings of the GTiCP. Furthermore, reference has been made in Chapter 6 to the attempt in Sheffield to map the IAPT-specific competences onto more generic ones. Of relevance to this is the linkage between therapeutic models of psychology and supervision models, and David Green's discussion in Chapter 5 is particularly pertinent. The future trajectory of these different approaches to supervisory skills remains to be seen.

Developing a curriculum for supervisor training

Within this book there has been a focus on the *introductory* training in supervisory skills. Further training has been identified as an area that would benefit from more input. Although it has been agreed by trainers that the supervisory competences that have been ratified by the BPS can be taught in an introductory block of around 3–5 days, there is acknowledgement of the need to develop and deliver further, more *advanced* training. Recipients of such training would benefit both from training in new topics and also from the provision of an opportunity to re-visit the original material, drawing on their further experience of supervising. In the North West of England the three clinical psychology training programmes are discussing the constituents of further or advanced training and are collaborating to provide a regular series of such training workshops.

In Chapter 8, Aitken and Dennis refer to the need to develop (self) reflective abilities within supervisors, and this may be just one example of a topic for further training. Another area for further supervisor training is training in formats other than one-to-one, such as group supervision. The competences for conducting supervision in a group format described in Chapter 10 (Roth and Pilling, 2008d) could usefully form the basis for developing this training.

Transferring training into practice

Just as important as the training provided to individuals in supervisory skills is the need to ensure that the training is transferred into practice and maintained subsequently. The content of supervisor training, and its links to competences, facilitates the evaluation of its transfer into practice. One of the learning outcomes for supervisor training is that an individual will 'Have knowledge of techniques and processes to evaluate supervision, including eliciting feedback' (BPS, 2010, appendix 5).

Clearly, as avowed scientist-practitioners, clinical psychologists will be interested in assessing the outcome of both supervision and training of supervisors. As was reported in Chapter 6, currently there are few efforts to monitor whether training in supervision skills is transferred into practice. In Manchester we have started (in 2010) to do this in a limited way. We are utilising the experience of colleagues across the Pennines on the Leeds–Hull–Sheffield training programmes, and that of the NHS Education for Scotland (NES) introductory module in supervision skills for clinical psychologists. We are aware of the limitations of this, and one criticism voiced of the accreditation process is precisely that it accredits attendance in training but fails to accredit subsequent practice.

This cannot be disputed and we have identified the processes that would improve this evaluation: in particular the repeated direct assessment of supervisory practice, probably through videotaping, would be a major contribution. Kadushin (1992) makes some telling comments about the limitations of self-report as the basic data for supervision, and in our training we ask people to consider the notion of one of Manchester's famous football managers failing to watch his team and subsequently relying on their impressions alone to help them to adjust their play and tactics!

Although using a more robust method of evaluation (such as that described above) should be considered, the resources for achieving this are considerable and likely to have significant implications for the local staff of the clinical psychology training programme. It might be interesting to consider whether this enterprise could be shared with local managers of clinical psychology services, and potential pros and cons can be seen for doing this.

What should we evaluate? When supervisor training contains the competences described above, transfer into practice arguably should bring about measurable changes in both supervisor and supervisee behaviour, and ultimately in clinical outcomes. Since the first edition of this book was written in 2002, there has been a growth in the number of instruments available for evaluating aspects of supervision. Many of these focus on aspects of the *supervisory process*, and this seems to us like a good place to start. Some aspects covered include: What happens in supervision? Is the supervisor's behaviour leading to 'Kolbian' learning (Kolb, 1984) in the supervisee? Can these aspects be operationalised and measured? Is the supervisory relationship satisfactory? Can we assess the manifestation of reflexivity within supervision?

What methods should be used for evaluation? There is an extensive and growing range of paper assessment tools available, usually to be completed by supervisor or supervisee. An example of one such tool is the Supervisor Relationship Questionnaire (SRQ), which was developed by Helen Beinart and described by her in Chapter 4 of this book. Importantly, this tool was developed specifically within the UK using a clinical psychology population. There is also an increased interest in the use of portfolios in which individuals present and describe evidence in support of competences, and they are often required to complement this with some reflective comments on their practice and how it links to theory. Additional and more resource-heavy methods include the use of videotaped recordings of supervision and live supervision. These can then be rated using structured assessments. Alternative uses of audio or videotapes include reviewing supervision within an interpersonal process recall framework (Kagan-Klein and Kagan, 1997).

Within this book there has been a demand for a closer examination of the role of power in supervision (Chapters 7 and 8). Logically, these issues should be addressed in any evaluation of the effect on practice of supervisor training. In addition to considering these more general issues of power, evaluation might also want to consider whether the more specific issues of difference and diversity are *consistently* addressed within supervision, and how this affects professional development.

Ensuring quality: The role of accreditation

It is clear that attempts to ensure that training is transferred into practice and maintained over time are part of an attempt to investigate and prioritise the quality of supervision. A further part of this process has been the progress towards establishing a form of accreditation for suitably trained individuals. With respect to the previous section, it is accepted here that training does not automatically confer improved practice, but it is a logical first step in professional skill development.

Since the first edition of this book was published in 2004 the BPS, the professional body for clinical psychologists has opened a register for suitably trained supervisors (the Register of Applied Psychology Practice Supervisors, RAPPS); this can begin to assure the quality of both training in supervision skills and the resulting practice.

The accreditation process attained for psychologist supervisors has been described in Chapter 6. It is a significant development and one that will be open to all applied psychologists. Membership of the RAPPS will not be a *requirement* for providing supervision, although it is hoped that membership will grow as individuals recognise the value accruing from accreditation. In its current form, membership is based on receiving training in supervisory skills and there are real limitations on the assurance of high quality supervisory practice. In the main, this will be provided by the requirement for 5-yearly re-accreditation, and the responsibilities for this will fall on local training programme staff (in the case of clinical psychologists) and equivalent 'commissioners' of supervision (in other branches of applied psychology). An acknowledged shortfall in this provision is the requirement for initial registrants only to be trained. It is quite possible, however, that an assurance of high quality practice will be introduced at a later date.

The entry requirements reflected a degree of *realpolitik*. Although the bulk of the initial membership is likely to come from within the Division of Clinical Psychology (DCP), the RAPPS is for all applied psychologists within the BPS. Arrangements for supervision and supervisor training vary across different Divisions (including Educational and Child, Forensic, Occupational, Counselling, Health, Neuropsychology, Sport and Exercise) and the requirements needed to be universal. Once again, as mentioned at the start of this chapter, the tendency towards conceptualising ourselves as applied psychologists might be considered here.

In developing the RAPPS a lot was learned from the form of accreditation used by some other professions. The identification of the professional organisation as the best body to accredit supervisors is consistent with other health professions (e.g. the Chartered Society of Physiotherapy). Since historically the primary role for supervision in clinical psychology has been in professional training, it was logical to allocate a central role in the accreditation process to the training providers who both provide training and organise placement supervision. The potential difficulties associated with training programme staff (with responsibilities for *pre-qualification* training) making evaluations of qualified clinicians has been discussed and may be exaggerated, although only time will tell, and there seems little evidence available from other professions with similar arrangements. Other health professions generally operate the accreditation scheme on a voluntary basis, although there are indications that in medical training accredited status will be a requirement for clinical supervisors (e.g. London Deanery, 2010). There is evidence from some professions of a slow growth in re-accreditation after the initial period.

It may be pertinent to ask whether the proposed advantages of accreditation by the BPS continue to exist following the recent move to regulation by the Health Professions Council (HPC). With the transfer in 2009 of professional registration and associated tasks from the BPS to the HPC, it is difficult at the time of writing to know how supervision will be affected. Interestingly, in the first edition of this book we predicted that the (then) planned introduction of statutory regulation of the profession would lead to a further increase in the importance and profile of supervision. It appears, however, that currently the HPC insists on minimal standards concerning supervision and the competences desirably associated with this. This would seem to be inconsistent both with the increased depth of understanding of and competence in supervision that clinicians have developed during the past decade and also with the strong view within the profession that supervision should be a key aspect of ongoing registration in order to further enhance public protection and patient safety. It seems likely that the role played by professional bodies will continue – at least in the short term – and will complement the registration role of the HPC. It is unlikely that the latter will perceive any conflict in this situation, and the longer history of involvement of other health professions would support this view.

The role of power in supervision: Issues of gender, 'race' and culture

The continuing importance of acknowledging and understanding the role of power in supervision has been highlighted by Nimisha Patel (Chapter 7) and Gill Aitken and Maxine Dennis (Chapter 8), who have updated their chapters from the first edition. They demand an acknowledgement of the importance of gender, power and difference to effective supervision. It is likely that their views of psychology will not be shared by all readers, and in the wider profession there are varying views about the importance to psychological practice of context and what is referred to as 'politics'. We are reminded, for example, of the difficulties involved in teaching about the importance of social inequalities to psychological enquiry to trainee clinical psychologists and the enthusiasm with which it was received (Fleming and Burton, 2001).

The BPS accreditation criteria for clinical psychology training programmes state that supervisor training will include 'an understanding of the issues around difference and diversity in supervision' (BPS, 2010, appendix 5). It is interesting to know what attempts are made to address the issues of gender within supervisor training. It is important to note that in the current BPS *Standards for Doctoral Programmes in Clinical Psychology* (BPS, 2010) there is a clear reference to clinical psychologists needing to 'understand the impact of differences, diversity and social inequalities on people's lives, and their implications for working practices' (ibid.: 2.3.7.3). No current data exist to confirm whether this is included consistently within supervisor training, although in 2004 52% of training programmes organised training for supervisors on 'race', culture and gender issues in supervision. A 2009 survey of training programmes in the UK found that 23 (93%) delivered introductory training to supervisors that included the professionally agreed learning outcomes (Fleming, unpublished). In Manchester we devote approximately half a day (out of a 5-day introductory training) to discussing issues of difference and diversity in supervision.

It is interesting to consider the anecdotal evidence that trainers may often seek external 'experts' to provide teaching on this theme, as if they feel devoid of expertise themselves. Also in Manchester, before we had an established programme of supervisor training and organised ad hoc individual events, the only workshop we had to cancel because of poor uptake was one with this theme. A conversation with a tutor from another programme (who, incidentally, was perceived as an 'expert' in this area) suggested that this was not unusual. We are reminded of Maxine Dennis's comment:

> If psychologists are working in an area where they have few referrals from black and minority ethnic people, it may be that issues of race and culture are less likely to be prominent. It becomes the problem of the 'other' whom they have little contact with and their own views and experience of difference can be excluded from conscious awareness. How this can be brought into the supervisory arena when the supervisor, supervisee or client may not be visibly different may be an issue.
>
> (Dennis, 1998: 28–29)

The importance of the supervisory relationship

Since the first edition was published there is increasing evidence of the importance of the supervisory relationship on the perceived outcome of the supervisory process, regardless of theoretical orientation. Moreover, we now have a much greater understanding of the constituents of that relationship, which are comprehensively discussed by Helen Beinart in Chapter 4; other authors in this book similarly emphasise the importance of the supervisory relationship to high quality supervision (e.g. Wheeler and Cushway, Chapter 2 and Green, Chapter 5) and this is universally agreed across all supervision developments, including IAPT (Roth and Pilling, 2008c).

It is interesting to consider the extent to which a supervisory relationship can be developed and maintained in forms of supervision that do not involve face-to-face contact, such as on-line and telephone supervision; indeed, is it necessary to establish a good working alliance for effective supervision in these formats? In Chapter 10, some seemingly contradictory information was reported upon. On the one hand, participants of an on-line peer supervision group, who used aliases and did not meet each other face to face, reported having felt more comfortable about disclosing information because of their anonymity (Yeh et al., 2008). In contrast, in a study that used video-conferencing technology for supervision (Marrow et al., 2002), participants reported that establishing a face-to-face relationship prior to the video sessions was important in aiding the disclosure of information. Kanz (2001) concludes his review of on-line supervision by advising that the supervisor and supervisee 'should attempt to establish a relationship before beginning work on supervisory issues . . . (in order) to develop a trust and a willingness to share' (ibid.: 419). We have some way to go before a clear picture emerges about the role of the supervisory relationship in these forms of supervision. As Scaife (2009) notes, there are advantages to not having face-to-face contact: for example, the participants 'will not be overly influenced by visible differences such as gender, ethnicity and disability' (ibid.: 240); on the other hand, the advantages of the supervisor and supervisee having met each other include the opportunity for both participants to develop their personal commitment to each other. Subjective reports from colleagues who use these supervisory formats (either as supervisors or as supervisees) suggest that there are advantages to having met the other participant(s), even if only briefly.

A further point to consider is whether the supervisory relationship is more important to some supervisory tasks than others: for example, is the educative role as dependent as the supportive role on an effective supervisory relationship? This is relevant to the later discussion below on the need for clarity in what is required in supervision.

It is clear also that an effective supervisory relationship will incorporate reflection and awareness of the potential impact on it of gender, and difference and diversity. As pointed out in Chapter 4, in the early stages of developing a supervisory relationship participants tend to rely on general socio-cultural information about roles, moving to a more individualised relationship over time. Moreover, several contributors, including Aitken and Dennis (Chapter 8), have noted that parallel processes can operate in the supervisory encounter, therefore it is important to have a clear contract about the parameters of supervision through which both supervisor and supervisee can be active participants in the supervisory process, thus aiding the development of a good supervisory relationship with clear boundaries that allow for the emergence of trust and a relational history.

Creative and practical approaches to supervision

Within both pre-qualification and post-qualification clinical psychology, the predominant modes of supervision are talking and self-report. Perhaps this is not surprising, given that this is the way in which the majority of clinical psychology work is undertaken. Hughes (Chapter 11) suggests that alternatives are available and can be useful. She describes a number of creative approaches that can be used to deepen the supervisee's knowledge and understanding and are applicable within a range of therapeutic orientations; these approaches include role-play, modelling and engaging in reflective exercises. In a similar vein, in Chapter 10 Steen refers to the work of Milne and Oliver (2000), who suggest that it could be advantageous to apply techniques from one supervision format to another. One way for supervisees to learn *how* to carry out clinical work (procedural knowledge) rather than simply learn *about* it (declarative knowledge) is to have the work demonstrated, followed by an opportunity to put that into practice for themselves (see, for example, Kolb, 1984). In line with this, Green (Chapter 5) advises that supervisors should use supervision to demonstrate the technique or skill to be developed, for example by means of role-play, so that it can be practised in a safe forum before the trainee has to apply it with clients. Anecdotal evidence from trainee clinical psychologists suggests that, anxiety-provoking though the idea of role-play might be, those who have experience of it very much value this as a means of learning in supervision. Often it is the supervisor rather than the supervisee who is reluctant to deviate from habitual ways of carrying out supervision, and this has clear implications for the initial training of supervisors.

Within clinical psychology training, the BPS stipulates that:

> . . . it is essential that the trainees and supervisors have opportunities to observe each other at work: the trainee can learn much more from this and it is essential in order for the supervisor to give the trainee accurate and constructive feedback. Placements differ in the most appropriate opportunities for such direct contact: some may use joint clinical work

of some kind; others may prefer audiotape, videotape or a one-way screen. Some form of mutual observation of clinical work is regarded as essential.

(BPS, 2010, appendix 4, 6.4)

Our experience is that although audiotape (and, to a lesser extent, videotape) is used, this is often infrequent and irregular; notable exceptions to this are examples of model-specific supervision, such as cognitive behavioural therapy. Direct observation of the supervisee does take place, often in the early stages of the trainee's clinical placement, and there can be occasions in which joint work is undertaken (incidentally, also providing excellent opportunities for a supervisee to directly sample the performance of their supervisor), but this is by no means a regular occurrence.

In our supervisor training at Manchester, we try to encourage more regular direct 'sampling' of supervisees' work, recognising that there are limitations to relying solely on self-report, and we use the following quotation to illustrate the issues involved:

If we apply what we know about human behaviour to the supervisee reporting on his own performance, we recognise the inadequacies of such procedures as a basis for either good teaching or valid evaluation. As a consequence of anxiety, self-defence, inattention, and ignorance of what he should look for, the worker is not aware of much that takes place in the encounter in which he is an active participant; some of what he is aware he may fail to recall; if he is aware of it and does recall it, he may not report it

(Kadushin, 1992: 447)

Another practical aspect of supervision that has been considered in this book is that of supervision *format*. In Chapter 10, it was concluded that choice of supervision format can be determined by a number of factors, at both the individual and the training and service level. It has been suggested that some supervision formats may be more suitable for some modes of therapy than for others, not least so that the dynamics of the supervision can more closely mirror the dynamics of the therapeutic work. One example of this is the use of group supervision for those practitioners running groups.

There are important practical aspects of supervision that apply regardless of supervision format and it is very helpful to have been reminded of these in Chapter 11. These include: beginning supervision with a clear contract, which takes account of the developmental stage, learning style and supervisory needs of the supervisee and covers the 'unwritten rules' of supervision; discussing the practicalities of the supervision, such as where, when and how often to meet, as well as the limits of confidentiality; clarifying the supervisor's and supervisee's responsibilities; introducing a system for monitoring, review and feedback.

Skills for research supervision: Are they different?

As has been noted elsewhere, this book has focused on supervision of clinical work. For clinical psychology trainees, whose programme of study includes carrying out two pieces of research (namely, a placement-based service-level project and a doctoral research project), another type of supervision is *research* supervision. Moreover, for many qualified clinical psychologists working in either clinical or academic settings, research is a key aspect of their work; here, supervision for research work is seen as being just as important as supervision for clinical work, as is reflected in the BPS guidance, which states that, aside from being used for discussion of therapeutic work, supervision can be used to discuss 'management, supervision, team working, research and teaching' (BPS, 2005: 3).

In pre-qualification clinical psychology training, whilst there are BPS guidelines that specify minimum standards for certain aspects of placement supervision, such as the amount of time that should be spent in supervision, the guidance about research supervision is less detailed, stating simply:

> Each trainee must have a research supervisor who is competent in research supervision. . . . Supervisory loads must be monitored and be such that adequate supervision is provided to trainees. There should be a research agreement between supervisor and trainee that covers matters such as a schedule of regular supervision meetings and progress reviews, written feedback on drafts and a timetable for the project.
>
> (BPS, 2010: 4.2.3)

Whilst it is helpful for guidance such as this to acknowledge the competence of the supervisor, this begs the question: What skills are needed to be a competent research supervisor? Many of the clinical psychologists who offer research supervision are the same people who provide clinical supervision on placements and it is interesting to reflect on whether the tasks of both types of supervision are similar and transferable.

At the University of Manchester there are two distinct opportunities for supervisors to receive training in research supervision. First, within the clinical psychology programme, regular 1-day workshops are provided for those clinical supervisors who also supervise trainees' placement-based research projects. These workshops, which are consistently well attended and very well received, provide information about the essential features of a placement-based project, giving participants opportunities to develop and discuss ideas for projects and discuss the supervisor's role and necessary skills. Within the wider university, training workshops are provided for supervisors of postgraduate research, such research including clinical psychology trainees' doctoral research. Apart from addressing practical requirements such as the format of theses and frequency of supervision meetings, they also cover such topics as: supervising cross-culturally and at a distance; establishing and maintaining good supervisory practice; supervisory roles and dialogues – empowerment or challenge. This certainly indicates that the role of research supervisor is being given more importance than it once was and, in keeping with this, within the clinical psychology programme at Manchester we are about to introduce a system for trainees to evaluate the quality of their research supervision, thus bringing it in line with clinical supervision.

Future perspectives

This book has reviewed the developments in theory, research and practice that have taken place since the first edition was written in 2002. Looking to the future, what might be important factors to consider?

Supervising other professionals

It is suggested that in future clinical psychologists will face increasing demands to provide supervision. This is already evident and has implications for both pre-qualification training and post-qualification (CPD). Newly qualified clinical psychologists are expected to supervise other professionals from an early stage in their careers and, in the North West of England at least (and there is no reason to suspect a different picture elsewhere in the UK), newly qualified clinical psychologists consistently identify 'supervising other professionals' and 'consultation' as two of their CPD training priorities. Given this, it will be important for some clarity to be established as to what is meant by supervision and indeed, as mentioned earlier in this chapter as well as in Chapter 10, how it differs from other forms of workplace support such as consultation, mentoring and coaching. Supervision is a much-used term within mental health services but it can be perceived in a number of different ways and the tasks involved in delivering effective supervision will vary accordingly. It is suggested that there are significant differences between, for example, clinical and managerial supervision and between case management and clinical supervision, which encourages reflexive learning. Moreover, whether supervision is viewed positively or has a more negative connotation will depend on the culture of the organisation within which the practitioners work.

The necessity (or advantage at least) of achieving agreement and clarity about the nature of supervision has implications particularly, though not exclusively, for interprofessional supervision. As was discussed in Chapter 10, it is not uncommon for practitioners to believe they are engaging in supervision when in fact the activity is more akin to *informal support*. The supervision contract takes a primary role here and clinical psychologists may need to combine negotiating and assertion skills to ensure that practice is effective. The fundamental issue would appear to be supervision for what? This has an impact on the discussions (e.g. in Chapter 3) of cross-functional supervision within a family of applied psychology and on the practicality of generic professional practice guidelines. These are not difficulties that cannot be overcome, but ones that require focus and attention.

What is the optimal time in a person's career for training to be a supervisor?

It is interesting to consider *when* clinical psychologists should be trained in supervisory skills. Historically, this happened some time before the second anniversary of qualification, the '2 years' criterion being linked to the BPS requirement for trainee clinical psychologists to be supervised by a clinical psychologist with at least 2 years' experience. The discussion in the chapters of this book suggests that supervisor training should start earlier and last longer. To prepare clinical psychology trainees both for their own super-vision and for supervisory activity with other staff (occasionally reduced to the competence in 'working through others'), training should start within the pre-qualification training period. These skills can then be developed in the immediate post-qualification period and refined over time. If clinical psychologists are to fulfil the supervisory roles ascribed to them in *New Ways of Working* (BPS, 2007b) they will need sophisticated skills in supervision and the opportunities to receive their own supervision for this work. As a dynamic process both parties have roles to play in ensuring that supervision is agreeable and effective. Wheeler and Cushway (Chapter 2) reminded us of the importance of enabling (through training and experiential learning) trainees to utilise supervision effectively. In their 'transitions' to becoming a supervisor, there are clear indications that individuals can benefit from reflecting on their own experience of having been supervised and the contributions that they made to this. Related to this, in Chapter 10 Linda Steen described the important role of peer group supervision in the development of supervisory skills during pre-qualification training.

Training in flexible formats for supervision

Generally, supervisor training is geared to a traditional one-to-one format. As noted in Chapter 10, for example, the BPS learning outcomes that guide supervisor training for clinical and other applied psychologists do not make explicit mention of other formats; this is not surprising when one considers that they were developed for the supervisory practice of those who supervise trainee clinical psychologists, one of the requirements of which is that trainees must always receive an 'appropriate amount of individual supervision' (BPS, 2010: 5.11.3). Moreover, as is acknowledged in much of the supervision literature, it is likely that new supervisors will find it easier to start by offering and learning about individual rather than group supervision, as the one-to-one format does not require the supervisor to consider the complex dynamics that accompany group supervision (see, for example, Scaife, 2009). As was also noted in Chapter 10, guidance to clinical psychology training programmes from the BPS includes the advice 'to establish supervisor workshops related specifically to team supervision' (BPS, 2010, appendix 4: 2.1). In practice, however, whilst clinical psychology training programmes do offer some teaching and training about formats other than one-to-one, resources usually limit this to being at a very basic level with little, if any, opportunity for experiential learning.

In post-qualification practice, both within and outside clinical psychology, we know that practitioners engage in a wide range of supervision formats, therefore it is interesting to consider how training in one-to-one supervision might need to be augmented to enable the development of competence to provide (and also to receive) supervision in alternative formats. A variety of external supervision courses are available, both as short (e.g. 1- or 2-day) courses and more in-depth ongoing training, and these include training in formats such as group supervision. It is fair to say, however, that for most clinical psychologists working within the NHS training in other formats is likely to be 'on the job' rather than by attending formal training courses, many of which have significant costs attached to them; exceptions to this might be for practitioners for whom a particular model of therapy and supervision, such as group psychotherapy and supervision, is part of their routine work. Other ways of beginning to learn to deliver supervision using alternative formats include co-supervising with someone from another discipline who has experience of different formats (Milne and Oliver, 2000) and, as mentioned in Chapters 6 and 10, enabling trainee clinical psychologists to have experience of alternative supervision formats (e.g. peer group supervision) during their training (e.g. Akhurst and Kelly, 2006) as an experiential route to gaining competence in supervisory skills.

Continuing research into supervision and supervisor training

As has been highlighted in this volume, there are a number of key areas for further research, particularly those that have received less attention to date, such as technological approaches and formats other than one-to-one: for example, Milne and Oliver (2000), in their review of flexible formats of supervision, concluded that 'this phase should be concerned with more rigorous evaluations of the efficiency of one or two of the more promising formats such as group and peer supervision' (ibid.: 303).

Moreover, surveys such as those carried out by Gabbay et al. (1999) gave us a very useful picture of the supervision practice of clinical psychologists at that time (and in one particular region of the UK), and the exciting developments reported in this book suggest that the time is right for another such survey to be carried out in order to give an accurate view of the supervisory practice of clinical psychologists.

A particularly valuable role in the future is likely to be played by The Supervision Practitioner Research Network (SuPReNet, www.bacp.co.uk/research/SuPReNet/index.php). The aims of this body are to promote good practice-based supervision research, both nationally and internationally, with the aim of improving practice. A series of meetings was held in 2010 on the themes *Outcome and Supervision* and *Supervision and the Therapist*, and an international conference is planned for 2011.

Retaining resilience in the supervisory role

In our supervisor training at Manchester we have noticed the process of change that ex-trainees go through as they adopt the supervisor role. Of interest has been the replacement of the feeling of being constantly scrutinised (and talked about) as a trainee, with similar anxieties about the public performance of a supervisor. We try to address this issue directly and, as reported in the Introduction, have found it helpful to refer to Kaslow's (1986) reflections about becoming a supervisor. We also use a long list of supposed attributes that should be held by a supervisor to 'flood' their anxieties! On a more serious note, there is an important issue about supporting supervisors and maintaining and enhancing their skills. What factors affect the *resilience* of supervisors?

Our experience suggests that the following are important to the supervisor's subjective experience of supervision: the fit with the supervisee; the ability of the supervisee to make progress, particularly when making judgements about failing supervisees; the general support of service managers for engaging in supervision; and the support provided by the clinical psychology training programme, particularly around any difficulties.

Feeling supported by the local training programme can be important and can manifest itself in many ways. Programmes can ensure that difficult decisions about a trainee's development or performance in supervision are handled sensitively. It is crucial that transparency and justice prevail in any decisions made arising from complaints or criticisms about supervision or supervisors. One proposal we are interested in offering locally is that of ongoing supervision for supervision. There is a nice illustration of what can go wrong in a training video (*Ethical Issues in Clinical Supervision*) produced by the Leeds Clinical Psychology Training Programme (University of

Leeds Media Services, 2004). An experienced supervisor who has suffered a deteriorating supervisory relationship and recommended that the supervisee 'fail' his placement is hung out to dry by the local training programme, who are afraid that minor procedural omissions might support an appeal to the university by the trainee. The supervisor is a fairly robust character with considerable experience, but when the decision to pass the trainee is conveyed to him (by a hapless clinical tutor), we get the distinct impression that his resilience has been affected.

Also, as Jan Hughes refers to in Chapter 11, the personal qualities of supervisors need to be acknowledged. A core quality of clinical psychology supervisors may be that of wanting to help others. Ensuring that this advantage does not move into the area of disadvantage in a desire to take responsibility for and rescue another, thus confounding the tasks of supervision, must be carefully considered. An example of this might be in the confusion of supervision with therapy, and an outcome can be difficulties in accurately assessing practice and ultimately failing poor performance. From medical education (Cleland 2009; Cleland et al., 2008) we can learn of the reasons given for supervisors finding it very difficult to fail poor performance.

Concluding comments

Within clinical psychology in the UK, the importance of supervision is recognised both within education and training and in routine clinical practice. As Beinart and Clohessy (2009) note: 'clinical supervision forms a substantial part of the professional training of clinical psychologists and is seen as having an important quality control function both during and after training' (ibid.: 319). As a profession, we are clear about what we mean by the term *supervision* and draw a distinction between clinical supervision and line management supervision (BPS, 2006a). Ideally it is recognised that these two types of supervision should be separated, both 'conceptually and . . . actually' (ibid.: 3), although our experience suggests that, often for practical reasons, it is not uncommon for clinical psychologists to receive both clinical and line management supervision from the same person.

In contrast to 2002 when the first edition of this book was being written, there is now a clear expectation from newly qualified clinical psychologists and their employers that both receiving and providing supervision will be an integral part of their role. It would appear that supervision is no longer seen as a luxury or indeed as an activity reserved only for newly qualified clinicians, but rather it is viewed as a necessity throughout a clinical psychologist's career.

We noted in our first edition that newly qualified clinical psychologists' choice of jobs was determined, at least in part, by whether they will have access to supervision (Lavender and Thompson, 2000). A straw poll of those newly qualified clinical psychologists who attend our supervisor training courses suggests that they all receive regular supervision, mainly one-to-one or peer group or, for those working within specialist services such as family therapy clinics, within formats that best fit with that mode of therapy. Moreover, far from being reluctant to supervise, as was sometimes the case previously, our experience shows that the majority of clinical psychologists are keen to embrace this role from an early stage in their careers.

One of our biggest challenges is related to the fact that we work within an ever-changing context in which clinicians are frequently 'stretched to the limits' (Morrison, 2005: 4); within this context, we need to guard against 'the paradox . . . that at the very time when supervision has never been more important to the process of change, it may also be one of its first casualties' (Morrison, 2005: 4).

Whilst we remain mindful of the need for more research evidence, particularly with UK populations, as well as for the continued sharing of information, we feel that the contributions in this book have shown that the practice of and training in supervision within clinical psychology is in a very healthy state. There is a great deal of knowledge, expertise and practical experience within the profession and there have been many important innovations and developments concerning supervision and clinical psychology since the first edition of this book was published. Importantly, our experience of working with trainee and newly qualified clinical psychologists has shown us that the next generation of clinical psychology supervisors and researchers are poised to take this work forward and view supervision as an activity that warrants the same attention as the development of clinical skills.

Summary

There have been many important innovations and developments concerning supervision and clinical psychology since the first edition of this book was published in 2004. These have included consolidation of a shared view of what should constitute introductory training in supervisory skills, increased sophistication of training models, a register for accredited supervisors (RAPPS) that is open to all applied psychologists and growth in research into all aspects of supervision. There is greater understanding of the centrality of the supervisory relationship and of what constitutes good practice in this regard, including the importance of a clear and careful contracting process.

One result of a service change has been a debate about whether generic supervisory skills are sufficient for working in a particular model, with the implications for a twin path approach to accreditation.

Although the demand for supervision has grown exponentially in recent years, there seem to be differing views about the purpose, process and outcomes of supervision. As well as the greater emphasis on clinical supervision within the profession, clinical psychologists receive increasing requests (rooted in policy changes) for providing supervision to others involved in psychological and more general healthcare. It is recommended that clarity and agreement about the nature of the supervision required are sought at the outset.

In the first edition of this book the Foreword stated that clinical psychology and clinical supervision have 'come of age'. Less than a decade later there is continued and growing interest within clinical psychology in all aspects of supervision, an interest that is both aware of developments in other professions and seeks out opportunities to develop across professions.

Future challenges will include responding to increasing and competing supervisory demands, both within and outside the profession; related to this, it will be important to continue to consider the advantages of moving away from a traditional one-to-one model of supervision towards more flexible models. There will be a continuing need to ensure that both pre-qualification and post-qualification supervision is of a good enough quality to aid supervisee learning and ultimately to lead to improved client outcomes. That this all needs to be carried out within a rapidly changing work context is one of the biggest challenges we have ahead of us.

There is clear evidence of considerable interest in both research to further knowledge and the development of practice. This encourages us to look forward with optimism to continuing developments in supervision and clinical psychology.

References

Adetimole, F., Afuape, T. and Vara, R. (2005) The impact of racism on the experience of training on a clinical psychology course: Reflections from three Black trainees, *Clinical Psychology* 48: 11–15.

Aitken, G. (1998) Working with, and through, professional and 'race' differences: Issues for clinical psychologists, *Clinical Psychology Forum* 118: 10–17.

Aitken, G. and Dennis, M. (2004) Incorporating gender issues in clinical psychology supervision. In I. Fleming and L. Steen (Eds.) *Supervision and Clinical Psychology: Theory, Practice and Perspectives* (1st edn), Hove: Brunner-Routledge.

Aitken, G. and Franks, A. (2009) *Cutting Through the Rhetoric: The Responsible Use of Authentic Self in the Coaching Relationship.* Paper presented at EMCC Annual Conference, Ashridge Leadership Centre, 6–7 April 2009.

Akhurst, J. E. and Kelly, K. (2006) Peer group supervision as an adjunct to individual supervision: Optimising learning processes during psychologists' training, *Psychology Teaching Review* 12: 3–15.

Allen, C., Bagnall, G. and Campbell, E. (2003) *Analysis of Education and Training Needs for Supervisors in Clinical Psychology across Scotland. Final Report to NHS Education for Scotland*, Edinburgh: National Health Education for Scotland.

Alliger, G. M., Tannenbaum, S. I., Bennett, J. R., Traver, H. and Shotland, A. (1997) A meta-analysis of the relations among training criteria, *Personnel Psychology* 50: 341–358.

Almeida, R. V. (1998) The dislocation of women's experience in family therapy, *Journal of Feminist Family Therapy* 10: 1–21.

Altfeld, D. A. and Bernard, H. S. (1997) An experiential group model for group psychotherapy. In C. E. Watkins Jr (Ed.) *A Handbook of Psychotherapy Supervision*, New York: Wiley.

Andersen, T. (1991) *The Reflecting Team: Dialogues about Dialogues about Dialogues*, New York: Norton.

Anderson, L. W., and Krathwohl, D. R. (Eds.) (2001) *A Taxonomy for Learning, Teaching and Assessing: A Revision of Bloom's Taxonomy of Educational Objectives*, New York: Longman.

Andersson, L. (2008) Psychodynamic supervision in a group setting: Benefits and limitations, *Psychotherapy in Australia* 14: 36–40.

Armstrong, P. V. and Freeston, M. H. (2006) Conceptualising and formulating cognitive therapy supervision. In N. Tarrier (Ed.) *Case Formulation in Cognitive*

Behavior Therapy: The Treatment of Challenging and Complex Cases, New York: Routledge.

Association for Family Therapy and Systemic Practice (AFT) (2007) *Information on Training* (http://www.aft.org.uk/training/documents/InformationOnTrainingSept 2007.pdf; accessed 31/3/10).

Aston, L. and Molassiotis, A. (2003) Supervising and supporting student nurses in clinical placements: The peer support initiative, *Nurse Education Today* 23: 202–210.

Atkinson, D. R., Marten, G. and Sue, D. W. (Eds.) (1993) *Counseling American Minorities: A Cross-Cultural Perspective* (4th edn), Dubuque, IA: Brown & Benchmark.

Babor, T. and Del Boca, F. (Eds.) (2003) *Treatment Matching in Alcoholism*, Cambridge: Cambridge University Press.

Bagnall, G. (2010) Preparing for clinical supervision in psychology: What can we learn from the Scottish experience? *Clinical Psychology Forum* 216: 15–20.

Bambling, M., King, R., Raue, P., Schweitzer, R. and Lambert, W. (2006) Clinical supervision: Its influence on client-rated working alliance and client symptom reduction in the brief treatment of major depression, *Psychotherapy Research* 16: 317–331.

Bandura, A. (2006) Towards a psychology of human agency, *Perspectives on Psychological Science* 1: 164–180.

Banks, A. (2001) Tweaking the Euro-American perspective: Infusing cultural awareness and sensitivity into the supervision of family therapy, *The Family Journal: Counseling and Therapy for Couples and Families* 9: 420–423.

Barkham, M. and Mellor-Clark, J. (2003) Bridging evidence-based practice and practice-based evidence: Developing a rigorous and relevant knowledge for the psychological therapies, *Clinical Psychology and Psychotherapy* 10: 109–327.

Barkham, M., Evans, C., Margison, F., McGrath, G., Mellor-Clark, J., Milne, D. L., et al. (1998) The rationale for developing and implementing core outcome batteries for routine use in service settings and psychotherapy outcome research, *Journal of Mental Health* 7: 35–47.

Barlow, D. H., Hayes, S. C. and Nelson, R. O. (1984) *The Scientist-Practitioner*, London: Pergamon.

Barlow, D. H., Nock, M. K. and Hersen, M. (2009) *Single-Case Experimental Design: Strategies for Studying Behavior Change* (3rd edn), Boston, MA: Pearson.

Barrett, M., Chua, W., Crits-Cristoph, P., Gibbons, M. and Thompson, D. (2008) Early withdrawal from mental health treatment: Implications for psychotherapy practice, *Psychotherapy: Theory, Research, Practice, Training* 45: 247–267.

Bassett, C. (1999) *Clinical Supervision: A Guide to Implementation*, London: Nursing Times Books.

Beck, A. and Steer, R. A. (1990) *BAI, Beck Anxiety Inventory Manual*, San Antonio, TX: A.T. Beck.

Beckwith, J. (Ed.) (1999) Power between women, *Feminism and Psychology* 9(4).

Beinart, H. (2002) An exploration of the factors which predict the quality of the relationship in clinical supervision. Unpublished DClinPsych dissertation, Open University/British Psychological Society.

Beinart, H. (2004) Models of supervision and the supervisory relationship and their evidence base. In I. Fleming and L. Steen (Eds.) *Supervision and Clinical*

Psychology: Theory, Practice and Perspectives (1st edn), Hove: Brunner-Routledge.

Beinart, H. and Clohessy, S. (2009) Supervision. In H. Beinart, P. Kennedy and S. Llewelyn (Eds.) *Clinical Psychology in Practice*, Oxford: BPS Blackwell.

Belfield, C., Thomas, H., Bullock, A., Eynon, R. and Wall, D. (2001) Measuring the effectiveness for best medical education: A discussion, *Medical Teacher* 23: 164–170.

Bellg, A. J., Borrelli, B., Resnick, B., Hecht, J., Minicucci, D. S., Ory, M., et al. (2004) Enhancing treatment fidelity in health behaviour change studies: Best practises and recommendations from the NIH Behaviour Change Consortium, *Health Psychology* 23: 443–451.

Bepko, C., Almeida, R. V., Messineo, T. and Stevenson, Y. (1998) Evolving constructs of masculinity interviews with Andres Nazario, J. Williams Doherty and Roberto Font, *Journal of Feminist Family Therapy* 10: 49–79.

Bernard, J. M. (1979) Supervisor training: A discrimination model, *Counselor Education and Supervision* 19: 60–68.

Bernard, J. M. (1997) The discrimination model. In C. E. Watkins (Ed.) *Handbook of Psychotherapy Supervision*, New York: Wiley.

Bernard, J. M. and Goodyear, R. K. (1998) *Fundamentals of Clinical Supervision* (2nd edn), Boston, MA: Allyn & Bacon.

Bernard, J. M. and Goodyear, R. K. (2004) *Fundamentals of Clinical Supervision* (3rd edn), Boston, MA: Allyn & Bacon.

Beutler, L. (2009) Making science matter in clinical practice: Redefining psychotherapy, *Clinical Psychology Science and Practice* 16: 301–317.

Bion, W. (1959) Attacks on linking, *International Journal of Psycho-Analysis* 40: 308–315.

Bion, W. (1962) *Learning from Experience*, London: Heinemann.

Bion, W. R. (1970) *Attention and Interpretation*, London: Maresfield.

Bloom, B. S. (1956) *Taxonomy of Educational Objectives: Handbook 1: Cognitive Domain*, London: Longman.

Bollas, C. (1994) Aspects of the erotic transference, *Psychoanalytic Inquiry* 14: 572–590.

Bond, M. and Holland, S. (1998) *Skills of Clinical Supervision for Nurses: A Practical Guide for Supervisees, Clinical Supervisors and Managers*, Buckingham: Open University Press

Borders, L. D. (1990) Developmental changes during supervisees' first practicum, *The Clinical Supervisor* 8: 157–167.

Bordin, E. (1979) The generalisability of the psychoanalytic concept of the working alliance, *Psychotherapy: Theory, Research and Practice* 16: 252–260.

Bordin, E. S. (1983) A working alliance model of supervision, *Counseling Psychologist* 11: 35–42.

Borrelli, B., Sepinwall, D., Ernst, D., Bellg, A. J., Czajkowski, S., Greger, R., et al. (2005) A new tool to assess treatment fidelity and evaluation of treatment fidelity across 10 years of health behaviour research, *Journal of Consulting and Clinical Psychology* 73: 852–860.

Bostock, J. (1997) Knowing our place: Understanding women's experiences and cause of distress, *Feminism and Psychology* 7: 239–247.

Bower, P. and Gilbody, S. (2005) Stepped care in psychological therapies: Access, effectiveness and efficiency. National literature review, *British Journal of Psychiatry* 186: 1–17.

Bower, P., Gilbody, S., Richards, D., Fletcher, J. and Sutton, A. (2006) Collaborative care for depression in primary care: Making sense of a complex Intervention, *British Journal of Psychiatry* 189: 484–493.

British Association of Art Therapists (BAAT) (2009) *Guidelines for Placement Supervisors*, London: BAAT.

British Association for Behavioural and Cognitive Psychotherapies (BABCP) (2008) *Course Accreditation Process for Courses Providing Training in Cognitive and Behavioural Psychotherapies*, Bury: BABCP.

British Association for Behavioural and Cognitive Psychotherapies (BABCP) (2009) *Guidelines for Full Accreditation* (http://www.babcp.com/silo/files/criteria-guide lines-for-full-accreditation-oct09.pdf; accessed 17/5/10).

British Association for Counselling and Psychotherapy (BACP) (2004a) *Guidance for Trainee Placements – Information Sheet T3*, Rugby: BACP.

British Association for Counselling and Psychotherapy (BACP) (2004b) *What is Supervision? – Information Sheet S2*, Rugby: BACP.

British Association for Counselling and Psychotherapy (BACP) (2010) *The Ethical Framework for Good Practice in Counselling and Psychotherapy*, Lutterworth: BACP.

British Association of Drama Therapists (BADT) (2006) *Standards of Ethical Practice for Registered Supervisors of Dramatherapy*, Cheltenham: BADT.

British Psychological Society (BPS) (1995a) *Clinical Psychology Training: Meeting Health Service Demand*, Leicester: BPS.

British Psychological Society (BPS) (1995b) *Guidelines on Clinical Supervision*, Leicester: BPS.

British Psychological Society (BPS) (2004) *Widening Access within Undergraduate Psychology Education and its Implications for Professional Psychology: Gender, Disability and Ethnic Diversity*, Leicester: BPS.

British Psychological Society (BPS) (2005) *Division of Clinical Psychology Policy on Continued Supervision. Discussion Paper*, Leicester: BPS.

British Psychological Society (BPS) (2006a) *Division of Clinical Psychology Policy on Continued Supervision*, Leicester: BPS.

British Psychological Society (BPS) (2006b) *Code of Ethics and Conduct*, Leicester: BPS.

British Psychological Society (BPS) (2007a) *Guidelines for the Employment of Assistant Psychologists*, Leicester: BPS.

British Psychological Society (BPS) (2007b) *New Ways of Working for Applied Psychologists in Health and Social Care: The End of the Beginning*, Leicester: BPS.

British Psychological Society (BPS) (2007c) *Good Practice Guide on the Contribution of Applied Psychologists to Improving Access to Psychological Therapies*, Leicester: BPS.

British Psychological Society (BPS) (2007d) *Leading Psychological Services: A Report by the Division of Clinical Psychology*, Leicester: BPS.

British Psychological Society (BPS) (2008a) *Generic Professional Practice Guidelines* (2nd edn), Leicester: BPS.

British Psychological Society (BPS) (2008b) *Committee on Training in Clinical*

Psychology: Criteria for the Accreditation of Post-Graduate Training Programmes in Clinical Psychology, Leicester: BPS.

British Psychological Society (BPS) (2009) *Code of Ethics and Conduct*, Leicester: BPS.

British Psychological Society (BPS) (2010) *Standards for Doctoral Programmes in Clinical Psychology*, Leicester: BPS.

Brosan, L., Reynolds, S. and Moore, R. G. (2007) Factors associated with competence in cognitive therapists, *Behavioural and Cognitive Psychotherapy* 35: 179–190.

Brosan, L., Reynolds, S. and Moore, R. G. (2008) Self-evaluation of cognitive therapy performance: Do therapists know how competent they are? *Behavioural and Cognitive Psychotherapy* 36: 581–587.

Brown, M. T. and Landrum-Brown, J. (1995) Counselor supervision: Cross-cultural perspectives. In J. G. Ponterotto, J. M. Casas, L. A. Suzuki and C. M. Alexander (Eds.) *Handbook of Multicultural Counseling*, Thousand Oaks, CA: Sage.

Brunning, H. and Huffington, C. (1994) The 'consultancy model': Empowering ourselves and our clients. *Clinical Psychology Forum* 73: 28–29.

Burnham J. (1992) Approach–method–technique: Making distinctions and creating connections, *Human Systems* 3: 3–26.

Butler, A. (2007) *Practice Teaching Annual Programme. SCW 329*, Plymouth: University of Plymouth Faculty of Health and Social Work.

Butler, A., Chapman, J., Forman, E. and Beck, A. (2006) The empirical status of cognitive-behavioural therapy: A review of the meta-analyses, *Clinical Psychology Review* 26: 17–31.

Butler, R. (2004) Childhood nocturnal enuresis: Developing a conceptual framework, *Clinical Psychology Review* 24: 909–931.

Butterworth, T. (2001) Clinical supervision and clinical governance for the twenty-first century. In J. R. Cutcliffe, T. Butterworth and B. Proctor (Eds.) *Fundamental Themes in Clinical Supervision*, London: Routledge.

Butterworth, T. and Faugier, J. (Eds.) (1992) *Clinical Supervision and Mentorship in Nursing*, London: Chapman & Hall.

Cape, J., Roth, A., Scior, K., Thompson, M. and Du Pessis, P. (2008) Increasing diversity within clinical psychology: The London Initiative, *Clinical Psychology Forum* 190: 7–10.

Carey, J. C., Williams, K. S. and Wells, M. (1988) Relationships between dimensions of supervisors' influence and counselor trainees' performance, *Counselor Education and Supervision* 28: 130–139.

Carroll, M. (1996) *Counselling Supervision: Theory, Skills and Practice*, London: Cassell.

Carroll, K. and Nuro, K. (2002) One size cannot fit all: A stage model for psychotherapy manual development, *Clinical Psychology Science and Practice* 9: 396–406.

Carter, R. (1995) *The Influence of Race and Racial Identity in Psychotherapy: Towards a Racially Inclusive Model*, London: Wiley.

Casement, P. (1988) *On Learning from the Patient*, London: Routledge.

Cassell, C. and Walsh, S. (1993) Being seen but not heard: Barriers to women's equality in the workplace, *The Psychologist* 16: 110–114.

Chambless, D. (2002) Beware the Dodo bird: The dangers of overgeneralization, *Clinical Psychology: Science and Practice* 9: 13–16.

Chartered Society of Physiotherapy (2004) *Accreditation of Clinical Educators Scheme Guidance*, London: Chartered Society of Physiotherapy.

Cherry, D. K., Messenger L. C. and Jacoby, A. M. (2000) An examination of training model outcomes in clinical psychology programs, *Professional Psychology: Research and Practice* 31: 562–568.

Chesler, P. (1974) *Women and madness*, London: Allen Lane.

Clark, D. M., Layard, R., Smithies, R., Richards, D. A., Suckling, R. and Wright, B. (2009) Improving access to psychological therapy: Initial evaluation of two UK demonstration sites, *Behaviour Research and Therapy* 47: 910–920.

Clarke, L. (2006) *It Takes Two. Perceptions on Supervisee Preparation*. Paper presented to DROSS meeting in Ambleside, York, 26 July 2006.

Cleland, J. A. (2009) *Are Clinical Psychology Supervisors Reluctant to Fail Students and Give Them Negative Feedback?* Paper presented at the Group of Trainers in Clinical Psychology Conference, Cambridge, 4 November 2009.

Cleland, J. A., Knight, L. V., Rees, C. E., Tracey, S. and Bond, C. M. (2008) Is it me or them? Factors that influence the passing of underperforming students, *Medical Education* 42: 800–809.

Cliffe, T. (2008) Making things compute: Developing an instrument that assesses competency in clinical supervision. Unpublished BSc thesis, Psychology Department, Newcastle University.

Clohessy, S. (2008) Supervisors' perspectives on their supervisory relationships: A qualitative study. Unpublished PsyD thesis, University of Hull.

Cohen, L. H. (1979) The research readership and information source reliance of clinical psychologists, *Professional Psychology* 10: 780–786.

Collins, P. H. (1990) *Black Feminist Thought: Knowledge Consciousness and the Politics of Empowerment*, Boston: Unwin Hyman.

Collins, S. (2002) Are clinical psychologists likely to be 'naturally' accurate appraisers of their own performance? In what ways can individuals develop and maintain critical appreciation of their strengths and weaknesses throughout their careers. Unpublished essay, University of Leeds.

Constantine, M. G. (1997) Facilitating multicultural competency in counselling supervision. In D. B. Pope-Davis and H. L. K. Coleman (Eds.) *Multicultural Counselling Competencies: Assessment, Education, Training and Supervision*, Thousand Oaks, CA: Sage.

Cooke, M. and Kipnis, D. (1986) Influence tactics in psychotherapy, *Journal of Consulting and Clinical Psychology* 54: 22–26.

Cross, W. E. (1971) The Negro-to-Black conversion experience: Toward a psychology of Black liberation, *Black World* 20: 13–19.

Cross, W. E. (1995) The psychology of nigrescence: Revising the Cross Model. In J. G. Ponterotto, J. M. Casas, L. A. Suzuki and C. M. Alexander (Eds.) *Handbook of Multicultural Counseling*, Thousand Oaks, CA: Sage.

Cuijpers, P., Van Straten, A. and Warmedam, L. (2007) Behavioural activation treatments of depression: A meta analysis, *Clinical Psychology Review* 27: 318–326.

Cushway, D. and Gatherer, A. (2003) Reflecting on reflection, *Clinical Psychology* 27: 6–11.

Cushway, D. and Knibbs, K. (2004) Trainees' and supervisors' perceptions of supervision. In I. Fleming and L. Steen (Eds.) *Supervision and Clinical Psychology. Theory, Practice and Perspectives*, Hove: Brunner-Routledge.

Cushway, D. and Tyler, P. (1996) Stress in clinical psychologists, *International Journal of Social Psychiatry* 44: 141–149.

D'Andrea, M. and Daniels, J. (1997) Multicultural counseling supervision: Central issues, theoretical considerations, and practical strategies. In D. B. Pope-Davis and H. L. K. Coleman (Eds.) *Multicultural Counseling Competencies: Assessment, Education, Training and Supervision*, Thousand Oaks, CA: Sage.

Darzi (2008) *High Quality Care for All* (The Darzi Report), London: DH.

Davis, D., Thompson, M., Oman, A. and Haynes, B. (1992) Evidence of the effectiveness of CME. A review of 50 randomized controlled trials, *Journal of the American Medical Association* 268: 1111–1117.

Davy, J. (2002) Discursive reflections on a research agenda for clinical supervision, *Psychology and Psychotherapy: Theory, Research and Practice* 75: 221–238.

Dennis, M. (1998) Is there a place for diversity within clinical supervision? An exploration of ethnic and cultural issues, *Clinical Psychology Forum* 118: 24–32.

Dennis, M. (2001) An integrative approach to 'race' and culture in supervision. In M. Carroll and M. Tholstrup (Eds.) *Integrative Approaches to Supervision*, London: Jessica Kingsley.

Department of Health (DH) (1993) *A Vision for the Future: Report of the Chief Nursing Officer*, London: DH.

Department of Health (DH) (1994) *Research and Development in the New NHS*, London: DH.

Department of Health (DH) (2000) *Making a Difference: Clinical Supervision in Primary Care*, London, DH.

Department of Health (DH) (2003) *Mainstreaming Gender and Women's Mental Health Implementation Guidance*, London: DH.

Department of Health (DH) (2004) *Agenda for Change: Final Agreement* (http://www/dh.gov.uk/en/Publicationsandstatistics/Publications/PublicationsPolicyAnd Guidance/DH_4095943 accessed 3/5/11).

Department of Health (DH) (2005a) *Health Reform in England: Update and Next Steps*, London: DH.

Department of Health (DH) (2005b) *New Ways of Working for Psychiatrists: Enhancing Effective, Person-Centred Services through New Ways of Working in Multidisciplinary and Multiagency Contexts*, London: DH.

Department of Health (DH) (2006) *Our Health, our Care, our Say: A New Direction for Community Services*, London: DH.

Department of Health (DH) (2007a) *The Competencies Required to Deliver Cognitive and Behavioral Therapy for People with Depression and Anxiety Disorders*, London: DH.

Department of Health (DH) (2007b) *Mental Health: New Ways of Working for Everyone*, London: DH.

Department of Health (DH) (2008a) *World Class Commissioning*, London: DH.

Department of Health (DH) (2008b) *IAPT National Implementation Plan*, London: DH.

Department of Health (DH) (2008c) *Supervision: The Key to Successful Patient*

Outcomes by Delivering IAPT Interventions of Proven High Quality and Fidelity, London: DH.

Department of Health (DH) (2009a) *Putting People First: Working Together with User-Led Organisations*, London: DH.

Department of Health (DH) (2009b) *Improving Access to Psychological Therapies (IAPT)*, London: DH.

Department of Health (DH) (2010a) *Equality and Excellence: Liberating the NHS.* London: DH.

Department of Health (DH) (2010b) *Confirmation of Payment by Results (PbR) Arrangements for 2010–11*, London: DH.

DeRubeis, R., Brotman, M. and Gibbons, C. (2005) A conceptual and methodological analysis of the nonspecifics argument, *Clinical Psychology: Science and Practice* 12: 174–183.

Division of Clinical Psychology (DCP), British Psychological Society (BPS) (1998) *Briefing Paper No. 16, Services to Black and Minority Ethnic People: A Guide for Commissioners of Clinical Psychology Services*, Leicester: BPS.

Division of Clinical Psychology (DCP), British Psychological Society (BPS) (2001) *Guidelines for Continuing Professional Development*, Leicester: BPS.

Division of Clinical Psychology (DCP), British Psychological Society (BPS) (2005) Challenging social inequalities: What can community psychologists do? *Clinical Psychology Forum* 153: 6–44.

Division of Clinical Psychology (DCP), British Psychological Society (BPS) (2006) Critical and community psychology, *Clinical Psychology Forum* 162: 3–33.

Division of Counselling Psychology (DCoP) (2008) *Guidelines for Supervision*, Leicester: British Psychological Society.

Division of Educational and Child Psychology (DECP) (2006) *Quality Standards for Educational Psychology Services*, Leicester, British Psychological Society.

Durham, R. C., Swan, J. S. and Fisher, P. L (2000) Complexity and collaboration in routine practice of CBT: What doesn't work with whom and how might it work better? *Journal of Mental Health* 9: 429–444.

Efstation, J. F., Patton, M. J. and Kardash, C. M. (1990) Measuring the working alliance in counselor supervision, *Journal of Counseling Psychology* 37: 322–329.

Ekstein, R. and Wallerstein, R. S. (1972) *The teaching and learning of psychotherapy* (2nd edn), New York: International Universities Press.

Ellis, M. V. (1991) Research in supervision: Revitalizing a scientific agenda, *Counsellor Education and Supervision* 30: 238–251.

Ellis, M. V. and Ladany, N. (1997) Inferences concerning supervisees and clients in clinical supervision: An integrative review. In C. E. Watkins (Ed.) *Handbook of Psychotherapy Supervision*, New York: Wiley.

Ellis, M. V., Dell, D. M. and Good, G. E. (1988) Counselor trainees' perceptions of supervisor roles: Two studies testing the dimensionality of supervision, *Journal of Counseling Psychology* 35: 315–324.

Ellis, M. V., Ladany, N., Krengel, M. and Schult, D. (1996) Clinical supervision research from 1981 to 1993: A methodological critique, *Journal of Counselling Psychology* 43: 35–50.

Equal Opportunities Commission (2004) *Delivering Quality Services, Meeting Different Needs: Promoting Sex Equality in the Public Sector*, London: EOC.

Ericsson, K. A. (2009) Enhancing the development of professional performance:

Implications from the study of deliberate practice. In K. A. Ericsson (Ed.) *Development of Professional Expertise. Towards Measurement of Expert Perform-ance and Design of Optimal Learning Environments*, Cambridge: Cambridge University Press.

Falender, C. A. and Shafranske, E. P. (2004) *Clinical Supervision. A Competency-Based Approach*, Washington, DC: American Psychological Association.

Falender, C. A. and Shafranske, E. P. (Eds.) (2008) *Casebook for Clinical Super-vision: A Competency-Based Approach*, Washington, DC: American Psychological Association.

Fernando, S. (Ed.) (1995) *Mental Health in a Multi-Ethnic Society: A Multi-disciplinary Handbook*, London: Routledge.

Fleming, I. (2004) Training clinical psychologists as supervisors. In I. Fleming and L. Steen (Eds.) *Supervision and Clinical Psychology: Theory, Practice and Perspectives* (1st edn), Hove: Brunner-Routledge.

Fleming, I. (unpublished) Analysis of ClinPsyD Programme replies to Aug 2009 enquiry about readiness for the Directory of Applied Psychology Practice Supervisors. Available from the author.

Fleming, I. and Burton, M. (2001) Teaching about the individual and society links on the Manchester Clin.Psy.D. Course, *Clinical Psychology Forum* 6: 28–33.

Fleming, I. and Green, D. (2007) Developing supervision within clinical psychology: The work of the DROSS group, *Clinical Psychology Forum* 175: 28–32.

Fleming, I. R. and Steen, L. (2001) Supervisor training with the Manchester Clin.Psy.D. programme, *Clinical Psychology* 8: 30–34.

Fleming, I. R. and Steen, L. (Eds.) (2004) *Supervision and Clinical Psychology: Theory, Practice and Perspectives* (1st edn), Hove: Brunner-Routledge.

Fleming, I. R., Gone, R., Diver, A. and Fowler, B. (2007) Risk supervision in Rochdale, *Clinical Psychology Forum* 176: 22–25.

Fleming, J. (1953) The role of supervision in psychiatric training, *Bulletin of the Menninger Clinic* 17: 157–159.

Font, R., Dolan-Delvecchio, K. and Almeida, R. V. (1998) Finding the words: Instruments of therapy of liberation, *Journal of Feminist Therapy* 10: 85–97.

Foucault, M. (1977) *Discipline and Punish: The Birth of the Prison*, New York: Vintage Books.

Foucault, M. (1988) Power and strategies. In C. Gordon (Ed.) *Power/Knowledge: Selected Interviews and Other Writings 1972–1977 by Michel Foucault*, New York: Pantheon Books.

Frawley-O'Dea, M. G. and Sarnat, J. (2001) *The Supervisory Relationship: A Con-temporary Psychodynamic Approach*, New York: Guilford Press.

Freeston, M. (2004) *How Will I Know if Supervision Works?* Paper presented at the Joint Clinical Conference, Ambleside, York, July 2004.

Friedlander, M. L. and Snyder, J. (1983) Trainees' expectations for the supervisory process: Testing a developmental model, *Counselor Education and Supervision* 22: 342–348.

Frost, K. (2004) A longitudinal exploration of the supervisory relationship: A qualitative study. Unpublished DClinPsych dissertation, University of Oxford.

Fukuyama, M. A. (1994) Critical incidents in multicultural counseling supervision: A phenomenological approach to supervision research, *Counselor Education and Supervision* 34: 142–147.

Gabbay, M. B., Kiemle, G. and Maguire, C. (1999) Clinical supervision for clinical psychologists: Existing provision and unmet needs, *Clinical Psychology and Psychotherapy* 6: 404–412.

Gaitskell, S. and Morley, M. (2008) Supervision in occupational therapy: How are we doing? *British Journal of Occupational Therapy* 71: 119–121.

Gatmon, D. (2001) Exploring ethnic, gender, and sexual orientation variables in supervision: Do they really matter? *Journal of Multicultural Counseling and Development* 29: 102–114.

Gilbert, M. C. and Evans, K. (2000) *Psychotherapy Supervision: An Integrative Relational Approach to Psychotherapy Supervision*, Buckingham: Open University Press.

Gillmer, B. and Marckus, R. (2003) Personal professional development in clinical psychology training: Surveying reflective practice, *Clinical Psychology* 27: 20–24.

Golding, L. and Gray, I. (2006) *Continuing Professional Development for Clinical Psychologists: A Practical Handbook*, Oxford: BPS Blackwell.

Goodyear, R. K. and Nelson, M. L. (1997) *The major formats of psychotherapy supervision*. In C. E. Watkins Jr (Ed.) *Handbook of Psychotherapy Supervision*, New York: Wiley.

Gopaul-Nicol, S. and Brice-Baker, T. (1998) *Cross-Cultural Practice: Assessment, Treatment and Training*, New York: Wiley.

Green, D. R. (1998) Investigating the core skills of clinical supervision: A qualitative analysis. Unpublished DClinPsych dissertation, University of Leeds.

Green, D. (2004) Organising and evaluating supervisor training. In I. Fleming and L. Steen (Eds.) *Supervision and Clinical Psychology: Theory, Practice and Perspectives* (1st edn), Hove: Brunner-Routledge.

Green, D. and Akhurst, J. (2009) *Structured Peer Group Supervision* (DVD), Leeds: University of Leeds (http://lutube.leeds.ac.uk/avsmas/videos/347).

Hagan, T. And Smail, D. (1997) Power-mapping – 1. Background and basic methodology, *Journal of Community and Applied Social Psychology* 7: 259–264.

Hall, J., Lavender, T. and Llewelyn, S. (2003) A history of clinical psychology in Britain: Some impressions and reflections, *History and Philosophy of Psychology* 4: 32–48.

Hansen, J., Pound, R. and Petro, C. (1976) Review of research on practicum supervision, *Counsellor, Education and Supervision* 16: 107–116.

Harris, T., Moret, L. B., Gale, J. and Kampmeyer, K. L. (2001) Therapists' gender assumptions and how these assumptions influence therapy, *Journal of Feminist Family Therapy* 12: 33–59.

Haslam, J. (2008) *NHS Direct NPO16 Clinical Supervision Policy* (http://94.236.79. 21/About/FreedomOfInformation/FOIPublicationScheme/~/media/Files/Freedom OfInformationDocuments/OurPoliciesAndProcedures/ConductOfBusinessAnd TheProvisionOfNHSDirectServices/010308_ClinicalSupervisionPolicy.ashx; accessed 22/1/11).

Hawkins, P. and Shohet, R. (1989) *Supervision in the Helping Professions*, Buckingham: Open University Press.

Hawkins, P. and Shohet, R. (2000) *Supervision in the Helping Professions: An Individual, Group and Organizational Approach* (2nd edn), Milton Keynes: Open University Press.

Hawkins, P. and Shohet, R. (2006) *Supervision in the Helping Professions* (3rd edn), Buckingham: Open University Press.

Health Professions Council (HPC) (2008a) *Your Guide to Our Standards for Continuing Professional Development*, London: HPC.

Health Professions Council (HPC) (2008b) *Standards of Conduct, Performance and Ethics*, London: HPC.

Health Professions Council (HPC) (2009a) *Practitioner Psychologists. Standards of Proficiency*, London: HPC.

Health Professions Council (HPC) (2009b) *Standards of Education and Training. Your Duties as an Education Provider*, London: HPC.

Helms, J. E. (1995) An update of Helms' white and people of color racial identity models. In J. G. Ponterotto, J. M. Casas, L. A. Suzuki and C. M. Alexander (Eds.) *Handbook of Multicultural Counseling*, Thousand Oaks, CA: Sage.

Helms, J. E. and Cook, D. A. (1999) Using race and culture in therapy supervision. In J. E. Helms and D. A. Cook (Eds.) *Using Race and Culture in Counseling and Psychotherapy: Theory and Process*, Needham Heights, MA: Allyn & Bacon.

Helms, J. E. and Richardson, T. Q. (1997) How "multiculturalism" observes race and culture as differential aspects of counseling competency. In D. B. Pope-Davis and H. L. K. Coleman (Eds.) *Multicultural Counseling Competencies: Assessment, Education and Training and Supervision*, Thousand Oaks, CA: Sage.

Henderson, C. E., Cawyer, C., Stringer, C. E. and Watkins, C. E. (1999) A comparison of student and supervisor perceptions of effective practicum supervision, *The Clinical Supervisor* 18: 47–74.

Henwood, K. and Phoenix, A. (1999) 'Race' in psychology, teaching the subject. In M. Bulmer and J. Solomos (Eds.) *Ethnic and Racial Studies Today*, London: Routledge.

Hess, A. K. (1986) Growth in supervision: Stages of supervisee and supervisor development, *The Clinical Supervisor* 4: 51–67.

Hess, A. K. (1987) Psychotherapy supervision: Stages, Buber, and a theory of relationship, *Professional Psychology: Research and Practice* 18: 251–259.

Hettema, J., Steele, J. and Miller, W. R. (2005) Motivational interviewing, *Annual Review of Clinical Psychology* 1: 91–111.

Hewson, D. (1999) Empowerment in supervision. Special feature: Power between women, *Feminism and Psychology* 9: 406–409.

Hill Collins, P. (1990) *Black Feminist Thought: Knowledge, Consciousness, and the Politics of Empowerment*, London: Harper Collins Academic.

Hogan, R. (1964) Issues and approaches in supervision, *Psychotherapy: Theory, Research, and Practice* 1: 139–141.

Holland, S. (1990) Psychotherapy, oppression and social action: Gender, race and class in black women's depression. In R. Perelberg and A. Miller (Eds.) *Gender and Power in Families*, London: Routledge.

Holland, S. (1992) From social abuse to social action: A neighbourhood psychotherapy and social action project for women, *Changes: International Journal of Psychology and Psychotherapy* 10: 146–153.

Holland, S. (1995) Interaction in women's mental health and neighbourhood development. In S. Fernando (Ed.) *Mental Health in a Multi-Ethnic Society: A Multidisciplinary Handbook*, London: Routledge.

Holloway, E. L. (1982) Interactional structure of the supervision interview, *Journal of Counseling Psychology* 29: 309–317.

Holloway, E. L. (1984) Outcome evaluation in supervision research, *The Counselling Psychologist* 12: 167–174.

Holloway, E. L. (1995) *Clinical Supervision: A Systems Approach*, Thousand Oaks, CA: Sage.

Holloway, E. L. and Neufeldt, S. A. (1995) Supervision: Its contribution to treatment efficacy, *Journal of Consulting and Clinical Psychology* 63: 207–213.

Holloway, E. L. and Poulin, K. (1995) Discourse in supervision. In J. Siegfried (Ed.) *Therapeutic and Everyday Discourse on Behaviour Change: Towards a Micro-analysis in Psychotherapy Process Research*, New York: Ablex.

Holloway, E. L. and Wolleat, P. L. (1994) Supervision: The pragmatics of empowerment, *Journal of Educational and Psychological Consultation* 5: 23–43.

Honey, P. and Mumford, A. (1984) *A Manual of Learning Styles*, Maidenhead: McGraw-Hill.

hooks, b. (1990) *Yearning: Race, Gender, and Cultural Politics*, Boston, MA: South End Press.

hooks, b. (1993) *Sisters of the Yam: Black Women and Self-Recovery*, Boston, MA: South End Press.

Horvath, A. and Greenberg, L. (1994) *The Working Alliance: Theory, Research and Practice*, New York: Wiley.

Howard, R. (2009) *The Cost of Training in Terms of Consultant Time* (http://www.rcpsych.ac.uk/pdf/What%20does%20training%20really%20cost%20(2).pdf; accessed 2/2/10).

Hughes, J. and Youngson, S. C. (Eds.) (2009) *Personal Development and Clinical Psychology*, Oxford: BPS Blackwell.

Humphreys, K. and Wilbourne, P. (2006) Knitting together some ripping yarns, *Addiction* 101: 4–5.

Huppert, J., Gorman, J., Bufka, L., Barlow, D. and Shear, M. (2001) Therapists, therapist variables and cognitive-behavioral therapy outcome in a multicenter trial for panic disorder, *Journal of Consulting and Clinical Psychology* 69: 747–755.

Iberg, J. R. (1991) Applying statistical process control theory to bring together clinical supervision and psychotherapy research, *Journal of Consulting and Clinical Psychology* 59: 575–586.

Inskipp, F. (1999) Training supervisees to use supervision. In E. Holloway and M. Carroll (Eds.) *Training Counselling Supervisors*, London: Sage.

Inskipp, F. and Proctor, B. (1993) *The Art, Craft and Task of Counselling Supervision. Part 1. Making the Most of Supervision*, Twickenham: Cascade Publications.

Inskipp, F. and Proctor, B. (2001a) *Making the Most of Supervision* (2nd edn), London: Cascade.

Inskipp, F. and Proctor, B. (2001b) *Becoming a Supervisor* (2nd edn), London: Cascade.

Jacobs, D., David, P. and Meyer, D. J. (1995) *The Supervisory Encounter*, New Haven, CT: Yale University Press.

James, I. A., Blackburn, I.-M., Milne, D. L., Freeston, M. and Armstrong, P. (2005) Supervision Training and Assessment Rating Scale for Cognitive Therapy

(STARS-CT). Unpublished instrument, available from the first author (ianjamesncht@yahoo.com), Centre for the Health of the Elderly, Newcastle General Hospital, NE4 6BE.

Johansson, P. and Hoglend, P. (2007) Identifying mechanisms of change in psychotherapy: Mediators of treatment outcome, *Clinical Psychology and Psychotherapy* 14: 1–9.

Jones, R. (2009) A movement led by Black service users in south London. In S. Fernando and F. Keating (Eds.) *Mental Health in a Multi-Ethnic Society: A Multidisciplinary Handbook* (2nd edn), Hove: Routledge.

Kadushin, A. (1968) Games people play in supervision, *Social Work* 13: 23–32.

Kadushin, A. (1992) *Supervision in Social Work*, New York: Columbia University Press.

Kagan-Klein, H. and Kagan, N. (1997) Interpersonal process recall: Influencing human interaction. In C. E. Watkins (Ed.) *Handbook of Psychotherapy Supervision*, New York: Wiley.

Kanz, J. E. (2001) Clinical-supervision.com: Issues in the provision of online supervision, *Professional Psychology: Research and Practice* 32: 415–420.

Kaslow, F. W. (1986) Supervision, consultation and staff training: Creative teaching/learning experiences in mental health professions. In F. W. Kaslow (Ed.) *Supervision and Training: Models, Dilemmas and Challenges*, New York: Haworth Press.

Kaslow, N. L., Borden, K. A., Collins, F., Forrest, L., Illfelder-Kaye, J., Nelson, P. D., et al. (2004) Competencies conference: Future directions in education and credentialling in professional psychology, *Journal of Clinical Psychology* 60: 699–712.

Kavanaugh, K. H. and Kennedy, P. H. (1992) *Promoting Cultural Diversity: Strategies for Health Care Professionals*, Newbury Park, CA: Sage.

Kazdin, A. (2008) Evidence-based treatment and practice: New ppportunities to bridge clinical research and practice, enhance the knowledge base and improve patient care, *American Psychologist* 63: 146–159.

Keen, A. and Freeston, M. (2008) Assessing competence in cognitive-behavioural therapy, *British Journal of Psychiatry* 193: 60–64.

Kenkel, M. B., and Peterson, R. L. (Eds.) (2010) *Competency-Based Education for Professional Psychology*, Washington, DC: American Psychological Association.

Kerlinger, F. N. (1986) *Foundations of Behavioural Research* (3rd edn), New York: Holt, Rinehart & Winston.

Kilminster, S. M. and Jolly, B. C. (2000) Effective supervision in clinical practice settings: A literature review, *Medical Education* 34: 827–840.

Kilminster, S., Cottrell, D., Grant, J. and Jolly, B. (2007) AMEE Guide No. 27: Effective educational and clinical supervision, *Medical Teacher* 29: 2–19.

Kilminster, S., Jolly, B. and van der Vieuten, C. P. M. (2002) A framework for effective training for supervisors, *Medical Teacher* 24: 385–389.

Kinderman, P. (2005) The applied psychology revolution, *The Psychologist* 18: 744–746.

Kirkpatrick, D. L. (1967) Evaluation of training. In R. L. Craig and L. R. Bittel (Eds.) *Training and Development Handbook*, New York: McGraw-Hill.

Kitzinger, C. (1991) Feminism, psychology and the paradox of power, *Feminism and Psychology* 1: 111–130.

Klein, M. H., Mathieu, P. L., Gendlin, E. T. and Kiesler, D. J. (1969) *The Experiencing Scale: A Research and Training Manual Volume 1*, Madison, WI: Wisconsin Psychiatric Institute.

Kolb, D. (1984) *Experiential Learning: Experience as a Source of Learning and Development*, Englewood Cliffs, NJ; Prentice-Hall.

Kraiger, K., Ford, J. K. and Salas, E. (1993) Application of cognitive skills – based and effective theories of learning outcomes to new methods of training evaluation, *Journal of Applied Psychology* 78: 311–328.

Ladany, N. (2004) Psychotherapy supervision: What lies beneath? *Psychotherapy Research* 14: 1–19.

Ladany, N. and Friedlander, M. L. (1995) The relationship between the supervisory working alliance and trainees' experience of role conflict and role ambiguity, *Counselor Education and Supervision*, 34: 220–231.

Ladany, N., Ellis, M. V. and Friedlander, M. L. (1999) The supervisor working alliance, trainee self-efficacy and satisfaction, *Journal of Counselling and Development* 77: 447–455.

Ladany, N., Friedlander, M. and Nelson, M. L. (2005) *Critical Events in Psychotherapy Supervision. An Interpersonal Approach*, Washington, DC: American Psychological Association.

Ladany, N., Hill, C. E., Corbett, M. M. and Nutt, E. A. (1996) Nature, extent and importance of what psychotherapy trainees do not disclose to their supervisors, *Journal of Counselling Psychology* 43: 10–24.

Lago, C. and Thompson, J. (1997) The triangle with curved sides: Sensitivity to issues of race and culture in supervision. In G. Shipton (Ed.) *Supervision of Psychotherapy and Counseling*, Buckingham: Open University Press.

Lahad, M. (2000) *Creative Supervision: The Use of Expressive Arts Methods in Supervision and Self Supervision*, London: Jessica Kingsley.

Lambert, M. J. (1980) Research and the supervisory process. In A. K. Hess (Ed.) *Psychology Supervision: Theory, Research and Practice*, New York: Wiley.

Lambert, M. J. and Ogles, B. M. (1997) The effectiveness of psychotherapy supervision. In E. Watkins (Ed.) *Handbook of Psychotherapy Supervision*, New York: Wiley.

Lammers, W. (1999) Training in team and group supervision. In E. Holloway and M. Carroll (Eds.) *Training Counselling Supervisors*, London: Sage.

Larkin, J. and Popaleni, K. (1994) Heterosexual courtship, violence and harassment: The public and private control of young women, *Feminism and Psychology* 4: 213–227.

Lask, J. (2009) *Update on Statutory Regulation and Supervision* (http://www.aft.org.uk/about/documents/Updateonstatutoryregulationandsupervision2009.doc; accessed 2/2/10).

Launer, J. (2007) Moving on from Balint: Embracing clinical supervision, *British Journal of General Practice* 57: 182–183.

Lavender, T. (2009) Reflections on the impact of New Ways of Working for applied psychologists, *Journal of Mental Health Training, Education and Practice* 4: 23–28.

Lavender, T. and Hope, R. (2007) *New Ways of Working for Applied Psychologists in Health and Social Care: The End of the Beginning*, Leicester: British Psychological Society.

Lavender, T. and Thompson, L. (2000) Attracting newly-qualified psychologists to NHS Trusts, *Clinical Psychology Forum* 139: 35–40.

Lawton, B. and Feltham, C. (2000) *Taking Supervision Forward: Enquiries and Trends in Counselling and Psychotherapy*, London: Sage.

Layard, R. (2005a) Therapy for all on the NHS. Sainsbury Centre Lecture, London, 6 September 2005.

Layard, R. (2005b) *The Depression Report: A New Deal for Depression and Anxiety Disorders*, London: London School of Economics Centre for Economic Performance and Mental Health Policy.

Layard, R. (2006) The case for psychological treatment centres, *British Medical Journal* 332: 1030–1032.

Leape, L. L., Berwick, D. M. and Bates, D. W. (2002) What practices will most improve patient safety? *Journal of the American Medical Association* 288: 501–507.

Leary, K. (1998) Race, self-disclosure and 'forbidden talk': Race and ethnicity in contemporary clinical practice, *Psychoanalysis Quarterly* LXVI: 163–189.

Leichsenrig, F. and Rabung, S. (2008) Effectiveness of long-term psychodynamic psychotherapy: A meta-analysis, *Journal of the American Medical Association* 300: 1551–1565.

Leslie, L. A. and Clossick, M. L. (1996) Sexism in family therapy: Does training in gender make a difference? *Journal of Marital and Family Therapy* 22: 253–269.

Liddle, H. A., Becker, D. and Diamond, G. M. (1997) Family therapy supervision. In C. E. Watkins (Ed.) *Handbook of Psychotherapy Supervision*, New York: Wiley.

Liese, B. S. and Beck, J. S. (1997) Cognitive therapy supervision. In C. E. Watkins (Ed.) *Handbook of Psychotherapy Supervision*, New York: Wiley.

Litrell, J. M., Lee-Bordin, N. and Lorenz, J. A. (1979) A developmental framework for counseling supervision, *Counselor Education and Supervision* 19: 119–136.

Llewellyn, S. P. (1988) Psychological therapy as viewed by clients and therapists, *British Journal of Clinical Psychology* 27: 105–114.

Lloyd, H. and Dallos, R. (2008) First session solution-focused brief therapy with families who have a child with severe intellectual disabilities: Mothers' experiences and views, *Journal of Family Therapy* 30: 5–28.

Loganbill, C., Hardy, E. and Delworth, U. (1982) Supervision: A conceptual model, *The Counseling Psychologist* 10: 3–42.

London Deanery (2010) *Professional Development Framework for Supervisors in the London Deanery* (http://www.faculty.londondeanery.ac.uk/global-news/files/news/minimum-training-specification-for-clinical-educational-supervisors%20FINAL.pdf; accessed 17/3/10).

Longmore, R. and Worrell, M. (2007) Do we need to challenge thoughts in cognitive behavior therapy? *Clinical Psychology Review* 27: 173–187.

Lorde, A. (1984) *Sister/Outsider: Essays and Speeches*, New York: Crossing Press.

Lucock, M. and Lutz, W. (2009) Methods for constructing and disseminating service level results in a meaningful way. In M. Barkham and G. E. Hardy (Eds.) *A Core Approach to Delivering Practice-Based Evidence*, Chichester: Wiley.

Lucock, M., Leach, C., Iveson, S., Lynch, K., Horsefield, C. and Hall, P. (2003) A systematic approach to practice-based evidence in a psychological therapies Service, *Clinical Psychology and Psychotherapy* 10: 389–399.

Magnuson, S., Wilcoxon, S. A. and Norem, K. (2000) Exemplary supervision practices: Retrospective observations of experienced counselors, *Texas Counseling Association Journal* 28: 93–101.

Manchester Mental Health and Social Care Trust (MMHSCT) (2008) *Standards for Clinical Supervision within Psychological Services (excluding Psychotherapy)* (http://www.mhsc.nhs.uk/pages/About%20the%20Trust/Trust%20Board/Board%20Meetings/2008/October/X%20-%20Clinical%20Supervision%20-%20Psychology.pdf; accessed 5/4/10).

Mannix, K. A., Blackburn, I. M., Garland, A., Gracie, J., Moorey, S., Reid, B., et al. (2006) Effectiveness of brief training in cognitive behaviour therapy techniques for palliative care practitioners, *Palliative Medicine* 20: 579–584.

Marrow, C. E., Hollyoake, K., Hamer, D. and Kenrick, C. (2002) Clinical supervision using video-conferencing technology: A reflective account, *Journal of Nursing Management* 10: 275–282.

Martinez, R. P. and Holloway, E. L. (1997) The supervision relationship in multicultural training. In D. B. Pope-Davis and H. L. K. Coleman (Eds.) *Multicultural Counseling Competencies: Assessment, Education, Training and Supervision*, Thousand Oaks, CA: Sage.

Mattinson, J. (1977) *The Reflection Process in Casework Supervision*, London: Tavistock Institute of Human Relations.

McKay, N. (1992) Remembering Anita Hill and Clarence Thomas: What really happened when one black woman spoke out. In T. Morrison (Ed.) *Race-ing, Justice, En-gendering Power*, New York: Pantheon.

McLeod, B. D. and Weisz, J. R. (2005) The therapy process observational coding system – alliance scale: Measure characteristics and prediction of outcome in usual clinical practice, *Journal of Consulting and Clinical Psychology* 17: 323–333.

McQueen, C. (Ed.) (2000) Women and Power, *Changes: An International Journal of Psychology and Psychotherapy* 18(4).

Mental Health Foundation (2006) *We Need to Talk*, London: Mental Health Foundation.

Miller, J. (1986) *Toward a New Psychology of Women*, London: Penguin.

Miller, J. B. (1991) Women and power. In J. V. Jordan, A. G. Kaplan, J. B. Miller, I. P. Stiver and J. L. Surrey (Eds.) *Women's Growth in Connection*, New York: Guilford Press.

Miller, S. and Binder, J. (2002) The effects of manual-based training on treatment fidelity and outcome: A review of the literature on adult individual psychotherapy, *Psychotherapy: Theory, Research, Practice, Training* 39: 184–198.

Miller, S., Duncan, B., Brown, J., Sorrell, R. and Chalk, M. (2007) Using formal client feedback to improve retention and outcome, *Journal of Brief Therapy* 5: 19–28.

Milne, D. L. (2007) An empirical definition of clinical supervision, *British Journal of Clinical Psychology* 46: 437–447.

Milne, D. L. (2008) *Introduction to Clinical Supervision: A Tutor's Guide*. Unpublished document available from the author (d.l.milne@ncl.ac.uk).

Milne, D. L. (2009) *Evidence-Based Clinical Supervision: Principles and Practice*, Oxford: Wiley-Blackwell.

Milne, D. L. and James, I. (1999) Evidence-based clinical supervision: Review and guidelines, *Clinical Psychology Forum* 133: 32–36.

Milne, D. L. and James, I. (2000) A systematic review of effective cognitive-behavioural supervision, *British Journal of Clinical Psychology* 39: 111–127.

Milne, D. L. and James, I. (2002) The observed impact of training on competence in clinical supervision, *British Journal of Clinical Psychology* 41: 55–72.

Milne, D. and Oliver, V. (2000) Flexible formats of clinical supervision: Description, evaluation and implementation. *Journal of Mental Health* 9: 291–304.

Milne, D. L. and Paxton, R. (1998) A psychological re-analysis of the scientist-practitioner model, *Clinical Psychology and Psychotherapy* 5: 216–230.

Milne, D. L. and Reiser, R. (2007) Supervison: Adherence and Guidance Evaluation (SAGE) manual. Unpublished document, available from Newcastle University via the first author (d.l.milne@ncl.ac.uk).

Milne, D. and Scaife, J. (2008) Master-class for supervisor trainers. Workshop held at the Northern Training Programmes Conference, Ambleside, York, July 2008.

Milne, D. and Westerman, C. (2001) Evidence-based clinical supervision: Rationale and illustration, *Clinical Psychology and Psychotherapy* 8: 444–457.

Milne, D. L., Aylott, H., Fitzpatrick, H. and Ellis, M. V. (2008a) How does clinical supervision work? Using a Best Evidence Synthesis approach to construct a basic model of supervision, *The Clinical Supervisor* 27: 170–190.

Milne, D. L., Britton, P. G. and Wilkinson, I. (1990) The scientist-practitioner in practice, *Clinical Psychology Forum* 30: 27–30.

Milne, D. L., Freeston, M., Paxton, R., James, I. A., Cooper, M. and Knibbs, J. (2008b) A new pyramid of research knowledge for the NHS, *Journal of Mental Health* 17: 509–519.

Milne, D., James, I., Keegan, D. and Dudley, M. (2002) Teacher's PETS: A new observational measure of experiential training interactions, *Clinical Psychology and Psychotherapy* 9: 187–199.

Milne, D. L., Keegan, D., Paxton, R. and Seth, K. (2000) Is the practice of psychological therapists evidence-based? *International Journal of Health Care Quality Assurance* 13: 8–14.

Mitchell, J. (1974) *Psychoanalysis and Feminism*, Harmondsworth: Penguin.

Molnar, A. and De Shazer, S. (2007) Solution-focused therapy: Toward the identification of therapeutic tasks, *Journal of Marital and Family Therapy* 13: 349–358.

Morley, S., Williams, A. and Hussain, S. (2008) Estimating the clinical effectiveness of cognitive behavioural therapy in the clinic: Evaluation of a CBT informed pain management programme, *Pain* 137: 670–680.

Morrison, T. (Ed.) (1992) *Race-ing, Justice, En-gendering Power*, New York: Pantheon.

Morrison, T. (2005) *Staff Supervision in Social Care* (3rd edn), Brighton: Pavilion.

Nadirshaw, Z. (2000) Professional and organisational issues. In N. Patel, E. Bennett, M. Dennis, N. Dosanjh, A. Mahtani, A. Miller, et al. (Eds.) *Clinical Psychology, 'Race' and Culture: A Training Manual*, Leicester: BPS Books.

Nelson, M. E. (1997) An interactional model for empowering women in supervision, *Counselor Education and Supervision* 37: 125–140.

Newcastle University (2009) Clinical placement outcome portfolio and associated guidance. Unpublished document, available from D. L. Milne (d.l.milne@ncl.ac. uk).

NHS Education for Scotland (2009) *Workforce Planning for Psychology Services in*

NHS Scotland Characteristics of the Workforce Supply in 2009, Edinburgh: NHS Education Scotland.

Norcross, J. (2002) *Psychotherapy Relationships that Work: Therapist Contributions and Responsiveness to Patient Need*, New York: Oxford University Press.

Norman, G. (2009) When will learning style go out of style? *Advances in Health Sciences Education* 14: 1–4.

North East London Strategic Health Authority (2003) *Report of an Independent Inquiry into the Care and Treatment of Daksha Emson and her Daughter Freya*, London: NELSHA.

Ofman, D. (2001) *Core Qualities: A Gateway to Human Resources*, Schiedam: Scriptum Publishers.

Okiishi, J., Lambert, M. J., Nielsen, S. L. and Ogles, B. M. (2003) Waiting for Supershrink: An empirical analysis of therapist effects, *Clinical Psychology and Psychotherapy* 10: 352–360.

Olk, M. and Friedlander, M. L. (1992) Trainees' experience of role conflict and role ambiguity in supervisory relationships, *Journal of Counseling Psychology* 39: 389–397.

Organisation Intersex International (undated) Cited in Planned Parenthood, Mid-Hudson Valley, Inc, Mental Health Association in Ulster County, Inc., University of Maryland Center for Mental Health Services Research and the New York Association for Gender Rights Advocacy (NYAGRA) *Enhancing Cultural Competence Welcoming Lesbian, Gay, Bisexual, Transgender, Queer People in Mental Health Services* (2nd edn). Unpublished Toolkit held at University of Maryland.

Orlans, V. and Edwards, D. (2001) A collaborative model of supervision. In M. Carroll and M. Tholstrup (Eds.) *Integrative Approaches to Supervision*, London: Jessica Kingsley.

Orlinsky, D. E. and Russell, R. L. (1994) Tradition and change in psychotherapy: Notes on the fourth generation. In R. L. Russell (Ed.) *Reassessing Psychotherapy Research*, New York: Guilford Press.

Page, S. and Wosket, V. (2001) *Supervising the Counsellor: A Cyclical Model* (2nd edn), Philadelphia, PA: Brunner-Routledge.

Palomo, M. (2004) Development and validation of a questionnaire measure of the supervisory relationship (SRQ). Unpublished DClinPsych dissertation, University of Oxford.

Palomo, M., Beinart, H. and Cooper, M. J. (2009) Development and validation of the Supervisory Relationship Questionnaire (SRQ) in UK trainee clinical psychologists, *British Journal of Clinical Psychology* 49: 131–149.

Patel, N. (1998) Black therapist/white clients: An exploration of experiences in cross-cultural therapy, *Clinical Psychology Forum* 118: 18–23.

Patel, N. and Fatimilehin, I. A. (1999) Racism and mental health. In C. Newnes, G. Holmes and C. Dunn (Eds.) *This is Madness. A Critical Look at Psychiatry and the Future of Mental Health Services*, Ross-on-Wye: PCCS.

Patel, N., Bennett, E., Dennis, M., Dosanjh, N., Mahtani, A., Miller, A., et al. (2000) *Clinical Psychology, 'Race' and Culture: A Training Manual*, Leicester: BPS Books.

Peckham, M. (1991) Research and development for the National Health Service, *Lancet* 338: 367–371.

Perepletchikova, F. and Kazdin, A. (2005) Treatment Integrity and therapeutic change: Issues and research recommendations, *Clinical Psychology: Science and Practice* 12: 365–383.

Petticrew, M. and Roberts, H. (2006) *Systematic Reviews in the Social Sciences: A Practical Guide*, Oxford: Blackwell.

Pidd, S. (2009) New Ways of Working for psychiatrists: The achievements and the challenges, *Journal of Mental Health Training, Education and Practice* 4: 18–22.

Pinderhughes, E. (1989) *Understanding, Race, Ethnicity and Power: The Key to Efficacy in Clinical Practice*, New York: Free Press.

Ponterotto, J. G. and Pedersen, P. B. (1993) *Preventing Prejudice: A Guide for Counselors and Educators*, Newbury Park, CA: Sage.

Priest, R. (1994) Minority supervisor and majority supervisee: Another perspective of clinical reality, *Counselor Education and Supervision* 34: 152–158.

Priestley, J. B. (1972) *Over the Long High Wall: Some Reflections and Speculations on Life, Death and Time*, London: Heinemann.

Procter, R. (2007) 'All you need is love': Is alliance the alternative explanation for successful supervision? Unpublished undergraduate thesis, available from the Psychology Department, Newcastle University, NE1 7RU.

Proctor, B. (1986) Supervision: A co-operative exercise in accountability. In M. Marken and M. Payne (Eds.) *Enabling and Ensuring*, Leicester: Youth Bureau and Training Community Work.

Proctor, B. (1997) Contracting in supervision. In C. Sills (Ed.) *Contracts in Counseling*, London: Sage.

Proctor, B. (2000) *Group Supervision: A Guide to Creative Practice*, London: Sage.

Proctor, B. and Inskipp, F. (2009) Group supervision. In J. Scaife (Ed.) *Supervision in Clinical Practice: A Practitioner's Guide* (2nd edn), London: Routledge.

Rabinowitz, F. E., Heppner, P. P. and Roehlke, H. J. (1986) Descriptive study of process and outcome variables of supervision over time, *Journal of Counseling Psychology* 33: 292–300.

Ramm, L. J. (2007) Clinical supervision: Enhancing fidelity through the development of a manual and scoring tool. Unpublished undergraduate thesis, available from the Psychology Department, Newcastle University, NE1 7RU.

Reese, R., Usher, E., Bowman, D., Norsworthy, L., Halstead, J. Rowlands, S. and Chisholm, R. (2009) Using client feedback in psychotherapy training: An analysis of its influence on supervision and counselor self-efficacy, *Training and Education in Professional Psychology* 3: 157–168.

Richards, D. A. and Suckling, R. (2008) Improving access to psychological therapy: The Doncaster demonstration site organisational model, *Clinical Psychology Forum* 181: 9–16.

Richards, D. and Whyte, M. (2008) *Reach Out: National Programme Educator Materials to Support the Delivery of Training for Practitioners Delivering Low Intensity Interventions*, York: University of York.

Ricketts, T. and Donohoe, G. (2000) Clinical supervision in cognitive behavioural psychotherapy. In B. Lawton and C. Feltham (Eds.) *Taking Supervision Forwards: Enquiries and Trends in Counselling and Psychotherapy*, London: Sage.

Ridley, C. R. (1995) *Overcoming Unintentional Racism in Counseling and Therapy: A Practitioner's Guide to Intentional Intervention*, Thousand Oaks, CA: Sage.

Robinson, J. (2005) Improving practice through a system of clinical supervision, *Nursing Times* 101: 30.

Robinson, V. (1936) *Supervision in Social Casework*, Chapel Hill, NC: University of Carolina Press.

Rosenzveig, S. (1936) Some implicit common factors in diverse methods of psychotherapy, *American Journal of Orthopsychiatry* 6: 412–415.

Roth, A. and Fonagy, P. (1996) *What Works For Whom? A Critical Review of Psychotherapy Research*, New York: Guilford Press.

Roth, A. and Pilling, S. (2007) *The Competencies Required to Deliver Effective Cognitive and Behavioural Therapy for People with Depression and Anxiety Disorders*, London: Department of Health.

Roth, A. D. and Pilling, S. (2008a) *A Competence Framework for the Supervision of Psychological Therapies* (http://www.ucl.ac.uk/clinical-psychology/CORE/compe tence_frameworks.htm; accessed 5/4/10).

Roth, A. D. and Pilling, S. (2008b) Using an evidence-based methodology to identify the competences required to deliver effective cognitive and behavioural therapy for depression and anxiety disorders, *Behavioural and Cognitive Psycho-therapy* 36: 129–147.

Roth, A. D. and Pilling, S. (2008c) *Competence Frameworks for the Delivery and Supervision of Psychological Therapies* (http://www.ucl.ac.uk/clinical-psychology/ CORE/supervision_framework.htm; accessed 5/4/10).

Roth, A. and Pilling, S. (2008d) *The Competences Framework For Supervision* (http://www.ucl.ac.uk/clinical-psychology/CORE/supervision_framework.htm; accessed 5/4/10).

Roth, A., Fonagy, P. and Parry, G. (1996) Psychotherapy research, funding and evidence-based practice. In A. Roth and P. Fonagy (Eds.) *What Works For Whom? A Critical Review of Psychotherapy Research*, New York: Guilford Press.

Roth, A. D., Pilling, S. and Turner, J. (2010) Therapist training and supervision in clinical trials: Implication for clinical practice, *Behavioural and Cognitive Psychotherapy* 38: 291–302.

Ryde, J. (2000) Supervising across difference, *International Journal of Psychotherapy* 5: 37–49.

Sabin-Farrell, R. and Turpin, G. (2003) Vicarious traumatization: Implications for the mental health of health workers? *Clinical Psychology Review* 23: 449–480.

Sayal-Bennett, A. (1991) Equal opportunities: Empty rhetoric, *Feminism and Psychology* 1: 74–77.

Scaife, J. (2001) *Supervision in the Mental Health Professions: A Practitioner's Guide*, Hove: Brunner-Routledge.

Scaife, J. (2008) *Core Challenges in Supervisor Training*. Paper presented at the Northern Training Programmes Conference, Ambleside, York, July 2008.

Scaife, J. (2009) *Supervision in Clinical Practice: A Practitioner's Guide* (2nd edn), Hove: Brunner-Routledge.

Scaife, J. and Walsh, S. (2001) The emotional climate of work and the development of self. In J. Scaife (Ed.) *Supervision in the Mental Health Professions: A Practitioner's Guide*, Hove: Brunner-Routledge.

Schon, D. A. (1983) *The Reflective Practitioner: How Professionals Think in Action*, New York: Basic Books.

Scott, S. and Dadds, M. (2009) Practitioner review: When parent training doesn't work: Theory-driven clinical strategies, *Journal of Child Psychology and Psychiatry* 50: 1441–1450.

Shadish, W., Ragsdale, K., Glaser, R. and Montgomery, L. (1995) The efficacy and effectiveness of marital and family therapy: A perspective from meta-analysis, *Journal of Marital and Family Therapy* 21: 345–360.

Shajanania, K. G., Fletcher, K. E. and Saint, S. (2006) Graduate medical education and patient safety: A busy – and occasionally hazardous – inter-section, *Annals of Internal Medicine* 145: 592–598.

Shanfield, S. B., Mohl, P. C., Matthews, K. L. and Hetherly, V. (1992) Quantitative assessment of the behavior of psychotherapy supervisors, *American Journal of Psychiatry* 149: 352–357.

Shepherd, C., Vanderpuye, N. and Saine, M. (2010) How are potential black and minority ethnic candidates being attracted into the clinical psychology profession? A review of all UK clinical psychology postgraduate websites, *Clinical Psychology Forum* 206: 1–6.

Sherwood Psychotherapy Training Institute (2010) *Codes for Graduate Members* (http://www.spti.net; accessed 8/3/10).

Siegler, R. and Crowley, K. (1991) The microgenetic method: A direct means for studying cognitive development, *American Psychologist* 46: 606–620.

Sloan, G. (1999) Good characteristics of a clinical supervisor: A community mental health nurse perspective, *Journal of Advanced Nursing*, 30: 713–722.

Society of Radiographers (2006) *The Approval and Accreditation of Educational Programmes and Professional Practice in Radiography. Clinical Education and Training: Guidance and Strategies for Effective Relationships between Education Providers, Placement Providers and Learners*, London: Society of Radiographers.

South Staffordshire PCT (2010) *Clinical Supervision Policy* (http://www.south staffordshirepct.nhs.uk/policies/clinical/Clin17_ClinicalSupervisionPolicy.pdf; accessed 19/3/10).

Spence, S. H., Wilson, J., Kavanagh, D., Strong, J. and Worrall, L. (2001) Clinical supervision in four mental health professions: A review of the evidence, *Behaviour Change* 18: 135–155.

Stedmon, J. and Dallos, R. (2009) *Reflective Practice in Psychotherapy and Counselling*, Maidenhead: Open University Press/McGraw-Hill.

Stedmon, J., Mitchell, A., Johnstone, L. and Staite, S. (2003) Making reflective practice real: Problems and solutions in the south west, *Clinical Psychology* 27: 30–34.

Stein, D. M. and Lambert, M. J. (1995) Graduate training in psychotherapy: Are therapy outcomes enhanced? *Journal of Consulting and Clinical Psychology* 63: 182–196.

Stoltenberg, C. (1981) Approaching supervision from a developmental perspective: The counselor complexity model, *Journal of Counseling Psychology* 28: 59–65.

Stoltenberg, C. and Delworth, U. (1987) *Supervising Counselors and Therapists: A Developmental Approach*, San Francisco: Jossey-Bass.

Stoltenberg, C., McNeill, B. and Delworth, U. (1998) *IDM Supervision: An Integrated Developmental Model for Supervising Counselors and Therapists*, San Francisco: Jossey-Bass.

Surrey, J. L. (1991) The 'self-in-relation': A theory of women's development. In J. V.

Jordon, A. G. Kaplan, J. B. Miller, I. P. Stiver and J. L. Surrey (Eds.) *Women's Growth in Connection*, New York: Guilford Press.

Taylor, C. (1984) Foucault on freedom and truth, *Political Theory* 12: 152–183.

Taylor, M. (1994) Gender and power in counselling and supervision, *British Journal of Guidance and Counselling* 22: 319–327.

Temperley, J. (1984) Our own worst enemies: Unconscious factors in female disadvantage, *Free Associations* 1A: 23–38.

Townend, M. (2005) Inter-professional supervision from the perspectives of both mental health nurses and other professionals in the field of cognitive behavioural psychotherapy, *Journal of Psychiatric and Mental Health Nursing* 12: 582–588.

Townend, M., Iannetta, L. and Freeston, M. H. (2002) Clinical supervision in practice: A survey of UK cognitive behavioural psychotherapists accredited by the BABCP, *Behavioural and Cognitive Psychotherapy* 30: 485–500.

Tracey, T. J., Ellickson, J. L. and Sherry, D. (1989) Reactance in relation to different supervisory environments and counsellor development, *Journal of Counseling Psychology* 36: 336–344.

Trethowan, W. H. (1977) *The Role of Psychologists in the Health Services* (The Trethowan Report), London: HMSO.

Trivedi, P. (2002) Racism, social exclusion and mental health: A Black service user's perspective. In K. Bhui (Ed.) *Racism and Mental Health*, London: Jessica Kingsley.

Trivedi, P. (2009) Black service 'user involvement' – rhetoric or reality? In S. Fernando and F. Keating (Eds.) *Mental Health in a Multi-Ethnic Society: A Multidisciplinary Handbook* (2nd edn), Hove: Routledge.

Turpin, G. (2009) The future world of psychological therapies: Implications for counseling and clinical psychologists, *Counseling Psychology Review* 24: 23–33.

Turpin, G. and Llewelyn, S. (2009) Clinical psychology and service organisation. In H. Beinart, P. Kennedy and S. Llewelyn (Eds.) *Clinical Psychology in Practice*, Oxford: Wiley-Blackwell.

Turpin, G. and Wheeler, S. (2008) *'Supervision: The Key to Successful Patient Outcomes by Delivering IAPT Interventions of Proven High Quality and Fidelity': Clinical Supervision Principles and Guidance*, London: Department of Health IAPT.

Turpin, G., Clark, J., Duffy, R. and Hope, R. (2009) A new workforce to deliver IAPT: A case study, *Journal of Mental Health Training, Education and Practice* 4: 37–46.

Turpin, G., Hope, R., Duffy, R., Fossey, M. and Seward, J. (2006) Improving access to psychological therapies Implications for the mental health workforce, *Journal of Mental Health Workforce Development* 1: 12–21.

Turpin, G., Richards, D., Hope, R. and Duffy, R. (2008) Delivering the IAPT programme, *Healthcare Counselling and Psychotherapy Journal* 8: 2–8.

United Kingdom Council of Psychotherapy (UKCP) (2008) *Standards of Education and Training: The Minimum Core Criteria Psychotherapy with Adults*, London: UKCP.

United Kingdom Council of Psychotherapy (UKCP) (2009) *Ethical Principles and Code of Professional Conduct*, London: UKCP.

University of Leeds Media Services (2004) *Ethical Issues in Supervision* (video), Leeds: ULMS.

University of Leeds School of Healthcare (2008) *Training the Trainers*, Leeds: ULSH.

Ussher, J. and Nicolson, P. (Eds.) (1992) *Gender Issues in Clinical Psychology*, London: Routledge.

van Ooijen, E. (2000) *Clinical Supervision: A Practical Guide*, Basingstoke: Churchill Livingstone.

Vize, C. (2009) New Ways of Working and the issue of responsibility and accountability, *Journal of Mental Health Training, Education and Practice* 4: 8–12.

Wainwright, T. (2004) Surveying the health of the profession, *The Psychologist* 17: 5–6.

Walker, G. and Goldner, V. (1995) The wounded prince and the women who love him. In C. Burck and B. Speed (Eds.) *Gender Power and Relationships*, London: Routledge.

Wampold, B. (2001) *The Great Psychotherapy Debate: Models, Methods and Findings*, Hillsdale, NJ: Lawrence Erlbaum Associates.

Wampold, B. E. and Brown, G. S. (2005) Estimating the variability in outcomes attributable to therapists: A naturalistic study of outcomes of managed care, *Journal of Consulting and Clinical Psychology* 73: 914–923.

Wampold, B. E. and Holloway, E. L. (1997) Methodology, design and evaluation in psychotherapy supervision research. In C. E. Watkins (Ed.) *Handbook of Psychotherapy Supervision*, New York: Wiley.

Waskett, C. (2009) An integrated approach to introducing and maintaining supervision: The 4S model, *Nursing Times* 105: 17.

Watkins, C. E. (Ed.) (1997) *Handbook of Psychotherapy Supervision*, New York: Wiley.

Weaks, D. (2002) Unlocking the secrets of 'good supervision': A phenomenological exploration of experienced counsellor's perceptions of good supervision, *Counselling and Psychotherapy Research* 2: 33–39.

Webster-Stratton, C. (2004) *Quality Training, Supervision, Ongoing Monitoring, and Agency Support: Key Ingredients to Implementing The Incredible Years Programs with Fidelity* (http://www.incredibleyears.com/Library/items/quality-key-ingredients-fidelity-04.pdf; accessed 5/4/10).

Weetman, J. R. (2007) Scrutinising supervision: 'Is there a RECEIPT for the supervisee?' Unpublished undergraduate thesis, available from the Psychology Department, Newcastle University, NE1 7RU.

Wheeler, D., Avis, J., Miller, L. and Chaney, S. (1986) Cited in A. Prouty (2001) Experiencing feminist family therapy supervision, *Journal of Feminist Family Therapy* 12: 171–203.

Wheeler, S. (2007) What shall we do with the wounded healer? The supervisor's dilemma, *Psychodynamic Practice* 12: 245–256.

Wheeler, S. and Richards, K. (2007) The impact of clinical supervision on counsellors and therapists, their practice and their clients: A systematic review of the literature, *Counselling and Psychotherapy Research* 7: 54–65.

White, M. and Epston, D. (1991) *Narrative Means to Therapeutic End*, New York: Norton.

Whiting, P. P., Bradley, L. J. and Planny, K. J. (2001) Supervision-based developmental models of counselor supervision. In L. J. Bradley and N. Ladany (Eds.)

Counselor Supervision: Principles, Process and Practice, Philadelphia, PA: Brunner-Routledge.

Wierzbicki, M. and Pekarik, G. (1993) A meta-analysis of psychotherapy dropout, *Professional Psychology: Research and Practice* 24: 190–195.

Wilkinson, J. (2007) Wilkinson's SWORD: An observational tool for measuring transfer from supervision to therapy. Unpublished undergraduate thesis, available from the Psychology Department, Newcastle University, NE1 7RU.

Williams, L. and Irvine, F. (2009) How can the clinical supervisor role be facilitated in nursing: A phenomenological exploration, *Journal of Nursing Management* 17: 474–483.

Wilson, M. (2007) Can experiences of supervision be quantified? My PETS: A new tool for measuring supervisees' perceived satisfaction with clinical supervision. Unpublished undergraduate thesis, available from the Psychology Department, Newcastle University, NE1 7RU.

Winstanley, J. (2000) Manchester Clinical Supervision Scale, *Nursing Standard* 14: 31–32.

Workforce Review Team (2009) *Migration Advisory Committee Shortage Report. Clinical Psychologists. SOC 2212. September 2009* (www.wrt.nhs.uk/Index.php/component/docman/cat_view/66-mac?strat=35; accessed 31/5/10).

Worthen, V. and McNeill, B. W. (1996) A phenomenological investigation of 'good' supervision events, *Journal of Counseling Psychology* 43: 25–34.

Worthen, V. and Lambert, M. J. (2007) Outcome supported supervision: Advantages of adding systematic client tracking to supportive consultations, *Counselling and Psychotherapy Research* 7: 48–53.

Worthless I., Competent, U. and Lemonde-Terrible, O. (2002) Cognitive therapy training stress disorder: A cognitive perspective, *Behavioural and Cognitive Psychotherapy* 30: 365–374.

Yeh, C. J., Chang, T., Chiang, L., Drost, C. M., Spelliscy, D., Carter, R. T., et al. (2008) Development, content, process and outcome of an online peer supervision group for counselor trainees, *Computers in Human Behavior* 24: 2889–2903.

Yerushalmi, Y. (1999) The roles of group supervision of supervision, *Psychoanalytic Psychology* 16: 426–447.

Young, J. and Beck, A. T. (1980) Cognitive therapy scale: Rating manual. Unpublished manuscript, Center for Cognitive Therapy, Philadelphia.

Youngson, S., Clarke, L., Hughes, J. and Jordan, T. (2005) *Preparation for Supervision Pre and Post Qualification.* Paper presented at the DROSS Conference, York, March 2006.

Yuval Davis, N. (1994) Women, ethnicity and empowerment, *Feminism and Psychology* 4: 179–198.

Index